Wayne Hussey Testimonial – S
legendary "Goth" Rock'n'Roll Band The Mission:

"Stevie Vayne was the real deal. A Punk-Rock'n'Roll Star, not just in his own head but to anyone that came into his orbit. He was legendary in Leeds among a cabal of late-night underworld dwellers, of which I was one. I've had the oft times dubious pleasure of meeting many fakers & frauds in my life who talked the talk but didn't dare walk the walk. Stevie was one of the very few that was genuine, authentic, who gleefully danced along the razor's edge in bare feet with a spoon & a set of works hanging out the back pocket of his ripped black leather pants. Stevie IS a Punk-Rock'n'Roll Star. Stevie IS the REAL deal."

Author's Note: It was always an honour and a thrill to go on tour with The Mission.

The band emerged from the "wasteland" born out of The Sisters of Mercy break-up – they took the music scene by storm all over the world.

The Mission put Leeds on the global music map like no other live band had done before - their gigs are more like an emotional epiphany, a ritual of positivity between band and audience, than just a Rock'n'Roll Show – and Wayne Hussey; the adorable Pied Piper "leading the hordes with a guitar in one hand and a bottle of Blue Nun in the other" - long live The Mish.

Nick Toczek Testimonial – Much loved and respected writer, poet, promoter and performer with a career stretching back 50 years – Nick is a fella who knows:

"Of all the many guitarists I've ever worked with, Stevie Hulme stands out as the unrivalled best – the real raw rock'n'riff raunchy deal. And here's the book that proves it. God alone knows how the drug-addled bastard even lived to tell this tale. But his isn't just an account of a demented descent into music's most messed-up mayhem; it's his amazing, anecdote-ridden record of how he was lured into that weird world and learned to embrace it. We see him sucked into it. He then name-drops his way through its siren seductions of sex, songs, success, and ceaseless narcotics. He even manages to make amazing music before crawling out of its cess-pit. I gigged with the man. We still argue like fuck about this, that, and the other. Perhaps we both learned to survive by walking away from working with arseholes like us. This is a great story in many ways, but maybe mostly because it charts a lifestyle that doesn't have many survivors. If I had his vanity, I'd have written a book as good as this myself."

Authors Note: Writer and performer Nick Toczek played a key part in my Punk-Rock'n'Roll genesis – in that he promoted some of my first shows when I was no more than 16/17 years old, he was also the guy that took me on my very first tour of Holland – a pivotal moment in my evolution from Stevie Hulme to Stevie Vayne.

Royston Langdon Testimonial – The enigmatic genius writer, singer and bass playing leader of the superstar rock band Spacehog:

"I met Stevie Vayne after he'd stepped away from the chaos of rock'n'roll - when he was managing the Corn Exchange in Leeds, as Stevie Hulme, and putting on some of the most amazing 'Raves' the city had ever seen - this was back in 1991.

But, I played with him once on stage — Stevie agreeing to do a 'one-off' guest appearance with my young band - singing Iggy's 'The Passenger' — I saw the spark that never left him. That raw, real energy, like lightning captured in a bottle. For the first time, I witnessed something true — not just music, but a life lived on the edge. That night, Stevie showed me what rock and roll really means. It was the moment I knew I had to leave Leeds and chase that fire all the way to New York.

Broke and in need of work, I picked up the White Pages and began calling all the studios in Manhattan looking for an internship. When I got to the B's, for Baby Monster Studios, Jill Wisoff — the manager at the studio, who had once played with Johnny Thunders, a man Stevie had opened for — answered the phone. When she heard I was from Leeds and that I actually knew Stevie Vayne, everything changed. That moment, that connection, gave me my first real chance in the city, which would lead to a whole new world opening up to me. I'm endlessly grateful — Stevie wasn't just a rocker. He was the real thing."

Authors Note: Royston Langdon is the closest I have ever come to knowing somebody with "pure musical genius" – in my humble opinion Roy is the single greatest songwriter and artist to ever come out of Leeds - watching him work "up close" you just know you're in the presence of somebody very very special. His band Spacehog broke the US market with consummate ease - their album *Resident Alien*, and the hit single from it, "In The Meantime", made them household names from East Coast to West Coast, invited on to all the late night talk shows, they were a phenomenon – but always, essentially, they were Leeds.

John F. Keenan Testimonial - Nobody has done more for the Leeds Music Scene than promoter John F. Keenan. From the Punk pioneering gigs of the F-Club, to the world famous Futurama Festivals and the highly respected live music venue The Duchess, John has put on just about everybody, and certainly anybody of any consequence; Nirvana, Oasis, Blur, Johnny Thunders, every Punk Band that mattered... the list of his gigs is as impressive as it is exhaustive – Icon, Legend, he has earned many names:

"Somewhere between the arrogance of the Sex Pistols and the swagger of the New York Dolls, The Vaynes were a popular fixture around the rock venues of Leeds (as well as in other parts of the UK and Europe), they were always guaranteed to pull a crowd. Frontman Stevie was on his way to becoming a Rock God... No one expected the sudden sidestep into Rave Culture and his subsequent escape to New York - but when his good friend and musical hero Johnny Thunders died, Stevie pulled the curtain on Vayne and moved with the times as Hulme. His success with iconic House Music brands like Subliminal Records and Pacha has enabled him to spend his later years on the paradise island of Ibiza, where he resides to this day.

Some say he was lucky, I say he was motivated - this is a must have book!"

Authors Note: Live Music and John F. Keenan – two elements that are as common to Yorkshire folk as Fish 'n' Chips, Sunday Roast with Gravy, or Bangers and Mash. "John F. Keenan and Live Music" is part of the everyday language "for bands and punters alike".

If John is promoting it, it's worth getting a ticket - it's that simple. John is the best promoter the City of Leeds has ever had – as the old saying goes, "he's forgotten more about putting on gigs than most other operators will ever know" – it's a thrill, and I am grateful beyond words, to receive his words and testimonial.

VAINGLORIOUS

A PUNK IN THE HOUSE

Stevie Hulme

#269

Big Love

Stevie x

ARMLEY
~PRESS~

Literary Agent USA
Marc Mikulich
Manhattan, NYC
marc@marcmikulichliterary.com

Literary Agent UK
Christopher Newson
London, England
chris@newsonwallwork.com

Credits:

Written By: Stevie Hulme
Edited By: Andy Buchan
Proofread By: Leda Immortelle
Overall Copy Edit & Proof By:John Lake
First Proof Motivation By: Linda Karlsson
Cover Photo By: Tony Woolgar
Cover Design: Mick Lake & Craig Sharp
Layout by Ian Dobson

Thank Yous & Dedications...

BAND MEMBERS & INSPIRATIONAL BUDDIES: UNCLE HAGGIS, Dil, Sir Harry Vayne, MICK VAYNE, Gerry Famous, Jessica Fischer, Nev, Martin S, Smelly, Richard Todd, Cyrus Murphy, Martin Aylward, CLAIRE MILLER, Ruth Franckel, Deb O'Connor, Ronnie Macrae, Skum, Flat Top Tom, Sid Cramp, Andy Moore, Mandy Brown, Kate McGuire & Cris, PAUL JOHNO JOHNSON, Steve Watson, Anthony Oates, Jez Webb, CRAIG ADAMS, WAYNE HUSSEY, SIMON HINKLER, MICK BROWN, Jeffrey Lee Pierce, Romy Mory, Jill Wisoff, Chris Musto, Stevie Klasson, Alison Gordy, Jamie Heath, JOHNNY THUNDERS, STIV BATORS, MATT DANGERFIELD, MICK WEBSTER, Dave Ryan, Shona, JOHN F KEENAN, NICK TOCZEK, MARK GOULDEN, Tom Needham, Tom Speight, Gwinny Punk, Chris & Kev Rushby, 'Evo(?)', Shepherd, Nelly, George Little, Janine, Wilkie, Johnny Copson, Emily, Antonia, Dave Baguley, Diane, ANDY PROWLER, MICK LAKE, Paul Barham, Paul Hazelgrave, JOHN LAKE, MICK McCANN, Graham Geldard, Shaun Slater, Romy and Cherry, Barbara Winston, Chris Carey, Danny Whittle, Keith Fuller, Tony & John Fallon, Dale &

Paula Joyce, Rob Welch, Claire Seed, Roger Turnbull, Dean & Lisa Hulme

I can't say for sure who captured the images - but the folk that took photos of the entire scene were: Iggi Demello, Tim Campbell, Tony Woolgar, Kari Ella Black Pearson and Others - A big appreciation sent out to all those "shutterbug-clickers"

(sorry if I missed anybody, you know who you are)

All From The Subliminal Family

All From The Pacha-Ibiza Family

Some cool folk from the Manhattan Crew: Yana, Cristina B, Stephanie P, Nick Marc, Martin Ewens, Brett, Griff & Ali

Special Peeps:

JANET WADDELL, ROYSTON & ANTHONY LANGDON, Johnny Cragg, Richard Steele, MATT GOSS, Mick Rock, SI STORER, SHELLY RAY, Jackie Moore, Ken and CHARLES "Charlie" SHEPHERD

FAMILY: Lila Parry, Gina Harris, Dean Hulme, Lisa Hulme

The final shout-out goes to my wife and boy: "YUSI & XABI...you saved me, changed my life and made me a better person - thank you"

FOREWORD

Is there life before death ?

You want a man like Stevie on your side
He gets things done
When the kid looked at Johnny he knew to get a crack at the
title he had to position himself a contender

Now you too are able to get ringside for a no holds barred
journey through the glittering gutters of Leeds 6 Punk-
Rock'n'Roll crisscrossing Europe on a shoestring all the
while with an eye on the top table of doing business in the
music business of London NYC & Ibiza

There's sex there's drugs there's violence all refracting
wildly through the prism of a charmed life

Come with me and join Stevie the kid who knew you gotta
live before you die

This is the story of the who what when how and why ?

From the pen of a ghost

Ms Leda Immortelle

PROLOGUE

Hats off to the Dead Men On Horses:
To all those who try — even while knowing that the possibility of failure is infinitely greater than the chance of success.

Let's hear it for the vainglorious, the innocent victims of failure — those who are saddled to the fast lane, riding hard until they finally find something that we might call "Salvation": it's a wonderful life, if you reach out and just go for it.

There was never any innocence, just mad curiosity, a desire to try — I tried it all:

Sex and Drugs and Punk-Rock'n'Roll — I drenched myself in it.

Hedonism, the High Life and House Music — I soaked myself in it.

"This is The Midnight Gun, And I'm Packing Silver Bullets Baby — Bang Bang"

Song for Mick Vayne, "Let's Ride":

Maybe we could talk all night
But even if we talked all night
I won't say goodbye
I'll say so long, but I won't say goodbye

Remember when…

On crazy horses we would ride
Packing silver bullets by our sides
On electric strings we'd fly so high
Like outlaw cowboys in the night

When you're rolling down the track
Once in a while just take a look back
One day you'll see me coming down the line

8

Vainglorious: A Punk in the House

You're gonna hear me cry one more time

Let's ride
One more time
Old friend of mine
Come on let's ride
Till the end of the line

So many years you stood by my side
I look stage left you're there with your red guitar
Sweet toxic twin you left a lifelong mark
A beautiful scar upon my broken heart

Remember when…

On crazy horses we would ride
Packing silver bullets by our sides
On electric strings we'd fly so high
Like outlaw cowboys in the night

When you're rolling down the track
Once in a while just take a look back
One day you'll see me coming down the line
You're gonna hear me cry one more time

Let's ride
One more time
Old friend of mine
Come on let's ride
Till the end of the line

INTRO: WHAT'S IT ALL ABOUT? WHAT KIND OF FOOL AM I?

I own an old motorbike. It's not a great bike, it's not a winner, but it runs well and it looks cool. It's a Chinese Kymco Zing II Custom 125. It seems to be based on some kind of classic cruiser model, like a Harley-Davidson Breakout, or some such similar model. I don't really know to be honest, I'm not a motorbike aficionado by any stretch of the imagination — it couldn't be called a proper bike, by which I mean, it's not a machine, or make, that would be considered fit for proper bikers.

I've known some proper bikers in my life. I've been on friendly terms with the some-time president of the Leeds Blue Angels for years, even to this very day. I also used to be on first name terms with one or two of the New York City Hells Angels. Well, I say first name terms, but in reality it was only for a brief moment back in the early 2000s when we all used to drink in a bar owned by mutual friends Jesse Malin and Johnny T; it was more just solid bar etiquette between regulars hitting up the same spot. Bar Niagara on Ave A & 7th Street was a great hangout that welcomed one and all. I even put a weekly party on in there myself for a while — so long as you were cool beans, Niagara was open to you. In an earlier life it had been known as A7 and was cited as the place that gave birth to the New York Hard Core scene. Co-owner Jesse Malin was also one of the main faces in the East Village from running the famous live venue Coney Island High, as well as being the main man in the punk band, D-Generation. He is also known in live music circles around the world under his own name too. Good times were had in that East Village, Alphabet City, Dive Bar in Manhattan.

I also have a very good friend who was with the pre-Charter South Coast Hells Angels in the UK too. Those are the kind of people you'd call proper bikers — I'm not one of them.

One of the founding members of The Dead Vaynes, Cyrus (RIP), was motorbike mad, just like another member of the same band who called himself Smelly and used to live in a shed with his motorbike. Other lifelong friends, also associated with The Dead Vaynes (a band I will introduce you to as we go along), Skum and Punk Elvis, have both been classic bike lovers for decades. But again, not me. I'm a tourist when it comes to motorbikes. I know little to nothing about them. That said, I ride around Ibiza in the sunshine thinking I'm Steve McQueen, with a little touch of Elvis, both wrapped into one. It's for show. It gets me from A to B. It's for fun, good times, and living life. I like my bike. But I'm digressing from the point I want to make, which isn't really about the bike itself. So let's get back to it: what kind of fool am I?

Just to set the scene, these days you'll find me living in Ibiza — and every day during the summer when I go to saddle up and ride my motorbike, which I call Elvis McQueen, I notice that there's a spider web built afresh each morning. I never disturb the web. I start up and roll off, leaving the web to stand or fall depending on the elements.

Anyway, one day, I had to take a ride from Ibiza Town to San Antonio. It would be a road trip from one side of the island to the other and back — maybe a 50km round trip — and the route would take me down the only proper highway on the island, where a speed of 100 km/h is occasionally allowed.

I set off in good spirits, looking forward to the ride, and as I got to the bottom of the first road, I pulled up for the red traffic light. That's when I noticed the spider, the one that built its web on the handlebars of Elvis McQueen. It was hanging upside down just below the ignition switch, and it dawned on me that I hadn't actually seen the spider before, I'd only ever seen its web. This was the first time it had revealed itself to me.

11

My first reaction was to pull over and coax it onto my glove, so I could place it safely in the shrubs by the side of the road, but the light turned green and I had cars behind me waiting to go. I rolled off again. But now, as I rode along, I found myself glancing at the spider and wondering if I should stop and help it off or if I should just go ahead and take it along for the ride.

I was hesitant to do the latter, strangely worried that it might blow off when the road got fast or bumpy. Falling off would mean it'd be away from its home somewhere in the handlebars of my motorbike. All of a sudden, I felt conflicted, responsible even. A little voice scolded me: "It'll definitely be away from its home if you help it off and put it in the shrubbery, you idiot!" A bit harsh, I thought. The voice countered: "No, not really. Look, why not give it an even chance? Just keep riding. If it manages to hold on for the journey, then it holds on. If it slips off in the wind, well, come on, it'll survive the fall anyway and live to build a web somewhere else. Go on, Punk, roll the dice for the little fucker."

It made sense, that little voice. The spider was small. It would be light enough, housed in a hard shell, to survive a fall at speed. And yeah, life would go on, different circumstances, but on it would go. I looked down at the spider, and I swear down, I'm sure it was looking right back at me, awaiting the verdict of my personal kangaroo court. I said: "OK, McQueen," (I know, double-dipping on the McQueen *legend*, but that's what I called it, call me lazy if you want). I said it again: "OK, McQueen, let's see if you can really do your own stunts." The line made me laugh out loud; I thought it was witty, maybe the spider did too? Anyway, I gave it a wink and pushed on — "Let's ride."

McQueen clung on, somehow holding tight to the underside of the ignition switch. I was impressed, especially as it was upside down. "Showing off, are we?" I ribbed McQueen playfully, but not for long — because once we got to the highway and I was gunning at a hundred, I noticed that

McQueen seemed to be clinging on with only three of its eight legs. The body and the other five legs were rocking hard in the wind.

I couldn't help myself; I pulled over to the hard shoulder and slowed all the way down to a stop. It was reckless behaviour, dangerous, because cars were screaming by just a foot or two away on our left. I didn't care; I felt obligated to the little bugger by now. I put my face close to where McQueen was hanging. "What do you want to do — give it up and jump off? Make a choice, McQueen."

Well, I kid you not, its little legs went into overtime, kicking out webbing and creating an anchor to set itself up nice and tight. The spider had moved position too — smart little thing. It went in front of a piece of plastic moulding that hung down around the handlebars, creating an additional layer of safety. It scrunched up into a tight ball as if saying: "OK, I'm set. Let's see what you've got. Come on, Punk, let's ride!" And that was it, we were off again.

I found myself talking to McQueen all the way through the outbound journey, just banter, and messing about: "What are we saying, McQueen, shall we overtake this one? Of course we will, let's have it." I was even singing songs to the little bugger. In fact, we got through the entire *Ziggy Stardust and the Spiders from Mars* album — I was having a fucking great time!

I landed at my destination and had to park up while I went and did my business. It might have taken me thirty minutes before I was on my way back to the bike. I swear, no lie and no joke, but as I got closer to McQueen the motorbike, I could feel myself getting anxious and excited to see if McQueen the spider would still be in the same place when I returned.

To my absolute delight, there he was, sitting pretty in the same place. "Snug as a bug in a rug, eh fella?" I was beaming. I fired up the Zing and we pelted it all the way back home. McQueen handled it without any problems, easy as pie. Arriving back, I parked up and thought about taking a photo of the spider. I didn't. I didn't really need a photo; the whole trip was etched inside me now forevermore.

It'd been a super-cool ride — rolling with my buddy McQueen. I'll never forget that wonderful moment in time — and isn't that the same for everybody, just enjoying moments in time?

Or maybe I'm made different from other folk…?

So, that's who I am, that's what it's all about. That little story is a metaphor for something… You can work out what it's a metaphor for once you've got through the book.

Dedicated with love:
Live Like Lila

1. START AT A MOMENT IN TIME

Russia, 2010: I'm in the DJ booth of Pacha Moscow, one of the best nightclubs on the planet. I grab the mic and prepare to say something momentous... I want to make an announcement.

But hold up a sec, spin back, I'll come back to this when I've filled in the story.

The resident DJ knows just how to work this room.

He knows just how to push this sound system, he knows just how to move this dance floor: this is "his house", these are "his people", and he knows exactly what he's doing as he slams the floor with the old school sound of my old mate Farley "Jackmaster" Funk and his classic track "Love Can't Turn Around".

It's a slick choice, designed to keep the room on its toes — and it works: it sounds like the best House music track ever made — which is debatable. Some House-heads believe that it's not only one of the first House anthems ever made but that it is also one of the best House tracks ever made.

Like I say, it's debatable, but right now, at this moment, me and 1,500 clubbers haven't got time to debate it. Right now, we have no choice but to raise our hands in the air and simultaneously sing along to Darryl Pandy's vocals, "Love Can't Turn A-r-o-u-n-d" — it's another ecstatic moment along a constant journey of moments in ecstasy.

I'm watching the crowd from the Pacha DJ booth, they're all wigging out and I'm feeling the music too, when out of nowhere I suddenly remember a bizarre meeting I once had with Darryl Pandy, it just pops into my head, and I get a mental picture of him hauling his massive frame out of a taxi.

It was years ago, maybe '97, in Marylebone, London. Darryl had arranged to come over to my office to talk to me about releasing one of his new projects.

I remember his big happy face, smiling and laughing, full of positivity and enthusiasm as he clambered out of the cab

15

and on to the street, where I was gallantly waiting to meet and greet him. His happiness didn't last very long. Less than fifteen seconds later, that same smiling face turned into a vision of contorted horror as he clapped his eyes on the steep staircase he'd have to climb in order to get to my office on the first floor — twenty gruelling steps stood between the street and the stereo.

Darryl Pandy had a lot of body to carry up that staircase, a real lot, and at first he even suggested that we have the meeting right there on the street. But as he wanted to play me a new track, it wasn't really a choice, and he quickly submitted to this reality: "Ok sweetie, you go on up, and I'll follow on behind."

I hurried up the stairs, taking the steps two at a time, which, to be honest, gave me a twinge of guilt once I'd got to the top. I made the mistake of looking back to see how he was getting along, only to see that Darryl was still at the bottom, and worse still he was looking back up at me seemingly in awe of my amazing act of agility — yes, I did feel a sense of shame about bolting up without even a pause for breath.

I hadn't realised Darryl was going to be so big or barely mobile either, but now I'd met him I knew I had to set about trying to find a chair that would be strong enough to hold him. None of my thoughts were negative, I was thinking of Mr Pandy and how I could make this meeting a little easier for him.

All I had for guests was a couple of standard plastic office chairs, or a very low-seated, soft-cushioned sofa that I would usually spread out on when listening to DJ mixes or tracks to consider for compilations — it was more like a chill-out and kick-back lounger than a sit up and take notes sofa.

So, thinking quickly, I re-positioned the two plastic chairs close to one another, not so it looked like I'd set up a "one chair, one cheek" combo on purpose, but rather so it appeared more like a natural accident upon which he could opt to share the load, or not; It gave him the option to spread over both chairs without making a big deal of it. I did it from a good place, I'd made the effort to think of how he might feel rather than being worried about my furniture.

Some minutes later, Darryl Pandy arrived, breathless and sweating, at the doorway to the office, leaning his big body against the solid door frame. He says with a smile, "Peeew, oh boy, I wasn't expecting gym class today," and with that line delivered, he lets out a long, loud, infectious, ice-breaking laugh. In an instant Darryl had us both laughing. He was cool beans, I liked him as if I'd known him for years, even though I'd never actually met him before.

I knew his partner in music pretty well though — Farley "Jackmaster" Funk. Farley was actually the artist listed on the classic "Love Can't Turn Around" anthem and he was also a legend in his own right as a DJ. I'd worked on a lot of shows featuring Farley on the decks: gigs at the Corn Exchange in Leeds, Maximus Nightclub in London, showcase events in Miami, and I'd even hung out with him in his hometown of Chicago.

But I didn't know Darryl personally. I'd seen the replayed TV clips of him from *Top of The Pops* taken from when the track was a hit in '86. He was a big guy even then, but one of those big guys that had energy to burn — he tore the room up on that memorable TV performance with his singing, shimmying and charisma. A big guy rolling around on the floor wasn't a normal *TOTP* performance back in '86, but now, more than ten years later in my London office, he was double the size, and sadly he was barely mobile.

The look of fear returned to Darryl's face when he saw the "sofa option" in my office, no doubt scared that he might not have the strength to get off again if he foolishly sat down there, so he opted for the plastic chairs. He hit them perfectly, one chair, one cheek, and they held the evenly-spread load without problem and without any drama: this wasn't his first rodeo, he knew how to saddle up.

I thought I'd handled it pretty well, better than well in fact — his being so big wasn't a problem for me, each to their

17

own, but it was a consideration that needed attention. So I'd done my best to make him feel "comfortable being comfortable" — know what I mean? We chatted, played some music, talked about the scene and where it was going, how he was a pioneer, yada-yada-yada, and about 45 minutes later we were done.

I was polite about his new track, but the harsh reality was that even though this guy probably had the first ever crossover hit in House music, there wasn't much we could do together, not on my side at least. But maybe for Darryl it was about keeping hope alive?

Even though we all know the game, you've got to take these meetings because sometimes they work out, and sometimes they don't. You never really know what can come of them — you've just got to suck it and see.

Darryl got himself up again, while I called a taxi to meet him downstairs: "Hey sweetie," he says, "ask them to come in about twenty minutes, please, I'm gonna have to take it real slow to get back down that staircase. It's pretty dangerous for me if I topple over, it's soooo steep!"

I told him I had to leave for another meeting — which was a dirty lie — but all he'd need to do was pull the general door closed at the bottom of the stairs as he left the building. I then reassured him, "By the time you're downstairs, your taxi will be arriving," and he was happy with the arrangements, "Oh that's great sweetie, I'll be just fine, you go on and take your next meeting, but call me right, don't forget" — he was still talking as I left the office ahead of him, not talking like "having a conversation", but more stuff like, "You get yourself along, call me, don't forget. OK sweetie, let's do something together", yada-yada-yada.

As I got to the door at the bottom of the staircase and stepped onto the street, the taxi was already pulling up outside, rather than coming over in twenty minutes as ordered. I let the driver know that he was too early and that the passenger would be a few more seconds. I looked back up the stairs to see Darryl had got himself sat on the top step

18

and was slowly bumping his way down one by one just like we used to do as small kids. An image of him falling forward, rolling down and flattening me in his wake ran through my mind's eye — death by rolling Pandy. It made me chuckle inside, and I think it would have made Darryl chuckle too. I called up to him, "Taxi is already here, Darryl, but you take your time; he'll wait for you."

As I got down to the pub on the corner of the block for my non-existent meeting I instinctively looked back towards my office to check on the progress of Darryl.

For fuck's sake: the shithouse taxi was already pulling off. "Fucking cabbie, can't you wait a few minutes, don't be a fucking wanker!" I shouted after the driver as he took the corner at speed; he was away — gone.

I went inside the pub and noticed Liam Gallagher from Oasis was with a couple of people sitting quietly in one corner drinking Guinness — it wasn't unusual to see one of the Gallaghers in this pub, given that their management offices were more or less located right underneath my offices. I didn't know Oasis, or the Gallagher brothers, not on a personal level, and I wasn't really a massive fan either. I mean, I really liked them, but I wasn't a follower. Bizarrely, I was strangely proud of them — it was probably because they were a council estate group, regular lads who had come from nothing to become the biggest band in Britain and threatened to become the biggest band in the world. I'd seen them years ago at The Duchess in Leeds when they were just getting started and now they were headlining festivals and dominating the newspapers — I had a massive respect for what they were doing: self-made, great songs and killer attitude.

I headed to the bar and — inspired by the sight of Gallagher's pint — ordered a Guinness of my own. So that was my meeting sorted. "I'm here, Guinness is here — let's sink a few for lunchtime. Happy days!" But I couldn't let what had just happened with Darryl and the taxi slide, I couldn't just let it go.

I rechecked the street and saw Mr. Pandy looking dejected and confused, I could almost hear him saying, "Why is my taxi nowhere to be seen? What's going on, he promised me it'd wait for me?" It was a sad sight to see, the big fella looking lost on the streets of London, a little heartbreaking really — I instantly knew I was in the wrong.

I wasn't naturally a bad-mannered kind of guy, and I recognised that I had to fix it. Darryl Pandy, the singer of "Love Can't Turn Around", a song that changed the course of House music history. He didn't deserve to be treated so shabbily: not by the taxi driver and definitely not by me!

It wasn't hard to put it right. I called the local taxi rank and explained the situation to the girl in the control office, who also wanted to make amends. We were in sync, doing what we could to rescue a genuine House music legend from his torrid ordeal in Marylebone.

Watching through the window, I could see the effort it took as Darryl squeezed himself into the cab, the vehicle taking the strain as he lifted his whole body weight to get himself in a position to leverage in his massive frame. "Love Can't Turn Around" sang in my head. "No love turning around in that cab, you big bugger," I said out loud to myself and let out a giggle. I wasn't being nasty, I laughed as I chugged down my pint. I figured Darryl would have laughed too. "One more Guinness please, love."

I half wanted to say hello to Liam, introduce myself and tell him about my Punk-Rock n Roll background. I thought we'd probably get along, or maybe not — I chalked it up as definitely maybe. Anyway, I didn't want to come over like a groupie, so I let it slide.

*

So, back to the Moscow DJ booth…

The resident DJ is on point, the music is on point and the sound system is fuck-off awesomely on point as we move in rhythm together like dead-brained morons, zombies in love, our faces a combination of idiot smiles and contorted grotesque expressions of happiness. Everybody looks

20

gorgeous — even the hideously ugly have taken on a previously well-hidden sheen of hot sexiness and raw animal attraction. Maybe it's the pills, maybe it's the cocaine, maybe it's the alcohol — maybe it's simply the music, but I feel sick.

On any other night like this I would be loving it, submerged in a cocktail of good times, good vibes, good drugs and good company. But right here, right now, I'm freaking out.

I want to go to the toilet for a quick nose-up, a couple more lines of good coke to shake my head up a notch, but I can't bring myself to go. I can't move from where I am; I can only dance on the spot and grin like a freak, gurning manically while grinding my teeth.

Instead, I managed to duck down in the DJ booth, my head almost stuck inside one of the tech cupboards underneath the decks.

I get about it, keying up a couple of good ones just as the resident DJ looks down at me. I want a cool vibe with him so I offer up the key, well loaded with snow white, along with a big "Aciiiiid" happy smile. "Fancy a sniff, fella?" I ask, assuming it was a rhetorical question — but his reaction catches me by surprise as he shakes his head, indicating a firm "No". He gives me a kind of artificial smile and turns his attention back to the decks as he gets busy setting up his next great mix, and I turn my attention back to the key as I get busy setting up my next great sniff.

This sniff refusal doesn't sit right with me. As far as I'm concerned — and I am, way too concerned, as you'll soon find out — he's been acting like a right prick, smiling like a smug-arsed cunt, usually while executing another perfect mix. And then he turns his nose up at a bit of nose-up? I mean who the fuck does that?

"That's because he knows — you daft prick!"

That's the sound of an internal voice — it's the mocking one that I call "Jam". It kicks in and starts pointing out to me that the resident DJ has been dropping great track after great track, simply incredible music, mixed with absolute precision,

21

"He's fucking amazing, no question about it, fucking amazing," Jam needles me, goads me, a constant barrage jabbing at me, seeking to unnerve me. What a little cunt Jam can be.

"Shut the fuck up!" I retaliate back at myself, but not internally. No, the words spewed out of my mouth with a tone of aggression, closer to an unhinged shout. "SHUT THE FUCK UP!"

The resident DJ looks at me, not sure of what he's just heard — that makes two of us to be honest — so I give him two thumbs up and a fresh grinning manic smile, as if I'd actually said something like, "That mix was sick, shut the fuck up, bruv."

I now feel even more sick.

By this point, you might ask, "Why are you feeling sick?" and "Why are you so down on the resident DJ, complimenting and killing him at the same time?"

Well, OK, here's the thing…

When this DJ finishes his set, that's when my own set begins — great, right? Well, I'll let you in on a little secret, the reason I feel sick is pretty simple — it's because tonight is my first ever live performance as a solo House DJ anywhere in the world.

How have I found myself in this position, where I'm booked as the Guest Star DJ despite never actually spinning a live solo DJ set before? That's a story in itself, we'll get to those details — but for now, just take my word for it.

Here I am, very much feeling like the victim. The victim of who and what I don't know and neither do I care, it just makes me feel better to blame something. Whereas in reality, being truthful, the "blagger's blag" has just come home to bite me on the arse.

Everybody here, except the suspicious and probably resentful resident DJ, thinks I'm an international touring DJ playing the hottest clubs worldwide every weekend, which I do, kind of — they think tonight is just another night in another super-club for me, which in essence, it kinda is.

22

So far, everyone is blissfully unaware that this is my first time playing out alone. But what they don't know is that the pressure on me is even more intense because it's not just any DJ set... I'm the headliner!

On top of that, I'm billed as "live and direct from Ibiza", which only adds to the sense of excitement in the capacity room, given that Ibiza is the universal capital of clubbing and any DJ coming from Ibiza is rightly expected to be shit-hot — rather than just shit.

The only reason I have this gig is that I've been up to my usual tricks for the last year or so, writing checks with my mouth that my actual DJ skills, most likely, can't cash.

The other reality I have to consider is that none of my personal problems matter one bit to the people in the club — they're all having a party in good faith that the DJ from Ibiza is gonna blow the roof off. Everybody wants to meet me. I must have shaken hands with just about everyone in the club over the past three hours since I arrived, glad-handing the owners, hugging strangers, drinking shots of vodka, toasting the night with champagne, slugging ice-cold beers and sniffing coke.

I'm living the life of the international superstar DJ, and everything should be cool — and it would be cool if only the resident DJ didn't seem to be so fucking suspicious, causing me to doubt myself.

"He knows, that you know he knows, that he knows — you're fucked mate!" taunts the inner voice of Jam, who — in my head — is voiced tonight by Steve Coogan's student-hating, pissed-tosspot, gloom-merchant, Paul Calf.

But thankfully, I also have another internal voice along for the ride tonight!

Step forward, and thank you, "Bravado".

"He's a fucking twat, this resident — there's always a fucking twat in the house; he's a fucking resentful resident DJ twat, fuck him!"

Maybe it's because Bravado's voice sounds like the mental London comic actor Paul Kaye, tonight, but it's having the desired effect on my consciousness.

"He's a resident DJ playing local clubs night after night — he isn't travelling the world living the life: he's stuck in one place, playing music for local money. He's just getting by while you're out and about, living wild, living the life, getting paid. Fuck that fucking cunting jealous wanking resident DJ twat!"

It's a good effort from Bravado, a really good effort — but in all honesty, what with the combination of everything I've taken tonight, (coke, vodka, champagne and beer, not forgetting the cheeky smarties), I think I might be about to throw up, or shit my pants, or both, right here in the DJ booth.

I find my feet and decide that the best thing to do is to make my way to the club's toilets — for a moment of sanctuary, if nothing else. I fumble my way through the room, hands patting me on the back, little one-liners expressing anticipation of the set they've come to hear by the Ibiza DJ.

Once inside, I marvel at the fact that these toilets are on another scale, so good that I'm double-glad that I made the trip. They're beautifully maintained and super-clean with expensive tile work, cool dark ambient lighting and doors that fill the entire frame of the cubicle for absolute privacy. Bliss.

Then there's the bonus feature — all of the stalls in these toilets have perfectly placed ledges, the height of each ledge being so perfect, so spot on, that I can only assume that they have been specifically designed for the act of chopping and snorting coke, a degree of comfort that is infinitely better than the usual alternatives. But they're also cunningly masquerading as a shelf to house various sprays, hand creams and tissues.

I take the opportunity to chop a line out onto the ledge inside my private cubicle, chortling and talking to myself as I get on with getting on it, "It'd be rude not to, kid, don't mind if I do, sir."

24

At the same time, I'm mentally saluting the owners of the club who have made a design so good that there's no need for me to get down on my knees and snort up off the toilet seat — what a classy joint. "The rich and famous of Moscow are out in force, and all their needs are pre-thought of and catered for," I think to myself as I go in for another snort. Bravado chips in: "You're one of them tonight, fella — you're the top shelf pick, mate, you're the star of the show." Good work, Bravado!

I get back to the DJ booth, still feeling sick, but... yes, feeling better.

It's an OK sickness now, a more natural nervous sensation of sickness, a heady mix of excitement, tension and anticipation. It's a challenge to see if I can pull it off, victory from the ashes of defeat — I don't mind that kind of sickness.

It's too late to stop the train anyway, there's no turning back, and I resign myself to acceptance. Feeling more in the zone, I decided I must have taken the resident DJ all wrong. In fact, I don't think he's a cunt anymore, especially as he drops the final track of his session, "Follow Me" by Aly-us — it's another classic and a brilliant final choice to close his set with, a killer old school gem.

On the other hand, I'm not 100% sure if he's just playing the cunt after all. "Follow Me" — is that a challenge?

"He's a cunting bellend fucking wanker!" Bravado reminds me casually with a whisper.

I can feel the shivers threatening to set in as the time to spin is upon me. My nerves are tweaked, I feel like jelly but also stiff, and my hands are tingling.

I wonder if I'm about to have a heart attack, or maybe faint at least.

"Love this fucking tune, man," I call out to the resident DJ over the too-high volume of the monitor speakers in the DJ booth. It's the kind of thing DJs say to one another whenever crossing over on the decks, but he doesn't hit me back; there's no acknowledgement of what I've said. He just looks at me without reaction: just a blank look.

The problem is, the resident can't hear a word I just said, but it's not because of the monitors — it's because all that comes out of my mouth is a croaking wheeze, like the sound a man makes when he's trying to tell someone he's choking to death, just a croaking, wheezing, wordless set of noises.

The combination of drugs and nerves have conspired to parch my throat of all liquidity — it's drier than the dunes of the Moroccan Sahara, and I know how dry the Moroccan Sahara dunes are, because I've been there and experienced them.

I also know the sound a man makes when he's trying to tell somebody he's about to choke to death — because I've heard it for real, many years earlier when I was living in the Bethnal Green area of East London, sometime around 1995 when Dutch Hal, an old mate, was visiting me from Holland for a few days.

*

Dutch Hal stood just over six-foot-six tall and was well cut on top of it. Dressed head to toe in leather, he cut an imposing figure. The fact that he rode a big loud Harley motorbike often gave regular folk the impression that he was something that he wasn't, a proper rider for life. He looked the part, the movie stereotype version at least, with his long lank black locks and an intense, dark-ringed, ice-cold, blue-eyed stare, so it was easy to see how people got it wrong.

In reality, Hal wasn't a biker, not a real biker — he was like my old pals Cyrus, Skum, Punk Elvis and Smelly. All five of them loved big bikes, and they all had a cool style about them, but none were actual bonafide riders.

Hal was a Punk-Rock'n'Roller, a fella who loved loud music and loud wheels. He was a great guy, a gentleman, and would do anything for his friends.

I'd met Dutch Hal some years earlier, sometime in 1982, when I was 18 years old and my band was on its first ever overseas tour. The first date of that tour was in a small pub in a little town called Schiedam — none of us had ever heard of Schiedam, never mind the small pub we were booked to play in, but as fate would have it, that small pub also happened to be Hal's local. I was more than happy to be there on tour, living the dream and enjoying the moments, but the rest of our touring crew seemed a little less enthusiastic. It was time to give the boys a pep talk.

"Everybody starts somewhere," I begin as I turn away from the jukebox and towards the rest of the band. "The Rolling Stones started in a boring pub somewhere in a boring London suburb, but look at us! Fuck me, we're in Holland, we're on fucking tour, and we're in a fucking pub too, but our pub's a Punk-Rock'n'Roll pub — and it's got a killer fucking jukebox."

I raised my beer bottle as the jukebox began to strike out the unmistakable opening riff of "Sonic Reducer" by The Dead Boys, my inspirational first selection. If any record is a game-changer, then this is it — it always has been and always will be. I still remember the first time I heard it in the local record shop; track one, side one — boom! I took it home and it changed my life.

And right here, right now, it's changing the atmosphere in this small Schiedam pub. Something positive was needed to drag the band out of their collective sulk.

"Lets fucking 'ave it!" I challenged them. And 'ave it we did!

The action started with the soundcheck, which we played in front of a load of local punks and oddballs. We rocked through classics like "Pills/Too Much Junkie Business", "Gloria", "Louie Louie" and loads more. We were proper killer in that afternoon soundcheck. The locals who hung around to watch were so impressed that they managed to convince every Punk-Rock'n'Roller in town to come on down for the real gig later that night, they banged the drum for us, "You've gotta check out the English band playing down the pub tonight."

That night the place was packed, so full that it felt like it was transformed into a *real* venue — I'd decided hours earlier that I would treat the show as if we were playing in

27

one of the Meccas of Punk-Rock'n'Roll: CBGBs in NYC, the old Marquee Club in London, or even The F Club in Leeds.

That first gig, in that little town, in that small pub, was magical! The room rocked, and we played for over two hours. I remember it like it was yesterday. There were no negative nerves that night, just an up and at 'em sense of raw emotion and bravado! I performed like the bastard son of Iggy Pop while also rocking out like the lost brother of Johnny Thunders on the guitar too — I was "Iggy Thunders". I even thought of changing my name, "Here comes Iggy Thunders," or maybe "Johnny Pop". In any case it was an incredible gig.

Hal was one of the locals we had met during the afternoon. Right away, he got the band because we played his kind of music, and before the night was over he had offered up his house for the after-party.

I didn't need to ask twice; this was one of the main reasons I had wanted to start a band in the first place. The idea of travelling to different cities and different countries, playing music, meeting new people and having unknown adventures — well, that was the flame.

The Dutch guys all seemed tall, but there was a giant of a man standing somewhere near seven feet and built like a brick shit-house who I found out was called "Long Johnny".

Like most of us there, Long Johnny was also a punk and challenged me to a drinking competition after the gig — I could hardly refuse, even if I'd wanted to, as it was more like a demand than a request!

The competition seemed to have no rules other than Long Johnny had to win. The only problem with that was that I could have been an Olympic Gold Medal Drinker. The sight of ten glasses of beer and ten whisky chasers set up on the bar for us to race through held no panic for me. In reality, the ten beers amounted to maybe three pints in a Leeds pub, and the ten shots were equal to about a quarter bottle of Johnny Walker Red.

28

I could have easily beaten him, but sometimes you have to be smarter than that. Taking candy from kids is easy, but when that kid is a giant like Long Johnny — who *needs* to be the alpha — there are other ways to play it. I was in Long Johnny's town, on his turf, and he was in front of his crew, so I let him believe he had won. I drank glass for glass, mindful to empty and put my glass down last. I knew, and he knew, that I was holding back.

Winning in his backyard made Long Johnny so happy that he invited me to break a wooden chair over his back to celebrate. I guess it was like a consolation prize for me, the vainglorious loser. It was obvious that this wasn't the first time he'd invited "the chair" — this was his party piece.

From that moment on, Hal and I were thick as thieves, and Long Johnny too — in fact, it was only a few weeks after first meeting Hal that I actually moved into his Schiedam apartment, then some years later he came to stay at my place in Leeds for a while too. In between times we always got together when I was touring in Holland, and eventually, when I moved to London, he came to visit me in the capital as well.

So, we're in London — which for Hal was like New York City for me, a place for dramas and dreams — sat in a local curry house in Bethnal Green's Brick Lane at 10.30pm. Hal was dressed head to toe in leathers with cut-off denim, all six and a half feet of him, looking for all the world like a lean, mean fighting machine.

We were tucking into our food as I recounted a tale about a trip I'd made across Europe years earlier. I was in full flow, enjoying Hal's audience, but then, all of a sudden, I noticed that he's stopped laughing, stopped acknowledging the comments, and stopped participating as an audience full stop. All that's coming back from him is a series of quacks, croaks and wheezes like the air is being sucked out of him.

He sits across from me, unable to breathe, unable to communicate, choking to death in front of my eyes. I could hear the sounds he was making but I couldn't register the reality of what they were warning.

Now usually I'm very reliable in a crisis, but on this occasion, I was too bladdered and blindly caught up in retelling the tales of our shared history. But basically, Hal is choking to death, and I'm not reacting to it — he was a few seconds from actually meeting his maker.

However, as unfortunate as Hal is to have me with him, he's infinitely more fortunate that in the same restaurant, right at that very same moment, there happened to be one of London's most well-known *naughty faces* — a proper underground player out with his wife for a quiet bit of supper.

I hadn't clocked him earlier, but he's one of the main players of an infamous London-Irish family. I look up and "Mr Big" comes striding over towards the table, moving quickly but unrushed, making a bee-line towards us — now I've realised who it is I immediately brace myself for a hard belt across the head. After all, the only reason I can think of for his approach is to tell us to stop making a racket and to give us both a poke for annoying him.

My worst fears seem to come true when he grabs Hal up from his chair by the scruff of his neck. I'm expecting blood and a monologue, something like, "Stop talking your filth in front of everyone, we don't wanna hear it…"

But, to my complete amazement, this well-known hard man only goes and uses a textbook Heimlich manoeuvre on my mate Hal.

Mr Big pulls it off perfectly, forcing Hal to gob up a ball of poppadom and naan bread. In an instant, he's back, normal and standing upright. Hal glugs down a whole pint of beer in one gigantic swallow. Putting the glass down, he pauses for a second and then turns to his good samaritan: "Thank you, I thought I was going to die!"

He offers his hand to Mr Big, who ignores it and looks up at Hal's black-ringed, ice-cold blue eyes: "I'll tell you what son, if you and him don't bottle your noise, I'll be back over,

30

and I'll choke you to death myself. Now think on, you pair of mugs. I'll not warn you again."

And with that, Mr Big turns to the waiter: "Their dinner's on me, give 'em whatever they want."

*

It's a cool story, but what's the point? Well: I genuinely know the sounds a man makes when choking to death, it's the same sounds that I'm making in the DJ booth of Pacha Moscow in 2010 as the resident DJ looks blankly at me.

Of course I'm not physically choking but the effect is the same, as the resident DJ can't understand the noise I'm making because it's just a series of croaks, wheezes and quacks.

The resident DJ's last track, "Follow Me", is coming towards the last minute outro — and when it ends, my headline peak-hour set will begin. Just to labour the point, we are in one of the world's best clubs, more than that, this venue represents one of the most famous brands in global House music and club culture — I have to find a way to deliver.

It feels a long way from Schiedam — and it's not as if I can just whip out "Sonic Reducer" to get me out of this jam. I'm bricking it, feeling very alone in a crowd of 1,500 high-rolling Muscovites — they're the richest of the rich, the coolest of the cool, people who have paid small fortunes to occupy the VIP tables — and they expect to be impressed.

So, it's just me and the voices in my head, and I'm feeling the pressure — even more so because the DJ booth is located in the middle of the room, meaning I'm fully exposed for everybody to see what the DJ actually does.

The image of Hal's choking face is flashing through my mind's eye, and the sound of his croaking, wheezing and choking is ringing in my ears as the twin voices in my head continue to battle with each other.

Bravado finally loses patience and shouts at me: "Get a fucking grip, you put us in this position, now fucking handle it. You're a fucking DJ, so just DJ. You've got great music, so

31

just play it. You've got big balls, so just wave them about. Think about the real shit you've faced in your life, you always find a way through it — just keep calm, do the simple things well and enjoy the moment, come on!!!"

Bravado is putting a proper shift in, his voice is pure manic, but there's still room for doubt to creep in too, as I ask myself: "Shouldn't you just come clean? Can you ball your way through and blag it? I mean, if the music isn't played right, the dance floor is gonna know, the resident DJ will know, the tech guy and the club manager will know, the owner will know — they're all gonna know. Maybe you should come clean?"

The club tech guy comes to the booth to make sure I'm all set to go — I'm not, but here we are. I'm staring down the barrel of a gun.

Using the technique of "advanced universal clubbers' sign language", I point, nod and wink, to let him know, despite me not speaking a word of Russian, and him not speaking a word of English, that I need to use a microphone for my set.

I start necking down as much water as possible, trying to soak my throat, a last-ditch attempt to clear out the sand dunes and limber up my vocal cords.

I test the mic: "Wow-wow... wow-wow... wow-wow." The sound comes out nice and loud through the system helped by me adding a massive echo effect to it. "All right, all right — OK, OK, OK" — syllables are bouncing all over the room, so much so that I think I sound like Alan Vega from Suicide. To my surprise everybody is cheering loudly and getting set to lose the plot with "the superstar DJ from Ibiza". The sound of my voice over the mic is like a dog-whistle for the room to get themselves set.

I fade Aly-us out and hold the resident DJ's hand up in the air, like a boxer giving a triumphant salute of respect to an opponent, letting him take his rightfully deserved applause.

But now, the moment in time has finally arrived...

I want to make an announcement...

2. BACK TO THE START

I was born in the upstairs bedroom of a back-to-back inner city terraced house in the capital of the north on November 4th, 1963. My birthday fell on what was known back then as Mischievous Night: "Ladies and gentlemen, welcome to Leeds, Leeds, Leeds."

We were the working class of a big industrial city at a time when the city, the country and the world beyond were experiencing a period of change. A change from old-fashioned grounded values to a new modernised desire to "break down the status quo of normal expectations".

Realistic expectations would be damned — we wanted more, more, more.

These cultural changes in the fabric of our day-to-day realities of life all happened in a relatively short period, just fifteen years!

What were these changes?

Well, the easiest way to put it would be to say that there was a shift in our everyday normalities; the way we thought, the clothes we wore, the way we played and the attitude we had. Old values were replaced with new ones, even if some of the old influenced much of the new. Change was marching on — it was a lot to soak up for everybody.

Bob Dylan warned of it in 1964 when he sang to the world: "So you'd better start swimming, or you'll sink like a stone, 'cause the times they are a-changin'."

The credo that our grandparents lived by was kind of like, "I'll get what I'm supposed to get and I'll not bother about the things I haven't." It was a way of thinking that had stood them in good stead, stable enough to have gotten them through tough times, and even the war years. But by the '60s, that kind of stoic wellbeing was laid to rest, abandoned by our parents and replaced by a more aggressive mindset, one based on desire: "I want more and I want it now!" There was an insatiable craving in the air "for everything".

33

In fact Iggy Pop was just as poignant as Bob Dylan when he summed things up in 1979 on his song "I Need More" as he demanded, "I need more than the ordinary grind, the more I think, the more I need, my life is going alright until now, even so, it's not enough for me, and I need more — more future, more culture."

As for me, I was too young to really appreciate the shifting sands around me, even though I was living in the eye of the storm — as all my generation were. I only recognised what had happened on a societal level, on reflection, some years later. All I can say for certain is that I was drawn towards music from the very start.

My earliest memories are all framed around something related to music, be it a song, a dance, an image of an artist, whatever. I embraced it and recognised that "life with music" was more colourful and more fun, it was a licence to thrill, a platform to be heard — I was "all in on music" from the get-go.

The formative years — the kid and adolescent ones — direct how a person will navigate their future lives.

Without coming over all pseudo-psychiatrist or holier than thou, the fact is that we are all influenced by the immediate events and realities that happen around us, be they near or far, happening in the first person, or as a third party voyeur — we soak up everything.

An old saying goes "Give me the boy at seven and I'll give you the man at fourteen"; It's a play on Aristotle: "Give me the boy at seven and I'll give you (the foundations of) the man", when people quote Aristotle they don't always include "the foundations of" and they don't home in on "age fourteen" either, but my mam did, and therefore, so do I. "Stuff" is essential during those seeding years, stuff like school, family, friends, trends, music, culture, curiosity and more, more, more — we have to make sure that we feed the right stuff to those we are looking out for, and as far as possible feed the right stuff to ourselves as well. My parents spoon-fed music to me and I gorged myself on it.

34

We were a decent-sized family: mum, dad, four kids, a dog, a cat, and sometimes even a budgie or a hamster. The house was always noisy with people making a racket, but mostly, it was always noisy with the sound of music.

My dad's job was the coolest thing in the world, so it seemed to my young eyes. He was an entertainer, a club and cabaret act, performing live shows to earn a living. He was good at what he did and was always in demand. He seemed so hip that I thought every kid in school must have wanted my dad to be their dad.

Other kids' dads went to work at places like the Barnbow factory at 8am in the morning, they'd come home again around tea-time at 6pm, all sporting nicely cut hair and wearing workman's overalls.

That's not to put that reality down, but my dad went to work at 7pm as the night started to come around, not returning until the early hours, or even the next day. His job was singing songs to the other kids' dads in one part of the country or another — his hair was long "like a popstar" and his clothes included satin type material shirts, tight pants and winkle-picker boots. He looked the dog's bollocks as he went on his way every evening; out the door, down the ginnel to his car, and off he'd drive to the next show — and even though it was my dad, I was as starstruck as I believed the other kids must've been.

He'd play a different place every night, travel up and down, far and wide, always on the road — not tied to a conveyor belt, a broom or a desk. He performed wherever the money was, be it the Working Men's Social Clubs or at plush cabaret venues, sometimes even in proper big theatres, as well as the annual summer season at a caravan campsite in Hopton, Great Yarmouth, the Norfolk Broads.

We moved to Norfolk each summer to live in a big caravan for a few months — we were even enrolled in the local village summer school. We loved it down there; the caravan, the holiday campsite, the cliffs, the beach and the sea, even the school was great fun with no real lessons. We just seemed to play out all day on the big fields with all the other kids — some, like us, were there for the summer "from somewhere else", and others were from the local area. It was like something in a book, idyllic — the sun always shone in Hopton.

Dad was so good that he was also booked to go and perform abroad in countries like Sweden, Malta and Spain. These foreign bookings were fixed contracts, usually for weeks or even months at a time. The best bit about those abroad bookings was that when my dad went abroad, we would visit him abroad too.

These seemingly far-off places — words on a map to most people down our way — were ours to see with our own eyes as Mum and Dad would find a way to combine his working commitments so that they'd cross over into a family holiday for us all.

Between the years 1970 and 1975 we'd jet out of the UK to wherever Dad was booked to perform. Keep in mind that flying abroad for holidays wasn't a casual whim back in the '70s. It was a taste of the high life, the good life.

Even when we travelled to Marbella in Spain by coach and ferry instead of flying, we still all loved it — we lived to be on the road and on our way "to somewhere".

The family plan was that one day we would all move away to live in the sunshine of Spain together, a dream that I bought into lock, stock and barrel. I wanted it, believed in it and trusted the game-plan.

Dad put the hours in, probably even more hours than the dads that worked regular jobs; he would play all night at his gigs and then practise all day at home, learning song after song, everything from the current hit parade of the day, through to renditions of old boppers from the '50s, or classics of the '60s. But mostly he would be belting out impressions of Jerry Lee Lewis on the piano, or singing like Elvis Presley while playing on his guitar. He worked hard at his craft, it wasn't just bright lights, it was also hard work perfecting his talent with practice practice practice — the essential part that an audience never sees, or even imagines is needed.

It was a good "lesson by example" — it showed me that unless you were a natural, or a genius, then flair and desire were only part of the recipe. Hard work was required to be good at whatever you were gonna do.

He was my hero. I'd hang around the piano with him at every chance I got, watching him recreate the music of Elvis and Jerry Lee Lewis, the two titans of Rock'n'Roll, right in front of my eyes, near perfect replicas of both talents. The Killer, Jerry Lee, and The King, Elvis Presley; heroes who have been in my life for as long as I can ever remember, and they still are today: some things you carry with you for good.

Out of all the other artists he would replicate, one that touched me right away was a "cowboy" called Hank Williams. I didn't understand why I could feel anything from a Country music artist like Hank, especially given that I was on the Whinmoor in industrial Leeds and he was singing songs about "Lost Highways" and "Lost Love" from somewhere in Nashville — but I did. His voice, the delivery, the vibe of the music — it all just hit me. As for his words, well, I sensed that he was singing songs that had depth and emotion to them, but in all honesty, as a young 'un, I couldn't claim the words made a mark. It wasn't until years later, once I'd experienced some life of my own, once I'd had a few ups and downs, that I could put Hank's personal story alongside his music and storytelling — then I'd transpose his words and reflect them on to my own experiences. That's when I began to understand why I got him. High times and heartbreak have no borders on a map, be it Leeds, Nashville or other: "The thorn on the beautiful White Rose of Yorkshire can cause you some pain if you don't handle it with care, and likewise, the gorgeous Purple Iris of Tennessee will give you a toxic rash if you don't handle it right." Philisophical Wisdom (?) from Stevie - Date Unknown.

I'd recommend anybody to invest some time in discovering Hank Williams — in fact I'd go so far as to say that Hank was the original Punk. His story is fascinating; born dirt poor, he learnt how to pick the guitar from his equally poor black neighbours, they also taught him something of the blues, the real blues. At the same time he was picking up on original American Folk. When these two elements fused together it gave him a distinctive swing when he played himself-written uptempo tunes — and at the same time it created a real sense of tangible emotion on the downbeat storytelling ballads.

He was dominated by his mother, who acted as his manager, tour manager and bouncer — at 14 years old, she had him playing night after night in any roadhouse willing to let her pass a bucket around for tips. He was so good that before long he was in demand, touring constantly on the road. But he was almost crippled in pain due to a badly diagnosed crooked spine; in fact he had a form of spina bifida, and that was his gateway to junk. On prescription painkillers, he would shoot the pain away with morphine and then come showtime he would shoot up a dose of amphetamine to give him the energy to get through the gig. Towards the end he had his own personal doctor on the road with him, although this doctor wasn't a doctor, he was a convict that had won a set of doctor's credentials in a jailhouse game of cards. But that was all he needed to write prescriptions for uppers and downers while on tour, lots of them, on top of the ferocious drinking. He was also a snappy dresser on stage in his made to measure Nudie Suits. He was rocking those threads long before Hendrix, The Doors, ZZ Top or The Stones — with his nasal vocal and his amazing songs, Hank Williams was the shit, pal.

But it all came to an end on New Year's Day, 1953, when he was taken badly while travelling in the backseat of a Cadillac en route to a show. His driver got him into a hotel in Knoxville where he died from a heart attack, induced by too much alcohol and outrageous levels of drug abuse: "Toxic in

Tennessee, remember the Purple Iris." He was 29 when he passed, the original "real wild-one" — at one stage he'd even been banned from the Grand Ole Opry itself because of the off-kilter way he ran his life. He also lost the twin loves of his life, his mother and his wife — who both equally drove him crazy, pulling at him constantly, often without any regard for the effect they were having on him and his mental state.

Hank actually married his wife multiple times in a row at the very same venue that banned him. Over one long day they repeated the ceremony over and over again so that the fans could line up in the street and file in to attend a version of the ceremony in shift rotation — such was the public's demand to see the event for themselves.

In the short time he was with us, he wrote countless classic songs that have stood the test of time. He was, in my humble opinion, the first Punk-Rock'n'Roller.

*

Going through school was never a problem. As young kids, we lived on the new Whinmoor housing estate; it was a shift away from the back-to-back, cobbled, inner-city, terraced streets of the Cardigans in Kirkstall. These new estates had massive open playing fields, giant black and white patterned footpaths, high-rise tower blocks of flats, maisonettes, rows of big family houses with front and back doors and gardens! It was the government's vision of a modern future in Britain. The Council Estate was born, and we were among the first of the new nuclear families to move in.

I couldn't claim to be academic as a lad at John Smeaton Comprehensive Middle and High School. School was more like a place where all my mates were; we focused more of our attention on games of football in the playground at break time than on caring much about class lessons. But with that said, I liked the lessons that included debate, and subjects like history, religion and social science.

I got on well enough with the teachers, was mates with the toughest kids and was also friends with the not-as-tough

39

kids — I played football for the school team, yada yada yada… but my preferred thing to do? Hang out with the girls.

I'd sing songs to them, act the fool to make them laugh, flirt with them, all of them; even as a real youngster in junior school, I loved the buzz of being around girls. It was the same through middle school; it continued into high school and stayed with me when I left school too.

I liked girls, and as I got older, I learned to love girls. Iggy Pop was on point, as usual, when he proclaimed, "I love girls, they're all over this world" — I thought the same, I got it, I love girls.

Now, here's a strange thing. Here I was in 1979 in Leeds, just finished out of school, a copy of the *New Values* LP already in my fan collection of Iggy albums. It would have been madness to think that years later I would live across the park from Mr Pop himself in the East Village of Manhattan, NYC.

But truth is often stranger than fiction.

By 1999, some twenty years after leaving school, I lived in New York City, on Ave A & 10th Street, feeling good perched up in a five-storey walk-up railroad-style one-bedroom flat with rooftop access.

At the same time, Iggy Pop was living on Ave B & 10th Street, only he was in the penthouse with elevator access and a private rooftop garden… We were neighbours!

But the story gets stranger, because by the turn of the millennium, the year 2000, I would be fucking, (from time to time), the same girl that "The Ig" was fucking (from time to time) too — Rita, the girl that loved a Margarita.

Iggy didn't know that Rita was "giving favour" to both of us at the same time — and even if he did know, he probably wouldn't have cared anyway, because Rita was basically his rebound girl after splitting with his "Avenue B" wife. She was also my rebound girl too, after splitting with the wonderful Molly from Burnley, a great girl who had moved to NYC with me — more on her coming later. I have to confess and admit, when I found out that we were both

40

sleeping with Rita it was a guilty pleasure of mine, I thought it funny, a cool beans twist of fate — you could say that we were all in a weird, "non-Iggy participating" ménage-à-trois kind of thing, Iggy, me and Rita too. I asked myself, "How the fuck has this happened? You, a nobody from Leeds, here in NYC and tapping the same girl as your teenage hero Iggy." The voice of Bravado couldn't let it slide: "Good work, fella, that's very good work — if they could see you now, kid."

This is how it came about. I bumped into Rita one day at a bar and we hit it off and before long we started casually fucking. Nothing serious, nothing more than that. I was seeing other people and she was seeing other people — it was cool, we weren't looking for a relationship. Then one time "it" came up:

Her: "Who else are you seeing?"

Me: "Well, who else are you seeing?"

And then she casually mentions: "Well, there's a guy I sometimes see who lives right here in the neighbourhood, but I've not been seeing him too much recently because he's been out of town touring with his Iggy Pop band."

"Whaaat!" (Fuck me — I nearly choked on my beer.) "*The* Iggy Pop?"

She looked genuinely surprised: "What do you mean, *the* Iggy Pop? Have you heard of him?"

It's not a joke on her part. She's a New York-Latino girl; she dances to Salsa and sings along to songs like, ironically, "Tu Son Rita" by Elvis Crespo. She doesn't even really know who Iggy is as an artist, and hasn't got a clue about "Punk" or "Rock n Roll" either.

"Do you know him?" Rita asks in stunned disbelief that her fuck-buddy, Iggy, is a hero of some kind to her other fuck-buddy, me.

"Rita, I spent most of my youth listening to his records — I actually met him once back home in Leeds. I've got T-shirts that I wear with his name on, one of them is even designed with his naked body on it!"

41

We eyeballed each other, maybe both in shock for our own reasons, because just like that — out of left field — we realised that we'd been in a non-participating "Iggy, Rita and Me" ménage à trois.

Funny to think, if she'd bothered to climb the stairs up to my apartment just once out of the few times I'd actually invited her up, she would have seen at least ten Iggy Pop records in the small collection of old vinyl albums I had, albums that have moved with me from home to home every step of the way — from when I first bought many of them (while still living at Mum's) through to when I first left home at age 16/17 — and then, no matter what city or country I have lived in, this bunch of vinyl has been with me all the way back to the period between 1976-1979.

It's actually true, what I told Rita, I did meet Iggy at The Warehouse Club in Leeds in 1981 after seeing him play at Leeds Uni earlier that night. I was a massive fan, and he was amazing live as usual — the greatest frontman ever, an electric ball of energy with great vocals and a great connection to the crowd, who adored him. I was right on the front row; Iggy wore tight jeans, a white cabaret-style shirt, and a soft-sparkling waistcoat — not sparkling in a Vegas way, but sparkling in a super-cool Punk-Rock'n'Roll way.

Before long, he was stripped down to his normal stage outfit of just jeans, his scrawny yet muscular body in full view for all as he strutted his stuff all over the stage.

During the rendition of his classic song "The Passenger" he came to the foot of the stage, and we all reached out for him; I held him in a star–fan-friendly hug and started singing the song's chorus down the microphone.

"La la la la la-la-la-la, la la la la la la la la" — repeat, repeat, repeat — I'm not sure if I can claim that I sang a duet with Iggy, but maybe it counts?

After the Iggy concert, I headed down to The Warehouse, the best club in town, where another band was playing.

I hadn't heard of the band before, but I could feel a buzz going around the room before they took to the stage. People said they were a local Leeds band that would be massive nationwide soon enough. The band were called The Sisters of Mercy, and rumour was that they were going to do a cover version of The Stooges' classic song "1969". I was glad I'd made the trek down after the Iggy Pop show, there was a great vibe in the air.

The Sisters of Mercy came on and were absolutely brilliant; they were different, enigmatic, dramatic, raw and totally hypnotic. Everybody there who witnessed them was blown away. We didn't realise it, right then and there at the time, but this show was to become an iconic moment in the Leeds music scene, talked about for decades to come, one of those "I was there" moments, where many people claim they were there, but in fact they never were.

Well, I was there, and so was Iggy Pop.

Iggy and his crew had cleaned up after their own Leeds Uni gig, then taken the short drive down to The Warehouse in their tour bus. The promoter of the show, an iconic promoter named John F Keenan, had rush-printed some invites to The Warehouse and had hopped up to the Uni to last-minute flyer the crowd. He went backstage and met Iggy and invited him down to see The Sisters at The Warehouse.

The Sisters of Mercy rocked through their set, I loved them right away, and most people there felt the same. Then, during their last song, I looked to the right of me, and to my utter surprise, there was Iggy standing right next to me and checking out the band.

As the Sisters finished their set we both clapped and whistled, showing our appreciation. Then I said to Iggy: "How did you like them?" not quite believing I had the nerve to actually ask him a question.

"They're just great," he said in his rich, baritone voice, beaming that big *Lust For Life* album cover smile; I guess it must be his real smile.

"I was at your gig earlier at the Uni," I offered.

Iggy took a step back to look me over: "Yeah, that's it, you're the guy on the front row…"

Then, one way or another, we both started laughing at the shared memory of me hanging on to him and hogging the mic for just a little too long.

"Thanks for coming to the show, I really love playing this city". Iggy is very gracious, I still can't believe I'm talking to him.

"I've seen you in concert a few times now — you're always brilliant — and I've got just about every album and bootleg that's ever been released with your name on it."

"Oh man, that's just too kind, I'm honoured to know that and grateful too."

What a guy! I loved Iggy. The chat went like this for a couple of minutes more, and then he said: "Well man, I've got to get out of here, thanks again for the kind words, thanks for the support — you take care of yourself." With that, we hugged it out, then he turned to leave the building.

I was made up! I'd met Iggy Pop, talked to him, and hugged it out with him without stalking him to do it.

I wonder if these two tales — *Rita, Iggy and Me*, and *Iggy Meeting Me at The Warehouse in Leeds* — are events that register in any way, shape or form in the memory bank of Mr Pop?

Probably not — but keep in mind the words of a song he wrote that went: "Tell me a story, And maybe I'll believe it."

*

OK, back to the family story…

We had three pianos, seven guitars, two drum kits, microphones and loads of other odds and ends in our house; the whole place was covered in instruments of one sort or another.

The whole family was into music — and, apart from Mum, we all played music too. It's worth noting that it was Mum who made sure that we got to take piano and guitar lessons, at least for those of us that wanted them, and she also had me and my brother attend the makeshift community hall dance school attempting to learn tap and ballet. We were never ridiculed for any of it by our mates; everybody seemed to accept the fact that because our dad was an entertainer, then it was natural for us to gravitate towards doing that as well.

In those days, kids grew up to do what their dads had done before them — if there is any one thing that I can thank my dad for, it's that he gave me the *music*.

From about ten years old, I was always trying to start a band, first with my sisters and brother, just strumming things out on acoustic guitars, singing old pop songs — all was going well for the "would-be Partridge Family" before disaster struck! My sister quit the band, she wanted to go play hopscotch and skip with her mates. 'Fuck, we could have been contenders!'

I knew entertainment was in my blood. My early claim to fame (not) was appearing on a TV program called *Junior Showtime*, where my character married a little darling blonde lass during a song-and-dance Fred and Ginger-type routine. That piece of film is probably sitting in a storage room. The program was massively popular at the time, probably sometime around 1970-1973. It'd be fun to see it again now… (Hmm, maybe not!)

I also teamed up with my brother at the Leeds Playhouse for a performance of *The Pied Piper*. He was the Piper and I was the Poor Crippled Child. We were like Olivier and Laughton, or maybe they said we were like Oliver and Stan? Either way, we enjoyed ourselves, and our beloved mother made most of our costumes for the performance too, making it a really cool family affair.

Then there was another time when three of us took to the stage together, again at the Leeds Playhouse. My brother, my older sister and me, with acoustic guitars, to sing three songs. "Knock Three Times", with the entire audience joining in on the banging and clapping parts the song called out for. Then there was "The Lion Sleeps Tonight" with me on the high-pitched yodelling lead vocal part. We'd also sneak in a slight change to the words; instead of singing "Wimoweh" we'd sing "Whinmoor Way" instead. He-he, tiny victories win big battles. And we also did "Bye Bye Love" by The Everly Brothers, where we sang a three-part harmony — which was funny as Phil and Don could only manage a two-part harmony on their version: "Ha! The Everly Brothers, we've shit 'em!"

Another time at another theatre, I played the part of a grumpy teacher who confiscates a bag of Midget Gem sweets from one of the kids in class, who's caught eating them during the lesson. It was supposed to be a comedy moment; the director had scripted the scene so that I would turn to the audience, nick one of the Midget Gems from the bag and pop it in my mouth. It was a scene designed to get a laugh "for the nasty teacher" — only I loved Midget Gems so much that I necked about fifteen of them all in one go. It meant that I couldn't get my next words out due to a gob full of sweets. The scene turned from a quick stolen laugh into a full audience in stitches.

I then found myself ad-libbing and milking it for more laughs, pushing it as far as it could go. A ten-second spot became a five-minute scene, and after the show it was heralded as "the highlight of the play". I took note of the experience.

From about the age of 12 or 13, I started playing with electric guitars, and a couple of years later I was putting together what I thought was a proper band. We wrote and played our own songs and even added in the occasional cover version of a Damned, Clash or Sex Pistols song.

The year was 1977 and Punk had arrived.

*

The Punk scene was sweeping the nation and would soon sweep the world.

The message ringing out was "Anybody can be in a band". Low and behold, every kid in school did just that and started up a band.

We were all seriously getting into music. It didn't matter how good or bad anybody could play an instrument; Punk was about attitude, about having something to say even if you had nothing to say, just say something, make a noise.

Our generation now had its own movement. We might have lost The King in 1977, but we found Punk! Viva La Punk Rock.

Thanks to a bit of divine intervention, I was already ahead of the curve when it came to playing an electric guitar. It's a fork in the road moment — you see my parents had bought me and my brother a chopper bike each for Christmas in 1975. They were all the rage, every kid wanted one. It was a push bike that had high, chopper-motorbike-style handlebars, a three-gear stick-change down on the chassis, a two-person curved seat and small, fat wheels, the back one bigger than the front one: they looked like the dog's bollocks.

Christmas morning, me and our kid were over the moon. We got straight out on the new bikes and raced all over the estate — we were out for hours.

On the way home, we decided to push the bikes up to the top of the road where the bus terminal stood. It was the start and end stop for the route between Whinmoor and Leeds town centre, our lifeline to the world outside of Whinmoor.

We pushed the choppers up the hill, took a breath, saddled up and rode back down the steep road at full pelt to the bottom — it felt like flying, so good that we repeated it again and again. On my final run I was feeling great, just as great as the first time, but somewhere near the bottom I started to lose control of the bike and crashed at full speed on the steep concrete road.

I looked up to see my brother racing down the hill towards me. I hoped he wouldn't crash out too, rather me than him, I was thinking. As he arrived at the bottom he threw his new bike to the ground and ran over to me:

"Are you OK?" I could see he had tears in his eyes for me. I looked up, probably in shock from the massive crash and said, "I think I've broken my hand," pushing my arm forward for him to see.

My right hand was snapped at the wrist; it was no longer on the end of my arm as usual but stuck directly below my forearm. It was a horrendous break.

While in the hospital my parents asked how I'd feel about them selling the chopper and replacing it with an electric guitar, the idea being that once on the mend, playing on an electric guitar would help the healing process.

I agreed, not because I was scared to get back on a bike — I'd always had a bike of some sort — but because I really wanted an electric guitar and to get a band going. It's such a strange twist of fate because everything else in my life has followed on from there.

Call it a lucky break, maybe. We all need a few of them along the way.

Half our estate and half our school were into the new Punk bands by the time we were 14 and 15. We'd go to as many gigs as we could get into, managing to see some incredible shows.

As I said already, it was a brilliant time to be a teenager. Change was all around us; we experienced it together and were influenced by it. Everybody knew each other down at the front of the life-changing gigs we went to — bands like The Ramones, Generation X, The Undertones, Stiff Little Fingers, Damned, Ruts, Iggy Pop, loads of bands, even Motörhead — collective experiences of vital bands, music and attitudes that shaped us, nights that have never left us.

It was good to be part of something; we were at the perfect age to soak it all up.

*

If it wasn't gigs or trying to write and play music or trying to cop off with girls that had our attention, the other thing we had in common was Elland Road and the Mighty Whites of Leeds United.

We were lucky enough to watch the glory team Don Revie built, led by the greatest ever — Billy Bremner, AKA King Billy, the Captain of Captains.

48

We were obsessed with Leeds United from the first moment we were old enough to recognise the club, maybe from around five or six years old.

From 1969, we started going down to what is referred to these days as Church to see the boys playing everyone off the park. At first, we went with parents, or adult neighbours. Then, as we got older, about 11 or 12, we'd go down with some of the older lads from school or off the estate. Then, finally, from 13, we'd go by ourselves.

We'd be there as often as possible. We were there for the good days, the bad days, the great days and the dark days, the immortal days and the want-to-forget-about-them days. It was a fantastic time to have Leeds United in your life.

It's a lifetime love too, Leeds United. And they fit in with that phrase I mentioned earlier in the Prologue, "God's Sad Boys". If any team fits that idea, it's Leeds.

How many times have we been close to glory with that team? How many titles or cups did we lose by tiny margins or by cheating refs? At least two European Cups.

Take the '73 Cup Winners Cup against AC Milan, which was refereed by a guy who later got banned for life for match-fixing. The crowd at that game in Greece pelted missiles onto the pitch during the A.C.Milan lap of honour as they knew it had been fixed.

Worse than that was the legendary '75 European Cup Final where the ref caused a riot with his blind calls that robbed Leeds of two clear penalties and ruled offside for a Lorimer goal. It would've put us even more in control than we already were, but instead, the title was stolen from us and gifted to Bayern Munich.

The Leeds fans went berserk, ripping the stadium up and rioting late into the night in the streets of Paris. The game gave birth to the chant, "We are the Champions, Champions of Europe" that still reverberates around Elland Road today and will do forevermore: "We will never forget Paris 1975."

49

When I think about how the lads have lit up the game, through the years, and brought that bit of "something else" to football, then compare it to the lack of trophies, it's enough to make you cry. And sometimes it does. God's Sad Boys indeed.

It's hard to be a Leeds fan, but we're Leeds for life.

*

Something else happened around the same time as Punk took off; my dad also took off. He upped and left us as he struck out for a new life in the rich man's playground of Puerto Banus in Spain.

He'd been doing extended stints as a resident piano bar entertainer over there for months at a time. We all thought it was the prelude to the whole family emigrating to the sun, as we'd all always talked about — but one day, during one of his short visits to us back home in Leeds, he announced to my mum that he was gonna be "fucking off" later that day and never coming back.

I remember it well — I was hanging out with one of my best mates from back then on the day it happened.

I was with a lad called Mick McCann, a legend amongst his mates even then, who grew up to become a writer and gave the world his fantastic books *How Leeds Changed the World* and his amazing debut, *Coming Out As A Bowie Fan In Leeds, Yorkshire, England.*

I was hanging out with Mick, playing records in the living room of his girlfriend Vicky's mum's house when I suddenly got this strange and intense sensation that I needed to telephone home. Vicky's mum let me make the call.

Dad answered the phone and started talking, nice and gentle, cool and calm, but something didn't feel right. Next thing, I could hear my mum in the background saying: "Tell him you're buggering off, go on, tell him, tell him you're leaving."

I asked him what she meant, and he said: "I've got to go back to Spain, it's work stuff. Don't worry, I'll be back home soon enough." All the time, my mum was calling out and contradicting him, "You're a bloody liar, don't lie to him, tell him the bloody truth!"

He said something about having to ring off as he was expecting an important call — but I wasn't buying it. I shouted out, "I'm on my way home. Hang on a bit, I'll run as fast as I can. I'm just down on the other side of Crossgates — I won't be long, don't do anything 'till I get there, right?"

But he didn't answer, he put the phone down.

Nevertheless, I started back home right away. It's about three or four miles from door to door, all uphill in that direction too, but I ran as fast as possible, didn't even stop to catch my breath. I was just thinking "If I can get there before he leaves the house, he won't be able to go"— I thought that my being there would stop him somehow. About twenty or thirty minutes later I burst through the door: "Dad?"

I hadn't been quick enough; he was already gone, he'd fucked off.

It turned out that he had decided to start a new life — without us, leaving us in industrial Leeds on the Whinmoor, while he'd made a run for the sun, making the dream we had all believed in come true.

Unfortunately, it was only gonna be a dream come true for him — we were excess baggage. He ran away to start a new life, and even begin a new family, with somebody else. It was an exit.

It was some wake up call for me too.

Given the old fella's sudden and final departure, and the fact that he didn't leave one penny, or send us one peseta either, it meant that the family was left living on welfare, scrounging various clothing handouts, applying for free school dinners and bus tickets. All while my mum worked as many jobs and hours as she could to make up the shortfall.

We found our way through it; my brother and I were 14 and 15, and at that age, we had a lot of distractions to deflect the pain. My younger sister didn't understand what had happened, so she avoided the heartache there and then. However, she felt it twice as bad as all of us combined as her birthdays passed one by one, while my older sister had already left home a couple of years earlier, so she didn't feel the jolt too hard.

But my mum, she went through the emotional mill.

On one hand, she was heartbroken — they'd been together since they were young teenagers, living in the Cardigans in Kirkstall. This was the fella she had brought up four kids with, had moved all over the country with, had married as a teenager, when they were barely adults — somebody she had planned for better days with — and now he was gone.

She was also furious and talked about tracking him down and sticking a giant hat-pin right through his heart.

Eventually, she got over the heartbreak, but she never, to this day, to her dying day, lost the anger — Mum was like a lioness; her cubs had been abandoned and left behind, something she could never forgive or forget.

Quite right, fuck that prick. It turned out dad wasn't cool after all.

*

In retrospect, I realise that our family in 1965-1966 were part of the first generation to lose sight of the extended family unit.

Gone were the uncles and aunts, grandmothers and grandfathers from day-to-day life because these new estates we lived on were usually built in the outlying areas of the city limits. This meant that mums, dads and kids were basically separated out to the suburbs — a long way away from the inner-city streets where everybody had traditionally lived side by side together.

For example, the entire families of both my mum's and my dad's sides all lived within spitting distance of one another on the same inner-city street in Kirkstall, if not even in the same house.

52

The support system of a traditional extended family had always been to the mutual advantage of everybody when living side by side in the old backstreet terraces. Kids were not just brought up by mum and dad; they were brought up by everyone who was around the neighbourhood. And with the new estates, all that glue disappeared almost overnight. Young parents with young kids were out on their own now.

By the time 1976-1977 arrived, so many social changes seemed to come about. Parents separating became a trend, and the dads were soon gone. Everybody on the estate seemed to be going through the same changing times of broken families, dads gone and mums left fending for themselves with a bag of kids in tow.

The next trend wasn't far behind. By 1979-1980, the girls from our classrooms would be young single mums at 16 years of age. Kids were having kids to get to the front of the housing lists. Bright lads, sporting lads, would become child-fathers, often having multiple kids all over the place. They were kids that they would hardly ever see. The trend of the "broken down family unit" started in those years, on those modern new estates. Society had quickly gone from the extended family to a broken nuclear family to a single-parent family.

The bright future those new estates represented for young parents in '65-'66, safe estates that would be full of fun for the kids, were now starting to decay, starting to turn grey. Young parents started divorcing and mums were left holding the baby; the future of these estates was to become a battleground for feral youths. Then came the new wave of single mums "getting pregnant to get a house key". They struck out on their own, "no dads required" — they got in bed with the state.

It happened fast, from 1965 through to 1980. Fifteen years was all it took for the rot to set in and the fabric of "the family" to be ripped to shreds.

When our dad left, we could have all fallen apart — we had idolised him every day — but we didn't. We kept it together. We just had to embrace it and grow older quicker.

Part of that was "losing my virginity" to a 19-year-old lass called Leslie.

I was 15, she was the older teenage woman, and me the younger teenage boy. All eight "in and outs" lasted maybe ten seconds, but the memory will live with me forever. She broke up with me after about a month and two more fucks, but a year later, I saw her out, down at the local estate pub, The Staging Post. It was a great pub just down from our house. It used to run loads of great live music gigs, and on weekends it would be a disco.

Leslie didn't live on our estate, where running into her would have been an almost daily occurrence. She lived over near Crossgates, so it was a surprise to bump into her at The Staging Post. Soon enough, we started chatting, having a laugh, getting touchy-feely and what-not — at the end of the night we went to the chippy next door.

We ate our chips around the back of the chip shop. It gave us a bit of privacy from all the other disco-goers, folks shouting and fucking about around the front. We hung out for a bit, having a laugh — and soon enough we got at it; a lot of kissing, some fumbling around inside her bra, working my hands down her body, going for a quick bit of finger, when she suddenly breaks the moment and says: "You know that first night when we did it?"

"Of course," I say, half embarrassed: "Sorry about that, but you were so hot, I could hardly control myself." I'm just trying to compliment her as an excuse for my "fast work" while still trying to move in for the digit dip.

Then she blurts out, "I got pregnant from that." I stop making my moves on her and make as if to pull away, like I recognise the seriousness of what she's just said and I'm gonna address it like an adult. She stops me from breaking the embrace, keeping a firm hold of me around the shoulders, and at the same time gives me a kiss on the nose. "I got rid of it and blamed it on somebody else."

"What? Why didn't you tell me? I would've stood by you," I said. Now believe me when I say, honestly I swear down, that as I said it, in that very moment, I believed that I meant it.

She giggled, a confident in-control giggle, then kissed me passionately. "You were too young." she started rubbing me, then unbuttoned me — we kissed, hugged, touched, our hands covered from sight under my giant vintage army coat. "It was better that way," she said in a whisper as she opened the gate and let me in, right there at the back of the chippy, just across from the Post and yards away from folk fucking about in the night. Somehow, it was a romantic moment — well, memorable at least.

I found out years later that she had lied to me. Yes, she had been pregnant and then she had aborted the baby, but no, she had never actually been pregnant to me.

*

I left school at 16 years old. It's 1980, and during the last week, there was a mandatory one-on-one careers adviser meeting to attend, with mine the last meeting on the last day of school.

"How do I get into the music business?" I asked the career advisor.

She pulled a pained face, looking like she was waiting for the punchline of a joke; maybe she forgot that most kids usually do what their dads have done before them. I wasn't joking, it was a serious question.

"I don't mean playing working men's clubs like my dad did," I started to explain, while updating her on my absent father. "And I can't ask him for advice, I haven't seen or heard from him for nearly two years." I tried to be crystal clear and let her know that I was being legitimate. "I mean, how do you get into 'the business' of the music business?"

55

I hoped that she would be able to see now that this was a serious question and I was looking for advice.

"Love," she sighed at me,"it's all a bit of nonsense, this, really, isn't it?" Her face looked at me with a wicked sadness, like she knew she was stamping on my dream, but was going to be brutal about it for my own good. "It's pie in the sky, this type of thing. You should be thinking of your future, not some pipe dream rubbish."

She paused a few seconds for effect and then looked out the window, away from me and into the distance of nowhere/somewhere.

"Stop dreaming silly stuff, it's real-time now, lad, forget all this music rubbish, you're not in the playground now. And you'll not be in the playground next week, that I can promise you!"

Turning back to face me, she says: "How about an apprenticeship up at the Barnbow factory, get yourself a trade — for life?"

Fuck that. I was going to do things my way.

"Love," she sighed at me,"it's all a bit of nonsense, this, really, isn't it?" Her face looked at me with a wicked sadness, like she knew she was stamping on my dream, but was going to be brutal about it for my own good. "It's pie in the sky, this type of thing. You should be thinking of your future, not some pipe dream rubbish."

She paused a few seconds for effect and then looked out the window, away from me and into the distance of nowhere/somewhere.

"Stop dreaming silly stuff, it's real-time now, lad, forget all this music rubbish, you're not in the playground now. And you'll not be in the playground next week, that I can promise you!"

Turning back to face me, she says: "How about an apprenticeship up at the Barnbow factory, get yourself a trade — for life?"

Fuck that. I was going to do things my way.

3. SCHOOL'S OUT, NOW WHAT, PUNK?

Bands like The Sex Pistols and The Clash, amongst many others, had brought social awareness into the musical landscape; they had opened our eyes to the politics of the world around us.

We had gone from singing along to "it's, it's, the ballroom blitz" with The Sweet, or "from Ibiza to the Norfolk Broads" with Bowie, to spitting out "Anarchy in the UK" by The Sex Pistols, or getting angry about "Career Opportunities" with The Clash. All while proclaiming "Babylon's Burning" courtesy of The Ruts.

By the end of 1979, I was 16 years old and my mind was open to everything — it was as good a time as any to start up my first proper Punk-Rock'n'Roll band. The line up included my brother and some mates from school who also lived on the Whinmoor. In truth, we weren't great, but we were willing triers.

I was attempting to write songs that mattered, probing for the right words that said something, pulling narratives based on the social fabric of the world around me.

One of the first songs I ever wrote was called "Teenage Disaster", which took on the "couldn't give a fuck" attitude around the issue of teenage pregnancy. It seemed to be almost endemic in school and around our way, with lasses from Smeaton and the Whinmoor getting themselves purposely "up the duff" to jump the council-flat waiting list on leaving school — not many from our way went on to further education, college or university.

I cribbed the vibe of the music on "Teenage Disaster". I used an all-downstroke, stubbed rhythm technique, played across a simple C–F–G three-chord trick. It wasn't very original, it was essentially the same as a lot of the other limited-skills Punk bands that were popping up all over the place in 1979-1980.

I also employed a chorus of sing-along "Ohs" which I'd ripped off from the original Leeds Punk-Rock'n'Roll band, The Boys. At one moment in time, The Boys were the only Punk band in Britain to hold a major recording contract, since The Damned, The Sex Pistols and The Clash were all either dropped and out of contract completely or just about to sign new deals. In any case, score one up for the mighty Leeds Punk-Rock'n'Rollers, The Boys.

> You've turned sixteen and you think you know everything.
> Rules and regulations don't seem to mean a thing.
> You've met a girl, and you think she's nice.
> You've just left school, and you don't think twice.
> And now she's pregnant, yes she's pregnant,
> So what you gonna do, what you gonna do?
> You're a teenage disaster, you're a teenage disaster
> Haven't you heard of CDDX? (Condom Durex)
> Didn't your dad tell you about the birds 'n' bees?
> You've met a girl, and you think she's nice.
> You've just left school, and you don't think twice.
> Now she's pregnant, yes she's pregnant,
> So what you gonna do, what you gonna do?
> You're a teenage disaster, you're a teenage disaster,
> So what you gonna do, what you gonna do?

I didn't know it at the time but some years later I would get to work with the main man himself from The Boys, the brilliant Matt Dangerfield, on some studio recordings that would eventually make it onto vinyl — but that's a few years down the road yet.

The words to "Teenage Disaster" might not have been super-smart, but they made a point, profound in their own basic way.

I couldn't claim to be as good a writer as Johnny Rotten from The Sex Pistols, Joe Strummer from The Clash, Jake

Burns from Stiff Little Fingers or Jimmy Pursey from Sham 69, but it was a start.

Now here's a funny realisation that came to mind at the time. It occurred to me that most people with something to say had a name that started with the letter *J*. John Lydon, Joe Strummer, Jake Burns, Jimmy Pursey, even Iggy's real name was James Osterburg. I considered using the name Jake Freeman for myself; well why not? It began with a *J*, and maybe it could give me an edge. In the end, I didn't use that name, but I sometimes wonder if that decision was the right or wrong choice? Did it have a good or bad effect on all that followed? Was it a seismic turn in the road?

"Teenage Disaster" was just the start of my songwriting efforts — the main thing was that the band was up and running. We busied ourselves playing at the local youth clubs around Whinmoor and the neighboring areas of Crossgates, Whitkirk and Halton, all local places really. In fact, usually we'd know every single person in attendance on first-name terms, they were "gigs for mates", but it was a start. And somehow we were soon offered a spot on TV, although recalling it now, it's so embarrassing that I can barely write it down…

Prince Charles and Lady Di were getting married, and the country was going nuts for it. I didn't even register it was happening, but our would-be-manager, an old Indian guy called Stuart who owned a small clothing shop in the Seacroft Centre, said, "If we do a song for the royal wedding I can get you on TV. And then I'll be able to get you a record deal."

I'm 16, still living at home and looking for a break — I'm thinking, well, maybe we can do something like The Sex Pistols did with "God Save The Queen".

It could have been the break we were looking for, but in reality, it was local TV and the video was filmed by one of the local news channels for either *Look North* or *Calendar*. It might not have been national TV but it was still a big deal around our way.

After much discussion within the group, mainly on the matter of band credibility and if doing this gig would ruin ours, we thought, "Fuck it, why not? Let's give it a go and try to make the most out of it!" I guess, looking back, we could be accused of being early-doors sell-outs. But so what? Life often only gives you one bite of the pie.

Unfortunately, it didn't help that I might have written one of the worst songs in songwriting history as an ode to the "not so happy" couple in celebration of the big day. I actually wrote a chorus that repeated the phrase, "It's the wedding of the year, it's the wedding of the year" over and over and over again. The verses were a little smutty, harmless innuendo like Benny Hill or a *Carry On* film. They went something like, "Prince Charles, the royal heir, Lady Di, what a lovely pair".

If the words to the song were bad, the music wasn't much better. But worse still was the video that the TV producer recorded.

My God, what a dog's dinner of nonsense! We looked so stupid dressed in our idiotic costumes, all covered in make-up. The quality of the film they used, and the editing itself, was another level of crap too. If we'd all sat down and designed the perfect clusterfuck of rancid rubbish, it still wouldn't have touched this steaming pile of dogshit. Everything was wrong with it. The only saving grace is that it happened so long ago, in the summer of 1980, that I can't remember what it sounded like, and hopefully, I'll never have to hear it again to find out.

When it was due to broadcast, it felt like the whole street was parked in our front room. We didn't know how bad it was right then as we hadn't seen the edit, so we were all thinking positive.

Ignoring the fact that the song itself was pants, and just being involved with the royal wedding felt completely bogus, it still felt like it was a big deal to us at that moment in time. It was the same for all of our friends, family and neighbours too; we all had a collective sense of slim hope. The thinking amounted to, "It's cheese, but what if?" Stuart kept telling us that the song was so insanely catchy that once it was exposed in Leeds and across Yorkshire word would soon spread and it wouldn't be long before it was getting played all over the country. He was a hype guy, and we were all hyped — he had us all excited and keen to see the debut of the video on local TV. But then disappointment crashed the party. The programme came on — and then ended — with no video in sight!

It turned out that we'd been bumped until the next night by a "breaking news" story that needed our airtime. What an anti-climax, but also a valuable lesson. Stuart explained. "That's the music business for you, highs and lows and waiting around, before action and chaos." I made a note to remember the feeling and understand the lesson.

So, the next night we all retook our places for the debut of, according to Stuart, our future hit record.

Fuck me but it was bad, oh my fucking-cunting-God was it bad — that bad that the whole house fell about laughing, mates, family, neighbours and us, the band, too. There was nothing to do but either laugh or cry, there was no other option in between. Our Punk credentials were shredded in bits while Stuart tried telling us it would definitely open loads of doors for us!

"Fuck off Stuart, there's the door, now get to fuck, get out of here, you're fired." We may have been laughing, laughing so hard we were shedding tears, but in reality we weren't best pleased.

"You can't tell me to fuck off, you can't fire me, we've got a contract." Stuart made an effort to stand his ground. We just looked at each other, laughed even harder and agreed to break up the band there and then.

Stuart did teach me a lesson that day however. His last resort was to argue that we had all signed the contract "jointly and severally", meaning that he had a contract with the band and also a contract with each of us as individuals. Naturally, we told him to fuck off again, and of course he didn't prosecute his contracted rights, probably fearing that we might burn his shop down if he pushed his luck. But this bit of cute contracting did feature in many contracts that I wrote myself years later, so at least something good came of this. I'd learnt my first valuable lessons in the business of the music business — always try to sign groups jointly and severally just in case they split up, so you get first dibs on the real talent. And always expect more lows than highs, it's a rough business.

*

Despite my obsession with breaking into music, I needed a regular job. My first job out of school was as a builder's labourer on a small four-house building site. I was doing anything and everything on the site; from carrying bricks and mortar in a giant hod to digging out garden plots, unloading lorries with various building supplies, helping out anyone on site who needed a hand, the joiners, plumbers, plasterers and so on. Strangely enough, even though it felt like hard labour to this workforce virgin, I loved it.

The guys on the site were much older than me, all great characters, funny as hell, and always up for a laugh. But you had to keep your wits about yourself to avoid being at the shitty end of all the jokes.

Everybody drank like a fish. Literally any excuse and Jim, the boss, would order us to down tools and retreat to the pub. A bit of rain would drop and that was all that was needed. And these builders, joiners, plumbers and plasterers, they knew how to booze.

I liked a drink, I liked it a bit too much — around two years earlier, aged only 15, I'd been rushed to hospital with alcohol poisoning after drinking a whole bottle of whisky in a washing yard at the back of my mate's maisonette flat. I'd passed out coma-style at the end of the underpass tunnel that connected Whinmoor to Seacroft Town Shopping Centre. My mum wanted the doctors at the hospital to wake me up for the stomach pump so I'd feel it and learn a lesson in pain. But they wouldn't do it. I was out cold, unconscious through it

62

all.

Another time, actually on the day I left school, walking out of *that* careers advice session, I jumped on a bus into Leeds City Centre and went on a massive bender. I went on my own — I wanted my own company and spent the afternoon just dossing around the crazy old pubs of Leeds getting properly loaded on lager with whisky chasers.

These old boozers were great places. You could learn more about life in those old hovels in an afternoon than you could from a year in school. That was if you could remember the lessons when you came back round from having passed out, of course.

These pubs had fantastic nicknames like The Mucky Duck, famous for the prostitutes that hung out there. There was The Snake Pit, famous for all manner of rogues, robbers and wrong 'uns. The Mad House, well-known for bar room brawls, and for being able to buy all kinds of stolen goods right there in the bar. There were loads of these booze dens in Leeds — then there was The Robin Hood, which was the place where "lags" would head to on release from Armley Jail.

I loved these places, and hit the lot of them on the afternoon I left school. Fuck knows how many, but I was found sometime later face down in a pool of my own vomit in The Scotchman, hauled to hospital for another stomach pump. Somebody asked me why I'd got into such a state, maybe a care worker of some kind up at the hospital. As I was hooked up to the drips for dehydration, I remember answering her by quoting something I thought I'd read Johnny Rotten say. "If we puke in the street, it's because we feel sick!" I can't be sure if it was Rotten who said it or not, but I liked the point that the quote was making.

Suffice to say, I wasn't a stranger to booze, but those building people were on another drinking level, and I learned fast how to hold my own.

Maybe it was the combination of doing proper hard work, the banter with the people working on-site, the million laughs together in the pub and getting hard cash wages each week in my hand to blow on whatever I wanted (after passing a few quid to Mum for board). Whatever it was, I loved that job, and any time I passed those houses up on York Road behind the petrol station, no matter how many years passed in between, I got a sense of pride that I had helped build them when I first left school.

I laugh to myself with the memories of hitting teenage adulthood alongside some fair people. It gives me a good feeling inside, innocent times, good times — and I could have stuck with the building life too if I'd wanted to.

After the four houses were finished, the boss asked me if I'd like to go to Australia and work with him building houses down there. He came out with it one day when we were building an old-fashioned stonewall as a fill-in job just down from where I was born on Kirkstall Road. A few days before we'd finished, Jim the Builder said, "Australia, it's the other side of the world, lad, but they're crying out for builders and their crews. You'd have a right life down under, shagging them Ozzie lassies, getting pissed with the blokes. Come on, son, I'm off. You come with me, it'll be the making of you."

He was a fantastic fella, Jim the Builder; he treated me like a son, taught me how to drink with the men and handle myself at work with the banter. And he was making the idea of Australia sound like heaven. "Lots of girls, lots of booze, an exciting far-off place…"

Almost all the elements were right, but the reality was, I wasn't born to be a builder. No matter how much I respected and liked the work, something else was nagging at me, something else was calling me.

"Sorry Jim, I can't do it, I've got my band and want to give it a proper go." I felt terrible, like I was letting him down. "I've got to stick at it, try to make it happen. It's my dream to work in the music business, not build houses. Sorry mate, but I've got to pass."

Looking back, it was a monumental decision, life-changing. It was a fork in the road choice — I was turning

64

down the chance to travel to a fresh new life in the sun. But I was determined to give my band the best shot I could, whatever the consequences. I had to try and follow my path. If I could make the band work, then I could get a foot in the door to the music industry proper and anything could be possible from there. Jim understood, possibly because his name started with a *J*.

My building site moment was over; it was time to look for a new job, and this time, I decided to try for one in an office. The thinking was: office hours, regular pay and easy work = lots of time to concentrate on the band.

I sent out a few applications for clerical work, and to my complete shock, I interviewed and got hired by the government, signed the Official Secrets Act, and went to work in the laboratory offices at the Ministry of Agriculture, Fisheries and Food (MAFF).

It turned out to be a strange job centred around me having to sniff the aroma of packets labelled as silage — or in layman's language, packets of shit labelled as silage. But still shit just the same.

Three times a day, I'd go through the ritual of smelling multiple packages of shit which had been delivered from farms all over the country — believe it or not, it was a job that was essential to the fabric and well-being of British life!

You see, the comments I made to describe each sniff of shit were, in fact, the first part of the process of identifying any problems on the farm.

The reality is that undetected problems can cause a national crisis. Be it good shit or bad shit, it's essential to identify one from the other because it affects the entire farming industry and the food produce it delivers to the country. Bad shit means unhealthy produce, which means bad food. Bad food means nobody eats, and then everybody gets ill and dies!

OK, it's an extreme synopsis, but in extreme circumstances, it's also spot on — it might have been a shit job, but it was an important job, an "unavoidable cog in the wheel" job. It was a dirty job but someone had to do it.

It reminded me of a lesson my dad had taught us before he fucked off: "Which job is more important: a brain surgeon or a dustbin man?"

Of course, I answered brain surgeon, knowing it was a serious job for super-intelligent, skilful people with education, while dustbin men lived on our estate.

He laid out his analysis of the question: "Well, maybe the brain surgeon is important; he uses his skill to save the lives of the few people with brain problems. But what if the dustbin man doesn't clean the streets? The rubbish would build up so high that rats would grow as big as cats, disease would spread into every household, and illness and death would follow on a massive scale. So, with that in mind, which job is more important?"

I got the point, and with that in mind I felt like a superhero, sacrificing my dignity, and sniffing shit for the benefit of everybody else. I'd ride the bus to and from the MAFF, Official Secrets Act signed like James Bond, and I'd think to myself, "If only this lot knew — me and my strange little job are at the front line in keeping the whole country free of disease, illness and death." Now, this wasn't the only time I'd affect the entire country; the next time would be much more consequential for the UK and even the world. I'll get to it and reveal it all later.

*

Musically, I still loved Iggy and still loved Punk, but I was starting to move more towards the reckless junkie bands, bands with a Punk-Rock'n'Roll sound. The vibe of these bands was more like a gang than a band, with cool names like The New York Dolls, The Heartbreakers, The Dead Boys and The Ramones. Loud guitars and Rock'n'Roll riffs played in a Punk style; they weren't singing about serious political or social issues but about regular day-to-day events and stories around them.

I loved the attitude and drug-fuelled adrenaline these

bands seemed to scorch through the world on. I especially liked Johnny Thunders from The New York Dolls and The Heartbreakers. He was like Elvis and James Dean all rolled into one. Maybe it was because I had left school, now in the wider world with a little bit of cash in my pocket, free to drink whenever I pleased, free to find and experiment with drugs and do whatever I wanted, but the reckless vibe of these bands seemed to match my own natural desire to be curious and reckless.

Johnny was the guy that mattered most. I could see the DNA of Punk-Rock'n'Roll, and it was clear to me that Johnny was the X-factor. I'll explain what I mean.

Johnny was the guitarist in The New York Dolls — they were Rock'n'Roll with a Punk attitude. The Sex Pistols creator Malcolm McClaren was also the manager of the Dolls before they imploded, so he created The Sex Pistols as a more political Punk version of the Rock'n'Roll Dolls.

The Sex Pistols debut album, *Never Mind the Bollocks*, has an amazing guitar sound to it. Steve Jones of the Pistols admits that his style is 100% influenced by Thunders, and in turn, Steve Jones has influenced thousands through that first Sex Pistols album. The Anarchy Tour featured The Sex Pistols and Johnny Thunders' post-New York Dolls band The Heartbreakers, along with The Damned and The Clash, both also influenced by Johnny Thunders' original band, The New York Dolls.

The Heartbreakers, for their part, influenced everybody. There are three great Punk-Rock'n'Roll bands to have ever existed, in my humble opinion — three bands with one killer Punk-Rock'n'Roll album each inside them, albums that sound as killer and vital today as they did when first released. None became household names, but that doesn't matter. Those that know, know — none were pure Punk, none were pure Rock'n'Roll, all three had a sound that I call Punk-Rock'n'Roll. Those albums are *L.A.M.F.* by The Heartbreakers, *Young, Loud and Snotty* by The Dead Boys — and I'll tell you the name of the other band, and the name of their album, later. I could go on and on about Johnny's influence, but I think you get it.

Johnny's important!

Back then, however, I only vaguely knew who Johnny Thunders was. I knew the name of his band The Heartbreakers and that they had been on the ill-fated December 1976 Anarchy Tour and had played the infamous gig at the Leeds Poly alongside The Sex Pistols, The Clash and The Damned, all-new Punk bands that me and my mates were all into by now. Especially The Damned, who were so Punk that they even got thrown off the rest of the infamous showcase tour.

My first musical introduction to Johnny Thunders was via The Dead Boys' debut album *Young, Loud and Snotty*, which I'd found in the rack at my local record shop. The cover just said something to me, it had an attitude, same with the band name and the album title. I took it without even having heard it, the shopkeeper had no idea who the band was either. It hadn't been on the market long, all he knew was they were from America.

When I got back to my bedroom at my mum's house, I opened the windows, even though it was a chilly November, and cranked it up.

The Cheetah Chrome guitar riff kicked off, Johnny Blitz drums hit it, and the band rocked a sound that was — well, how can I describe it? Vital. It sounded urgent and vital. And then Stiv Bators started spitting out words about not needing anyone, devil machines and electronic dreams... "Sonic Reducer, ain't no loser, I'm a Sonic Reducer, ain't no loser."

Whaaaat! I didn't have a clue where those words came from; they were angry, dramatic, snotty, defiant, independent, and proud, and as I listened more, it just got better! Do yourself a favour and go look up the lyrics for yourself — then thank me later once you're done.

I was hooked, even if I didn't really understand what I was hearing and didn't know where words like that came

68

from — at least not back then.

I didn't know anybody else who had this album. The Dead Boys felt like they were my personal thing, even if I shared it with the street at full blast. I still have the original vinyl, and it still sounds brilliant today. That Dead Boys album was my gateway to finding Johnny's own album, *L.A.M.F.*

From '79 onwards, Johnny Thunders was on a par with Iggy. So far as my adoration went, by '82, he was surpassing Iggy as an influence. Eventually, it all culminated together on Tuesday, 28th August, 1984.

That was the first date that I met and played a support show with the icon that is Johnny Thunders. The first thing I heard him say to me was, "Hey, what's that you're cooking up?" Billy Rath and Jerry Nolan, the other members of Johnny's Heartbreakers band, came into the small dressing room at The Warehouse where they found me and my band preparing some drugs to shoot up in our arms. It was a great first line, better than any other I could have expected.

This would be the start of a firm friendship that would see us Tour the UK and Europe multiple times together over the next six years. In fact, Johnny even ended up living in my apartment for a short time and we would stay friends through to his tragic and mysterious death on April 21, 1991 in New Orleans.

*

So, I was sniffing shit at work while sniffing shit of a different kind outside of work — by now, I had left the Whinmoor estate and the family nest, in late 1980; and 1981, 17 years old by now, I started living in Bedsit Land, where nothing was off limits.

The house I moved into had six rooms and was famous for its wild parties, loads of smoke, poppers, speed, acid and alcohol. We would spend just about every night partying in that place, and just about everybody in The Warehouse Club scene seemed to follow us home to party alongside us.

Even though drugs were all around, it never seemed to

mean more than the vibe of being part of a scene. Drugs were like an add-on to the scene, rather than the scene itself. I mean, if we smoked, then it was a casual toke rather than burning through a block of hash. Something like acid was maybe once a month when everybody felt up for a trip. Speed we would snort little bumps of off the back of our hand as a pep-me-up. Poppers were used more than any other drug, but only because the trendy thinking was that it made sex better. And alcohol was consumed as a supplement rather than grogged down like a drunkard — I grogged it, but, then again, I didn't have any sophistication; I wanted it all, everything now and more, more, more…

I think it was probably because there were so many gay people around the scene, who were more obsessed with dressing up and acting over the top in a cabaret kind of style, that drugs and whatnot were more like fun add-ons, decadent props, rather than anything else more sinister. Somehow, it all balanced out perfectly.

The house was always over-occupied with random bodies sleeping wherever they fell or wherever they were fucking — men with men, women with women, boys with girls, girls with boys, all combinations. You could say it was hedonistic.

It was also the home of electronic duo Soft Cell, a more accessible version of a band called Suicide. Suicide, the original electronic duo from NYC, were a groundbreaking band that worked with a mixture of weird electronic–rockabilly sounds and a spaced-out Elvis type of vocal. Just as important, they had a "fuck it all" attitude.

David Ball was the keyboard and electronics side of Soft Cell. He had one of the bedsits at 27 Leicester Grove. He gave me a Suicide LP and also a solo album by that band's vocalist, Alan Vega.

I don't know if Dave remembers it, but I can't thank him enough for the musical education in those two albums. This music crossed multiple frontiers: Punk, Rock'n'Roll and electronic sonic effects mixed with Elvis-styled vocals swamped in an over-the-top reverb and echo. When all those

70

elements were wrapped together, raw and uncompromising, Suicide and Alan Vega were the fucking coolest cats in town.

I saw Vega play live at The Warehouse a couple of years later in 1983; of course, he was magic. I also saw Suicide perform in NYC around 2004 and had a funny experience with one of the cast members from the New Jersey mob show *The Sopranos* — maybe I'll get to that story later.

Soft Cell of Leeds were massively influenced by Suicide of New York, but while Suicide remained at the cutting edge of underground sounds throughout their whole career, influencing many artists through the decades while remaining unknown to the wider public, Soft Cell became massively, internationally successful as hit record followed hit record on both sides of the Atlantic.

We couldn't believe that these guys who lived around us became top-selling bonafide pop stars within a year or so of getting started. It all began at 27 Leicester Grove and The Warehouse, and that's where I had landed on leaving home.

As I said, this was predominantly a gay household. The whole scene at that point in Leeds seemed to be gay, with Marc Almond as the singer of Soft Cell, the cloakroom attendant at The Warehouse, the DJ at The Warehouse and the main face driving it all.

I was a permanent fixture on the front room sofa throughout most of 1980. Then somewhere during Soft Cell's 1981 releases, club anthem "Memorabilia", global pop chart hit "Tainted Love" and their debut album *Non-Stop Erotic Cabaret*, Marc gave up his Housing Association room at 27 Leicester Grove, and I took it over.

Everything was amazing at 27: mind-expanding stuff, sexual times, drug times, crazy times, all the times. Experiences that could only bring out the artist inside me that I believed I was.

It was a time of Non-Stop Erotic Everything. This was a time when vicious sexual diseases weren't even a thing. We were the last of the lucky ones who could fuck without fear.

I met a sensational woman at The Warehouse, she was the

DJ's girlfriend. One night she came up to me and said that I looked ill, and that she was gonna bring me a bag of fruit the next night "to help me get better". I didn't feel ill, didn't think I looked ill either — I looked cool as fuck in my eyes. But she was smoking-hot, so I was only too willing to play along. I'm not lying when I say that she was the most striking girl I'd ever seen up until that point in my life, she was the pick of the top shelf down at The Warehouse, a real stunner, dressed most nights in a faux-fur cavewoman bikini, or a leather bikini, or some other wildly revealing costume. She looked like she should be on TV. Whatever she wore, its prime function was to show off the incredible figure she was rocking.

The first time we hooked up, I followed the sexy cavewoman out of the club — and when I say cavewoman I mean she looked as good as Raquel Welch did in the film *One Million Years BC*.

We walked down the street against the tide of the massive queue waiting to get inside. When we got to her small car, parked down a side street that was next to the emergency exit door of the club, she pulled me to her as she perched herself on the bonnet. She kissed me, a gigantic wide open-mouthed kiss, I was surprised as her tongue was wild all over my lips, it was like a kiss I'd only ever seen before in a movie. Then before I knew it we were fucking right there in the street over the bonnet of the car. Let's leave it there, I'll not say much more about her, because later in life she became a very famous household name, a TV soap star, and I wouldn't want any stories about us, from so many years ago, to negatively affect her career or personal life today.

*

Somewhere, in amongst everything — leaving home and moving on to a sofa until my room became free, sniffing shit at the MAFF, sniffing other shit at 27, partying hard at The Warehouse, and sleeping with any girl that was willing — I'm also keeping a focus on the band.

In this particular band incarnation, I was the guitarist, the writer of the music and also the writer of some of the lyrics. I had an amazing friend from my school days as the frontman, primary lyricist and singer — he'd been the first person to introduce me to the music of Iggy Pop and the real David Bowie. The lyrics he wrote were like poetry, they were just brilliant. He could have been and should have been a real star, but that isn't where his future turned out to be; we all called him Zowie — and that's his own story to tell.

I wanted to make a record but I had no idea how to do it. Regardless of having no real plan, I booked a recording studio, managed the session and oversaw the production of the recording itself. Zowie also delivered a piece of artwork, an elephant foot resting on top of a baby chick's head — it represented the cliff-hanger "To Be Continued", as in, what comes next, death or glory? The rest of the band contributed to the studio session with loads of musical improvements to the general songs delivered by Zowie and me — we were all on the same page, and we were now in possession of a finished studio recording, complete with cool artwork. So what next?

I was told about Pinnacle Distribution, a music company based somewhere down London way. They were the best distributor for independent bands and labels. So armed with a couple of pounds worth of change for the public telephone box, I decided to call and chance my arm.

"Hi, Pinnacle Distribution, who can I connect you to?" the receptionist answered.

"I don't know who I need to talk to, but I've got a band, and we've recorded some great songs, so I'd like to chat with someone about making a record. Is anyone there who can help with that?"

I could almost see her smiling at my industry innocence down the telephone — if she could understand my Leeds tones, that is. She could!

"Hold the line, my darling, I'll connect you to someone who can — just one moment."

Who knew it'd go so well? I was expecting to be blown

73

off, yet before I knew it, I'd been connected to a really friendly fella who seemed interested in what I was telling him. The call ended, as my change was running out, but with an appointment made to go down south and meet these guys in their offices.

I was well made up, and the band were too. I had a date to go to London, which was a massive event for a young lad from Leeds.

On the appointed day, I bought a return ticket on the National Express bus for a day trip straight down in the morning and back again later the same night.

It was my first time going to London on my own. I had been before as part of a family trip, but I was so young, a little kid, I couldn't even remember it.

But, this trip today to Pinnacle was a real trip to London, a business trip, in fact, to the Borough of Bromley — which alone had me excited as that is where the infamous Bromley Contingent came from. They were the original followers of The Sex Pistols, you could say the original Punks. They were famous as a group of people and became famous as individuals — Billy Idol, Siouxsie Sioux, Steve Severin, and even weird visionary Philip Sallon.

Siouxsie Sioux and Steve Severin were part of the Sex Pistols v Bill Grundy television interview in December '76, where Rotten said the word "shit" and Jones called Grundy a "dirty sod, dirty old man, dirty fucker, fucking rotter". It was the first time anybody had heard swearing like that on early evening TV, and it caused a national uproar.

In the actual meeting, I just talked and talked — non-stop. Just bollocks, I suppose, given that I didn't know what I was talking about in the first place, but it seemed to make sense to me; talking about how my guitars on these songs were like Bauhaus guitarist Danny Ash on their album *In the Flat Field*. I told them that the vocalist was massively influenced by Bowie and was a great performer, but we were basically a Punk band with a twist.

74

Then we played the music, which sounded great and cranked up loud on their fantastic system. The A&R guy and the product manager said they liked what they heard; they could hear some great elements across the three songs. Then the label manager said, "OK, we will give you a P&D deal to carry your label."

The first thing was, I didn't know I had a label, but apparently that's what I would now be: the label.

"How exactly will the P&D deal work?" I asked, giving the air that I knew what P&D even meant.

"Well, with all production and distribution deals that we do, we're prepared to pay all the upfront costs for the production and manufacturing of the record. We'll distribute it across the UK and export abroad, and we can help with the marketing to retail if you want. But we'd have to take a higher percentage on the sales. The main thing is that you need to get out on tour to support the record in the market. We can give you our standard terms and conditions contract to take to your lawyer today" — (who!?) — "and you can sign and send it back to us when you're ready to start, OK?"

"OK. Fucking OK! Fuuuucking OK!!! You bet it's fucking OK!!!"

OK, I didn't say that out loud, I said something like, "OK, that sounds fair enough, but I'll talk it over with the band and have our lawyer take a quick look over it too, if that's good with you? But honestly, I think we're good to go. I've brought the master tapes and artwork with me. I can leave them now if you want."

That was that — I was now running a record label. I had my foot in the door, a fucking P-and-fucking-D deal, and not a real clue what any of it meant.

I signed the agreement and sent it back to Pinnacle.

"Yes, our lawyer (who?) says the agreement is fine." And after a few weeks, we received about a thousand 7-inch promo vinyl singles to an address in Leeds. We couldn't believe it: a proper record of our music — but we were keeping it Punk by doing it as a DIY independent label.

75

The reality is that we didn't have a clue what to do with the copies of the record we had — we had no gigs in Leeds or any tour dates across the country to promote or sell them at, nor did we have one single contact in the music press or on the radio. But we didn't care; we just loved having this record in our hands. And so we gave loads away to friends, family and complete strangers — until they were all gone, one way or another, all gone.

Then, one day soon after, Zowie, the true star of the band, announced, "Sorry, lads, I can't be in the band anymore. I'm off to work down the pit with my dad," and that was that. The band was over. He followed in his father's footsteps, as most down our way did, and became a coal miner.

Looking back, it was simple what went wrong. I didn't know my arse from my elbow so far as the business of the music business was concerned and had no idea about touring or promoting — the main things the guys at Pinnacle had told me I needed to do. It seemed so easy for Soft Cell.

4. THAT'S COOL BEANS, MATE

Life in bedsit land was like being in another world, just like The Only Ones sang on "Another Girl, Another Planet".

People told me that The Only Ones were singing about drugs in that song, and their lyrics do set the tone: "I always flirt with death, I look ill, but I don't care about it". The writer, Peter Perrett, said it was probably about addiction to sex and an infatuation with a space cadet girl from Yugoslavia.

My life would soon become like that opening Only Ones lyric, whichever way you took it, sex or drugs, as dark and wild days lay ahead.

But for the time being at least, life was fun, more in line with the words that Marc Almond from Soft Cell wrote in a song called "Bedsitter" — a song he actually wrote while living in the room that I had now moved into. The chorus said it all: "Dancing, Laughing, Drinking, Loving, And now I'm all alone in bedsit land, My only home." It's another song with great lyrics. Again, I recommend you hunt them down in full — they really capture a moment in time.

When I took Marc's room, he had left a strange paper-mâché sculpture shaped like a full-size torso hanging on the wall. It was painted black but had transparent hollow parts that were filled up with different pills: everything from Paracetamol to Valium, Green Eggs to Cough Drops, and loads of other goodies of various shapes and colours. He said it represented how he felt on the inside, "darker, sometimes up, sometimes down, sometimes wanting to feel better, sometimes embracing the worst". Marc was something more than he seemed to be on the outside.

I kept the torso on its hook, painted the walls blood red and fashioned a mural of blue skies and white clouds, with a giant golden sun shining sunbeams across the roof. It looked bohemian with the contrasting colours across the walls and the ceiling like heaven and hell, good and bad, or mischievous but nice.

77

Woodhouse, where the house was located, was tucked between the city centre of Leeds on one side and the Hyde Park and Headingley student-dwelling meccas on the other. I'd never known Leeds was such a big university city until I moved there.

People from all over Leeds, from all over the country and all around the world gravitated to this area, be they students, musicians or thrill-seeking freaks. It was brilliant to be around it — I hadn't known that such a metropolitan part of Leeds existed.

It was different from the Whinmoor. Here, it was hedonism, attitude, music, sex and culture — those commodities were the currency. It was so new to me. Where I came from, the currency was a sense of humour, a willingness to chance getting caught when up to no good, an openness to have an argument or a fight, football, Punk and birding it.

The crew at 27 Leicester Grove were positively millionaires in this new-to-me social currency. They were the city's movers and shakers, especially down at The Warehouse. And I was now a fully participating member of the cast — it turned out that I was a natural when it came to bohemia and hedonism, drugs and sex.

The people in the house were incredible creatives, so I'll quickly introduce you to them.

Annie Hogan lived in one of the rooms. She was a super-talented musician, particularly an accomplished pianist; she worked for years with Marc & The Mambas after Soft Cell took a break. She was also a brilliant DJ with a vast music collection — all kinds of great music would seep out of her room, from Nico to The Normal, Bauhaus to B52s, Cure to John Cale. Later, she lived in London and hung out with some of the Bromley Contingent, like Siouxsie Sioux and others.

Just a quick aside; It's dawning on me that there seems to be a small degree of separation between Siouxsie and myself.

According to somebody's book, we are all a maximum of six degrees of separation away from each other. Well, let's test it.

I knew Annie; she knew Siouxsie, so that's me two degrees separated from the Banshee. And now I'm thinking about it, I'm also two degrees separated from Siouxsie via Johnny Thunders. Lastly, I'm three degrees of separation from her via PJ Proby and my long-disappeared "fuck 'em and feed 'em beans" old fella, given that PJ Proby and Siouxsie once recorded a (never released) duet together, and my dad also shared the bill with the "famous pant splitter" himself at a show they both appeared on. Isn't it a wonderful life that we live in!

Another room was occupied by Tim/Chester, a bass player in the fantastic rockabilly band Pink Peg Slax, who would soon have the attention of radio legend John Peel. They'd also be releasing their music on vinyl by 1984. I would spend hours in his room listening to very cool, obscure old rockabilly records from his collection. He had so many incredible tunes, including the real stuff: greats like Wanda Jackson, Jimmy Lloyd, Carl Perkins, Gene Vincent, Elvis Presley, Eddie Cochran and The Johnny Burnette Trio. His records truly rocked, and I'd happily spend whole afternoons with Tim/Chester listening to good music.

And we still had Dave Ball, the electronics wizard in Soft Cell, in another room. The sound system he set up in his room was created by him to give a unique sound that only he would have access to. I remember him having a multi-channel equaliser hooked up to manipulate the tones, which was impressive, like having a small studio to play his records.

His music collection ran through so many genres, from Northern Soul to Kraftwerk, Suicide to Giorgio Moroder. I still play the two albums by Alan Vega and Suicide that Dave very generously gave to me as a "welcome to 27" present so many years ago. As soon as the needle hits the vinyl I'm transported back to those times, down at The Warehouse, where I would dominate the dance floor whenever "Jukebox

Babe" by Alan Vega would come on. I could never resist the urge to put on a show for the rest of the room — I was an accidental Warehouse Hero and Performer. It was like the DJ would put it on and will me to put on a show for the room. Obligingly, I always did.

Some thirty-odd years later, after first being properly introduced to his music by Dave Ball, I would actually work with Giorgio Moroder, the disco-electro maestro himself, as I booked him to play two shows at the world's most famous dance music club, Pacha in Ibiza, during the summer season of 2014 when I was the music director at the venue.

On both shows, he played all the hits he'd produced, from Donna Summer to Blondie and everything in between. The 3000-capacity club was rammed on each date and decorated with spectacular props. We had canons of confetti, dry ice and smoke systems, freaky-costumed dancers and random creative animation all over the main room, including things like flash-mob performers interacting with the crowd without them knowing. It was an incredible audio-visual experience.

The July night Giorgio played was during the height of the season. It was a super-packed and spectacular affair, made even more memorable for me because my mum had come to Ibiza to celebrate her 72nd birthday. She wasn't a stranger to Pacha; I'd taken her down a few times before on previous visits. But on this night, I set her up in a special VIP section that I'd occasionally put together right next to the DJ booth. As the night rocked on, she got involved with the room's spirit, the drinks flowed and everybody in the area fussed over her. Then, out of the blue, Moroder danced himself over to the partition rope separating his working space from our VIP party space, unlatched the rope, took Mum's hand and started dancing her back into the DJ booth with him. She didn't need a second invitation, off she went, boogying alongside the man they simply call "Giorgio". The crowd cheered, throwing their hands in the air to the oldest swingers in town. What a brilliant moment it was for Mum, and Giorgio seemed to get a kick out of it too. You could feel the love in the room.

Back to Leeds. The other two bedsit rooms were taken up by the two gay Andys — not to be confused with the two "fuck any girl with a pulse" hetero Andys who were well known for having the ability to seduce just about any girl who came around the scene. We had "Original Gay Andy' and "New Gay Andy" — they were like the VIPs of the gay contingent down at The Warehouse. Both were hugely popular, with their dead-white, bleached, crimped hair and super-trendy wardrobes full of Worlds End or Vivienne Westwood sex clothing, bought from a shop run by — ironically enough — the two hetero Andys.

I loved being around so much creativity, whether in the house, around the area or down The Warehouse. It didn't matter what creativity it was — musicians, artists, writers, fanzine editors, freaks or chancers. It was inspiring.

I started as the fish out of water. It took a little while for me to find my feet, as it was my first time living away from my mum and the Whinmoor. But I dived into everything, drank a lot, smoked a fair bit, sniffed a lot of poppers, sniffed a bit of speed and bedded as many women as I could. It was cool beans, really cool beans.

I wasn't neglecting the band, either — I hadn't lost focus on the goal. In reality, everything happening around life at 27 was playing its part, generating experiences. I was seeing life through another lens, through a multicoloured kaleidoscope lens that had a combination of close-up or long-range vision, as well as narrow or wide-angle views. It wasn't what I saw but how I saw everything around me. My mission was to experience everything, and I didn't hold back in going forward to seek new thrills; I didn't set boundaries.

*

By now, I'd reshaped the band once more, becoming both the lead guitarist and the vocalist–frontman, and writing a load of new songs.

81

We played gigs at various pub spots around the city, but not as frequently as I'd have liked. Some of these places weren't that friendly towards a Punk band, but we got on with it and were generally well-received. People started following us a little bit, and we were happy — for a short while — to play and get paid in beer, a free bar for the night. But once we'd played a few times, venues found it cheaper to pay us a few quid and throw in a small amount of pre-agreed drinks on top — it was much cheaper than letting us go hell-for-leather on the beer taps.

The scene in Leeds was something else in '80-'82 — maybe it was the same all over the country, too?

The original Punks had been joined by the second wave of Punks. They dressed in leather jackets covered in studs, topped off with dramatic multicoloured mohicans for an almost cartoon-looking image. Somebody coined the phrase "If you're gonna be unemployed then you might as well look unemployable".

Bands like The Exploited were getting massive, GBH or Discharge were pulling big crowds and selling records. Still, my favourite from the new lot was Leeds's very own Abrasive Wheels, not just a Leeds band but a Crossgates band.

The Wheels became serious players in the second wave of Punk and had an army of fans who would follow them to shows nationwide. Shonna, the lead singer, was a brilliant frontman — so effortlessly a proper Punk, no filter and no play-acting with him. Dave Ryan had a right arm like Popeye's, nobody could chop the Gibson Les Paul copy like he could. Harry and Nev were drums and bass, two great lads who would eventually leave Abrasive Wheels and join me in my real proper band, which you'll read about soon.

They were local champions for us, and we were proud as punch for them. The Abrasive Wheels were great people, a great band, and inspirational in showing us what was possible on an indie Punk level, while on the commercial side, Soft Cell showed us what could really be achieved. I was studying it all, a natural sponge, learning from everything.

The Wheels were the first band I knew personally to go on tour in America. They returned telling stories of how fledgling heavy glam rockers Mötley Crüe would cruise around Sunset Strip on giant custom-made motorbikes or in super-colourful limos — which all sounded fake and glitzy to me, rather than real glitter in the gutter. Of course, the Crüe went on to become multi-million-selling superstar icons, but I never liked their sound, although I did meet Tommy Lee in Ibiza years later. And he was cool beans.

Talking of years later, when I was living in NYC the Wheels reformed and came to America on tour again, somewhere around 2002-2003. They landed in New York to play at the legendary CBGBs and were fucking fantastic! The crowd went mental all the way through. I couldn't help but think they could've been massive if only Harry and Nev hadn't left the Wheels to join me. But that's the rub, my friends.

Meanwhile, back in Leeds, 1980-1982, there was a new set of electronic synth artists coming out and vying for attention. They attracted a growing number of people who were into dressing up, preening like gorgeous peacocks, men and women, dressed in elaborate, elegant robes and designer threads, hair crimped and back-combed for extravagant head-turning effect, or greased down flat like an old silent-movie star. Artists like Gary Numan, Depeche Mode and Soft Cell supplied the soundtrack alongside Ultravox and A Flock of Seagulls.

Another new strain of music and style was also breaking through — a new, darker sound. Under the radar to start with, it was a mix of Rock'n'Roll guitars married to programmed electronic drum-machine beats. Its followers dressed exclusively in black, and it was the start of what became known as Goth, led by the soon-to-be inspirational trio of Leeds bands The Sisters of Mercy, The March Violets and Red Lorry Yellow Lorry. I became friends with individual members of these bands over time, some more than others, with friendships lasting until today. This sound and style eventually grew bigger than the confines of Leeds, it ultimately took root all over the world, and Leeds was ordained as Goth City.

I didn't mind any of the bands in this melting pot of new music, be it the second-wave Punks, the electronic synth stuff, or the new underground Goth sounds — it all had a value, everything contributed to the mixed-up eclectic scene. But, despite that, nothing touched Punk-Rock'n'Roll in my eyes.

There's no uniform required for Punk-Rock'n'Roll, at least not past what I'd call regular stuff. Things like worn-out, naturally ripped jeans, zip-up ankle-length boots with jeans pulled over the boots, not tucked inside unless you were wearing cowboy boots, but the cowboy boots had better be fucking snazzy and black, or just fuck off!

Winkle pickers were cool shoes, or sometimes Ramones-style baseball sneakers. Up top, you'd wear a cool T-shirt: bands we liked included MC5, the Stooges, Ramones, Iggy, the Dolls, The Damned, The Dead Boys — and "Viva La Punk". Quick side note: what the hell happened to Ramones T-shirts over the years? Every Tom, Dick and Harry seems to wear a Ramones T-shirt now, forty-fucking-plus years after the event.

Anyway, another good look was to find the cleanest dirty shirt from your closet — or from off the floor — and cover it over with a slick waistcoat or black leather jacket. Sometimes, I'd wear a long Crombie overcoat in winter or a funeral coat if you could find one in summer. I also didn't mind wearing a woman's fake fur coat now and again too — if the Dolls could, I could! Often, my hair would be simply left loose on top, not too long, but at least down to the collar. It wasn't really in a style, more a "just woke up" thing.

Like I said, the Punk-Rock'n'Roller was a good and easy natural look that you could accentuate with a few little add-ons, like pocket chains or skull rings, neck-scarves, studded belts, odds and sods. Whatever felt good, whatever was around — we were generally skint, so we grabbed whatever we could. The only real rule was to wear what the fuck you want — it's who you are and how you stay true-hearted that counts, so far as I'm concerned anyway.

I felt like I was the star of a movie, band or no band, a house full of people living beside me or not. I had plenty of attention from the club girls, which was fine for me. I was a one-man show, mainly, and I liked it like that, I liked my own company. But after a while, and not by design, a co-star entered into the act.

*

Somewhere at the start of '82, I made a new friend. He went under the name of Evo, a name earned from his excessive glue-sniffing school days. I don't actually know which part of Leeds he came from, and I wonder if he ever even went to school.

Evo was a rat-like twat. Every word he ever uttered was undoubtedly a lie. In fact, another mate told me that there was some graffiti scrawled on a wall about him that read, "Evo stinks of shit like a two-faced bastard".

It didn't take long, knowing him, to understand what the sentiment meant. But I liked him; I liked him right away as soon as we got together.

He was as big a fan of Johnny Thunders, Iggy Pop, Dead Boys, Alan Vega and Suicide, as I was, and I didn't know anybody else who was also into the same things as much as me, at least up until I'd met Evo. He was a kindred spirit right from the get-go, and that was good enough for me — he didn't give a fuck about anything, other than getting fucked up mainly and Punk-Rock'n'Roll music. It was a bit like looking in a mirror, to be honest.

I'd heard about him when I started occasionally sleeping with a great lass called Doris, who was great mates with him

85

and his sister, Sister C. So, it was Doris who encouraged us to get together. Eventually, it was arranged that we'd meet.

I don't know why we'd never met before. We'd both been to many of the same gigs at The F Club in Leeds. The F Club was just about the only place in Leeds where the Punk bands would come to play, a tiny place where it was hard to miss people. And Evo was a regular at The Warehouse, not just attending the odd gig but hitting the club at least two or three times a week. We had both been to see Iggy every time he played a concert in Leeds — but somehow, despite our "unknown connection" through attending the same venues, we hadn't met. We hadn't even been aware of each other until I'd copped off with Doris. She played matchmaker for us.

When we did meet, it was at The Warehouse — of course — and it was an instant attraction. While everybody else was dressed in outrageous threads, peacocks looking great, shadows in black, or spike-headed second-wave Punks in leather studded jackets, me and Evo were in our natural shit. You know — Punk-Rock'n'Rollers, tight pants, a cleanish dirty shirt, black waistcoat on top, cool beat up leather jacket, zip-up ankle boots, hair plopped on our heads, unkempt "just got out of bed" style, the odd neck-scarf, chain and other odds and sods. We'd come as ourselves.

We spent that first night drinking beer with whisky shot chasers, reciting over and over at each other the Iggy ad-libs from the bootleg of the live Stooges concert *Metallic KO* — each trying to top the other as the biggest Iggy fan, and then the same with famous Johnny Thunders one-liners.

We became big mates. Evo started coming over to my bedsit at 27 all the time. God knows where he was living — there was no point asking either, he'd only tell a lie. He'd show up around 7pm after I'd get back from work at the shit-sniffing factory, and we'd buy a 12-bottle crate of Royal Dutch Beer and a bottle of Jack Daniels or vodka, or both, from the corner shop on the end of the block, get back up to my room and start drinking by 7.30pm.

If we had some dope, we'd burn it on a badge placed under a glass and suck the shit up to get a proper hit. The record player would belt out The Stooges, The Heartbreakers, etc., as loud as my six speakers would allow. Then, by 9.30pm, we'd be over to The Fenton pub across the small park, sink a couple of pints there, then walk up to The Faversham pub, which was always busy with student girls and loads of people in great local bands. Every part of the pub would have a different band in it — some went on to do really well, some went nowhere and some were doomed for the not-quite-made-it path of the God's Sad Boys — which meant more to some than others. By midnight, we'd be down to The Warehouse, where we got really, really, really good at stealing pints, cocktails, anything in a glass, from the top bar.

People would rush to the dance floor with a too-trusting confidence that they were in a non-drink-stealing safe zone. But as they would camp it up, wigging out in amazing outfits, swinging away to Grace Jones or something from one of the New Romantic bands, us two were grabbing momentarily abandoned pints, bottled beers, gin-and-tonics — whatever we could get our mitts on in the slipstream.

Other times, we'd plot out a group from different directions. I'd distract them by launching into a wild Iggy-style shake-about in front of them, getting right up in their faces — not in an aggressive way, more a nutty, harmless madman, freaky way. Attention engaged, Evo would grab what he could from the other side, then I'd dance off and meet him down at the bottom bar, where we'd grog it down before setting off on the next alcohol-hunting trip.

The nights at The Warehouse would finish at about 2am in those days. (Years later, I would single-handedly be responsible for extending Leeds to 4am licences, and from there on to all-night 6am licences, too. You'll read about it later, I don't want to stop the Evo flow right now.)

If I'd copped off, we'd say our goodbyes there and then in the club. Evo didn't seem too interested in copping off with girls but I was, and I'd take my lass home if I had, and he'd go off to LS6, Hyde Park, Headingley, or somewhere, anywhere, probably to rob one of the student houses, and eventually, he'd land wherever he used to, most likely at Sister C's.

On the nights I didn't cop off with a girl, then we'd both focus all our attention on copping drugs instead. Now Evo really did like copping drugs. Our favourite drug was speed, so we'd head back to mine, grab some beer from one of the kebab shops. Once home, we'd set about sniffing up the gear, drinking down the beer and draining whatever JD or vodka was still left over from earlier, finally passing out at about 5am during weekdays and not sleeping at all during weekends. It's hard to believe, but on school nights, we'd be up again at 8am, me going off to work, and him going wherever.

At first, we'd carry on like this a couple of times a week. Soon, it was three, then five, then eventually every night. We didn't have much time for anybody else, we loved our own vibes the best. Weeks and months flew by with us just busting our guts, laughing in each other's company, drinking, smoking and sniffing speed. We were relentless.

Inevitably, all we wanted was more, more, more of the fast stuff.

At first, we'd have a wrap of speed between us. Then we progressed to one wrap each, keeping us both high and happy for the whole night. Then we added a third wrap that we would go half each, saving it as a "get me up" for the morning, with enough left over for a "pick me up" at midday. Which I'd snort up while sitting at the same workstation as where I'd sniff the shit for the MAFF.

The next stage was we wanted more bang for our buck. And that's when we decided that sniffing wasn't enough; we needed to inject to get the most out of what we had. We had no trepidation about it and didn't need to debate it. We knew what we wanted, so we went for it with eyes wide open — or maybe eyes wired open.

We took our first injected shot of amphetamine speed together in my bedsit at 27 Leicester Grove. Encouraged by our shared stupidity, we set off head-first on a more intense attack on drug abuse.

So, here is where I'm gonna try to tell the story of the first shot; if you've not done it, it's like remembering your first fuck, that's how powerful the memory is for me.

We got hold of some amphetamine speed, which we were relieved and happy to get, as we considered it a cleaner regular speed, rather than methamphetamine, which was super-strong and had a dirt-like vibe to it.

So this was it; we were about to embark on needles, the direct inject, armed with a wrap of amphetamine and a needle and syringe, a set of works that I'd got from a student nurse I used to sleep with from The Faversham. We were set — Billy Idol's vocals were rocking through my head, "Ready, (ready) Steady, (steady), Goooooooo!"

Ready

The preparation of the injection, also known as The Dig, was a process that soon became a ritual. The ritual became almost as addictive as the mental addiction the speed would become — speed isn't really a physically addicting drug, but it's a proper mental one.

We copied what we'd seen in the movies — *Panic in Needle Park* starring Al Pacino, was pretty good as a teaching manual. We'd get a spoon, add some water, put maybe the equivalent of a phat line's worth of gear in, hold a lighter underneath to heat the water and watch the speed dissolve. Then — and thinking back, this was disgusting — we would break a cigarette butt off from a Marlboro and add that on top of the water. That would be our filter.

Nobody seemed to be talking about chemicals in cig butts back then. We would strain the liquid through the needle until it was all inside the syringe: the Barrel, the Gun. Next, you would push the liquid up to the rim of the needle so the plug, plunger or Trigger and the Barrel of the Gun had no air bubbles inside.

89

We would act like nurses — Rock'n'Roll nurses, of course — and flick the barrel to be sure no air was inside, as we had heard an air bubble would kill you if it got in your vein and bloodstream. Who knows if that's even true? Either way, it made us feel like we were being careful and not being stupid or reckless.

Hahahaha, you gotta laugh, right?

Part one of the set-up complete, we tossed a coin for who goes first. I won. I was ready.

"OK, Evo, you do me and then I'll do you."

I pulled the bootlace around my left arm above the elbow as a tourniquet, pulled the string tight and flexed a few times to pump up the virgin veins. They popped up nice, fat, easy to see, and easy to hit.

Steady

Evo had the works in his right hand, tapping on my already pumped-up veins with his left hand, just going through the motions rather than affecting anything. He then took a piece of toilet paper in his grubby fingers, dabbed it in a cup of salted water and rubbed it over the inside of my elbow to help keep it clean and germ-free. At least we were making an effort!

Then he came towards the vein, the biggest one that crosses downwards from right to left, rather than the harder-to-hit straight one that runs up on the left. The needle goes straight in, but it goes too far and heads straight through the other side of the vein before he pulls it back just a bit.

I note the sensation of steel embroidering my arm, but he's hit the spot now. He holds the Gun still and steady and rests the Barrel in his left hand while his right slowly pulls back on the Trigger. Red blood flows into the Pistol, not a lot, just a little bit, enough to tell us we're nearly there.

I release the tourniquet as his right thumb pushes the plunger an the liquid starts to enter. I can feel it. I'm not sure if it feels hot, or cold, or if it feels like nothing. Slowly, but not too slowly, he drains the Gun, picks the damp piece of toilet paper back up off the Heartbreakers *L.A.M.F.* classic

90

album cover where he'd left it, places the paper over the needle, pushes down and starts to slide the needle out of my arm.

Go

"Go, go, fucking go!"

Before the needle is out, I can already feel the drugs running fast into my body, and a sense that the liquid is racing up to my head comes over me. He's out now, and almost in one movement, at the very moment when his prick-penetration is released, I'm already rising from the small two-seater sofa at the end of my mattress-on-the-floor bed.

"Oh my God, it's like fucking rocket fuel," I shout.

"Are you rushing?" he asks.

"Yeah, it feels like I could jump right through the fucking ceiling, Evo, it feels fucking brill. Fuck me, this is it, Evo, come on, build one for you, I've got to move about a bit!"

I sit down, stand up, turn the record player up and drink a cup of water.

"Give me a fucking cig, Evo, fuck me, you're gonna love it." This might have been my first hit, but I was already thinking about the next shot later on.

Now I'm speeding like a mother fucker. Everything is moving quicker than usual, but I'm also focused on whatever has my attention. It won't always be like this. Sometime down the line, focusing on one thing for a moment will be impossible, but right now, I'm focused — focused like a focused fucking motherfucking focused cunt!

I get on my knees. Evo is now sitting on the two-seater sofa in front of me. I return the favour for him, plunging the needle into his vein.

Evo starts to rev. "Woooooooaaaahhhhhh, fuck yeah, cam'on, cam'on, cam'on, yeeeeessss, I'm rushing, I'm fucking rushing!"

The music is playing loud, Johnny Thunders and the Heartbreakers are on deck, Walter Lure sings, and I sing with him, "Tie it up, shoot it up, bang your head, and throw it up."

All together now.

91

"Too much junkie business, too much junkie business, too much junkie business, don't wanna fuck around with you."

This high-as-hell feeling went on for a while. We were buzzing good and grinding teeth, rabbiting on about anything and nothing, non-stop yap yap yap. It wouldn't always be like this, but it was this time, the first time. We'd broken our duck and were ready for another night out. We knew it'd be different this time, though, new senses had been awoken — we were already looking forward to getting back home before we'd even walked out the door.

Now, if that sounded like glamour, well, it is what it is. I've never advocated for anybody to go the same way. I've always said, "Walk this way by your own volition, or run away as fast as you can in the other direction." All I know is that we both loved the drama of proper drug taking. We didn't care where it would take us or what kind of trouble might be down the track.

I've always been adamant about drug stabbing, though. It isn't glam, it's dirt, and it isn't for everyone — but it was fun for me and Evo. A lot of fun. We went at it fearlessly, copping what we could, when we could, every day if we could.

The reality was that drugs for injection were not on tap, especially not from our crap dealer. We wanted more and more. Still, the lack of a daily supply didn't stop the Dum Dum Boys, no, not at all. Without speed to shoot up, we would resort to going into the medical trash skips that were hidden behind the old LGI hospital, not too far away from my place, actually en-route from The Warehouse. In those late-night skip raids, we'd find these sealed tins and run back to 27, rip them open and inject any remnants of any liquid we found inside — small medical bottles half full of something or other; we hadn't a clue what. It could have been deadly, but we didn't think twice, we felt invincible anyway.

If we didn't find anything in the skips, we would shoot up vodka and whisky instead — we'd literally try anything that was at hand. I couldn't even say if any of these concoctions made us medically high; the ritual was the same, and it was definitely dangerous. We lived on Iggy's words, "Give me danger little stranger".

Medically high or not, we were fucking flying, running around like cunts, causing chaos with a feeling of complete entitlement to do as we pleased. And the more fucked we got and the more ill we looked, bizarrely, the more people seemed to find us appealing, sexy, charismatic, like no matter how brattish we were, we were forgiven every misdeed. I think that was probably because we weren't malicious or nasty or aggressive, we were just "couldn't give a fuck Punk-Rock'n'Rollers" who found everything exciting. That excitement rubbed off on people around us; it made us strangely magnetic, good–bad but not evil.

Eventually, we found a proper regular — good — dealer who was always on point. But being so good, he was always in demand by serious underground players — that meant we couldn't always get him to come over if it was just for a couple of wraps. He suggested we buy quantity so we could start dealing wraps ourselves. If we did it right, then we could skim enough from the weight to get fucked for free too. So that's what we did.

We'd get a quarter bag, which usually splits into eight nice bags. But we'd split it into ten bags, giving us eight slightly smaller wraps to sell and two free wraps to use ourselves. Then we'd buy two more back from our stock, leaving six to sell and make our money back. We dropped the price to counter the tiny shortfall, too. We were good guys like that; well, I was; Evo was a rat.

Speed started catching on as something around the scene. More people were getting into sniffing speed all the time, so we could sell quickly and dig at will. The more we shot up, the more we liked it. Pretty soon, the non-stop drugging was taking the place of the non-stop fucking, which didn't seem to matter to Evo, and truth be told, even I was becoming a little less bothered about it too. After all, we had each other, brothers in arms, and we really, really couldn't give a fuck about much else.

We wanted to test our limits, wanted to see how fucked up we could get, how much we could take, what we could handle. We weren't on a death wish; we were living for the moment, every moment.

Sometimes, we'd wake up and find blood all over the walls — blood-stained, blood-red walls. The first time it happened, we didn't immediately remember how it had got there, then bit by bit, we realised that we'd pulled barrels of blood out of our arms and squirted them all around the room. There was blood on the ceiling, blood up the walls, blood on the sofa — all over the place. We worked out that we'd had the idea to shoot a bullet of each other's blood into the other one's arm — but I don't know if we actually did it: maybe we did, maybe we didn't, I really couldn't say. But at a guess…

I remember us laughing at the sight of the "blood art" in the morning. The paper-mâché torso that depicted "Dark Marc" was a target of our "art", substituting the pills we'd liberated and swallowed with our own "Life's Blood". It was symbolic: we were alive, curious cats — we were rocking on "Raw Power"; "Street-walking cheetahs with a heart full of napalm". Yeah, I understood The Stooges.

During this period of discovery, quite unbelievably, I was still going to work. My strange shit-sniffing job was mainly based down in the lab, which kept me away from other staff. So I'd take my works with me and build a dig up in one of the bathroom cubicles, flushing the pot and pulling some "clean" water out from the new flow, cooking it up in a bottle top and banging one off right there in the MAFF toilet stall, before returning to the lab for an afternoon of save-the-world shit-sniffing — it was all strangely addictive.

5. NEW HORIZONS

I was home alone, playing around on my guitar and trying to map out a song — working on chord sequences, top riffs, hooks and looking for something that might stick. It wasn't going well, so after a couple of hours of just banging my balls against a wall, I decided to cook up a dig and crack The Stooges on to my stereo, the *Funhouse* album.

I set up the Gun and shot myself with a Silver Bullet. I'm smoking, hanging out with myself, blissfully rocking away to "Down on the Street" along with Iggy's great band. Then, out of nowhere, a little voice popped up inside my head. Now, like most people I'd had plenty of little chats with myself over the years, but this time it was different. This little voice was chatting at me — with a force that I hadn't experienced before. Not only was it uninvited, but it was dishing out a proper rat-a-tat-tat verbal assault!

"Hey! what's going on, you've got the girls, you're living with the gays, how about that new freedom in bedsit land, you like that, right, you know, free to hit the drugs, free to get fucked up, well done Punk, you're doing some living, hey, it might kill you but don't worry about that, "so what, whatever", isn't that what you like to say… Come on, Punk, you've got it going on, so you better write it down, go on, get it down, put it on paper, play your guitar, get picking with the old-broken hand, do something, do it now!"

I wasn't sure what was really happening to me, the voice just kept going on rat-a-tat-tat:

"Hold up, what's that? You're playing The Stooges again, maybe some Johnny Thunders next, then a few songs by The Dead Boys? Hey, it's all good fella, but just one question; where's *your* fucking album? Don't you want your own *L.A.M.F.*? Your own *Young, Loud and Snotty*? Can you be arsed to put a bit of work in? Don't you want to write something good enough to sit right up there on the top shelf next to those classics? Come on now, step up, be somebody, be you, don't just sit about Getting Totally Fucked, Get To

95

Fuck with that shit, come on, 'Down To Kill Like A Mother Fucker', well how about 'DTK–LAMF' or go home, you snotty brat? Do Something, Do It Now!"

Well fuck me, I was exhausted after hearing all that, but I pushed back against the voice:

"Shut up, I've been researching, it's all good." But the voice wasn't having it, and off it went again:

"Say what? Researching, you say you're researching, oh for fuck's sake, get your fucking shit together or ship out — because this shit's not for kids, Punk! It's adult entertainment, so have at it, get about it, or fuck off home and don't bother hanging around here no more."

I knew that this inner voice, tormenting me, goading me, was actually spot on, it was coaxing me and pushing me. It wasn't trying to be nasty just for the cunt of it, it was trying to help me:

"Alright, alright, shut the fuck up, fella." I turned off The Stooges and picked my guitar back up: "I'm on it."

I'd had some control over the usual back-and-forth chit-chats with myself up until then. It was usually like two of me chatting things out together, like me and my best mate. I generally welcomed an internal chat, invited it even, but this time it was almost like I needed it, I was giving myself a kick in the arse regardless of whether I'd invited or welcomed it. I recognised that I needed it — a hard pep-talk, like a Don Revie halftime bollocking to the players in the glorious Leeds United team.

The Don would usually give his bollockings to the lads down in the dressing room, after first spending a few minutes with his back to them — combing his hair while scanning the room via the mirror — then, he'd turn around and let rip with hellfire.

That's what this was like, a self-administered, "Kick out the Jams" hard foot up the ass, from me to me.

I grabbed my guitar again, having inadvertently let it slip back on to the bed while processing what was going on — I didn't want to hear any more. I told the voice calmly:

96

"Alright, I get it, now pipe down and fuck off, will you?" I was just giving it a little bollocking back, just keeping it in check. It cut out and I got to work writing these lyrics for a song called "Tonight".

"Tonight"

Goodbye, you know that I said goodbye…
I don't need your tension, I've got mine!
Under the street lights, you steal my pride
But the truth is, you'll never take me down.
I've got a feeling deep inside me, I think I'm justified…
Oh yeah, you know I wanna, I wanna let it out!
Hey straight man you need saving, I recommend sedation tonight…
I said tonight, c'mon tonight, genocide tonight…lift off now.
You seem to forget that you never passed the test
You gave me a bad time once, you had no regrets.
Well my gun is waiting to fire silver bullets, how many times did you put me through it?
You want my soul, you want it heaven sent, but you can't afford to pay the rent…tonight, I said tonight, c'mon tonight, genocide tonight, lift off now.
Well, you've been talking
for so long now, and I ain't sorry, no not at all!
You're cheap and trashy
And you take the bait
You gave me a bad time once, and now it's all too late…lift off now…

I was well pleased with it; the words and music were all completed in that one session: "That'll stand up to scrutiny once it's recorded and put on an album — how do you like that!?"

I was challenging the voice to say something negative, I dared it to: "Go on then, have a go at slagging that off, a

97

proper Punk-Rock'n'Roll song, say something bad about that then!"

The voice was silent, it knew I'd done good, I'd written a little snapshot of something, put it down in writing, put it to music and delivered a song.

The words to the song might not have been Shakespeare, maybe they were more word salad than poetic prose — I didn't really know and I didn't really care, so long as they made sense to me. I was sure they'd make sense to other people like me too, but even if they didn't, "so what, whatever!" I think the song was really no more than a personal expression, my view of the social war zone and how it was better to deal with shit while high on drugs… "hey straight man you need saving, I recommend sedation."

It was also a confirmation, a call-out to junkie town: I was a Punk-Rock'n'Roll Junkie and it didn't phase me — I wanted to be what I knew I was.

"It's the dog's bollocks, pal," the voice spoke up at last. It was good to hear that we were in agreement.

It'd go on like this with the voice from here on in — an everyday feature of life now, and to be truthful, most of the time it did pipe down and fuck off if I asked it to. I had a pretty good degree of control over it. Well, at first I did.

*

My reputation around the music scene in Leeds had started to take shape. I'd already had a record out, and by now I'd done quite a few Leeds gigs as well.

I was becoming a well-known "face around town" and was "almost famous" at The Warehouse. Not famous like Marc Almond and Dave Ball from Soft Cell, or infamous like the notorious "fuck 'em all" Andy Riley from the two straight Andys, nor like the famed "weirder than the rest" Roxy, whose dress-up style was outrageous even by the most outrageous standards.

I wasn't famous like many others in the club were, the Leeds version of the Blitz Kids or the Bromley Contingent, but I was almost famous down there at The Warehouse. It seemed like most people knew who I was — "the Iggy Thunders guy", "the Jukebox Babe fella" — and of course not forgetting I was one of the 27 Leicester Grove Crew.

Me and Evo were always together: "Here they come," people would say out loud, probably half in compliment and definitely half in disdain. Between us we had forged proper drug-abusing credentials.

So far as I can remember, it was only us two sticking needles in our veins right then, and our capacity to get fucked night after night, yet still always able to rise to the challenge of the next day, the next night, was already becoming *admired* around town.

We felt like we were the unquestioned top-dog Punk-Rock'n'Roll drug abusers on the scene — well, the scene as we perceived it to be, which was probably made up of just us two idiots anyway: we were two vainglorious little pricks!

But others were curious about us, some people would even gravitate to be around us, to be in our niche druggie scene, rather than run away from us. (Maybe they should have.) But for us two, we were in it for the long haul, drugs was a lifestyle we actively embraced. We weren't bystanders; we were shooting from the hip, like outlaw cowboys in the night. Well, not just in the night, in the morning, in the afternoon, early evening — anytime, all the time. We wanted to be Kings of the Junkie Punk-Rock'n'Rollers.

I wrote more new songs, songs about nothing, the attempts at political–social commentary were gone. I wasn't clever enough to write that stuff, not informed enough, or interested enough — not at that point anyway. Writers like Joe Strummer and Jimmy Pursey could have that. Johnny Rotten had re-set himself as John Lydon by now, and he had taken things to new levels on those social–political themes. The Three Js were brilliant dissident aggressors, brilliant writers: I bailed on that style of writing, it wasn't my bag.

I was mostly writing about being drug-fucked. The cunty voice said: "You lost your respect, you did — and that's Rock'n'Roll." I wrote it down as a song:

"You Lost Your Respect, You Did!":

Well, a good friend sold me a pistol…
You know I'm the type who really likes to get things fixed!
And I've been working down in the graveyard
I'm just digging holes 'cause it's how I get my kicks
I said: "Hey, you lost your respect." I said: "Hey, you lost
your respect"
Now my best friend, you know that he's been vacant…
And my girlfriend, she's just fixed another line!
I'm not eating, but it ain't called starvation…
I guess maybe that's why everything falls down!
I said: "Hey, you lost your respect," I said: "Hey, you lost
your respect"

I was writing from a more personal viewpoint, an emotional place full of colourful storytelling. Tales of the real life that was going on around me — a life I was creating for myself, using analogy and symbols to portray a version of my reality. It didn't need to have a message.

I liked to think of this style of writing as "real". I was becoming a dirty street poet, talking about gutter-glitter culture, pouring out a nosebleed of verbiage: "Whatever the fuck that meant, that's what I thought it was."

It made me feel unique in my immediate musical surroundings. Nobody else was writing like this in Leeds, or the UK, not that I knew of anyway. I was penning colourful, black-and-white glimpses of a life less boring, putting it to Rock'n'Roll chord sequences and playing it out with a Punk "so what, whatever" sensibility and honesty.

Maybe it was even me who coined the tag "Punk-Rock'n' Roll". I hadn't heard anybody else say it, and I'd not seen it written anywhere either, not back then at least. Usually, it was "Punk" or "Rock'n'Roll" that people referenced. Neither was accurate for what I was starting to produce, so I put them together as "Punk-Rock'n'Roll" — this was 1981-1982. If

100

you can show me a Punk-Rock'n'Roll reference that pre-dates '81, then fair go, but until then, I'm claiming it for myself.

One thing I was clear about though: it was my aim to be sat on a par with the crew of artists that spoke to me: Stiv Bators, Johnny Thunders, Iggy Pop, Alan Vega, all those guys. I wanted to match their efforts in personal nonsense — I wanted to leave something behind that bled.

*

One way or another, I managed to work through the days and do drugs with Evo through the nights.

Back at the MAFF shit-sniffing lab I took advantage of the solitude, caught up on sleep for an hour here and there, sketched out song ideas, sniffed the shit, and in between time, once or twice a week, I'd get over to Whinmoor to see me mum and rehearse with the band. It was like living three separate lives but sharing one body. I never felt tired. I was still young, 18/19 years old. Just a lad really. I got myself into a rhythm where I could do it all, no sweat, no problem.

I arranged a gig in Leeds down at another local hot spot called Le Phonographique.

Annie Hogan, from 27, was one of the DJs there alongside Claire Shearsby. Claire was the girlfriend of the guy who was the singer for The Sisters of Mercy and she'd also been the DJ at The F Club — the music was always top-notch wherever these two girls played. I loved the fact that it was the girls who were spinning and getting us vibed up, it just fit, they were both great. But I can't mention The Phono without saluting the star of the show down there who was an incredible DJ known as "Big Jim".

He was the best-loved DJ in the scene, always armed with a great bag of music to play from. He was a very tall, bleached-blond gay guy, very flamboyant. He could be fun or feisty. He would often jump down from behind the DJ booth and physically bounce somebody out of the club himself if they were causing a problem.

He was a character and ruled the roost — he wasn't a shrinking violet, that's for sure. The only other place you'd see Jim would be up at The Faversham, having a beer and holding court with a gaggle of impressed followers, all hanging on his every word. Various groups of flamboyant guys'n'gals seemed to worship Big Jim be they straight, gay, Punk, Goth, Electronic New Romantics, or even me and Evo, the Punk-Rock'n'Rollers — he was just massively popular around the scene and we all loved him. He was enigmatic, that's the word for Big Jim.

Anyway, The Phono was a tiny 100-200-capacity club — a really fun place, that had its dance floor set up in the middle of the room, built around a mirrored column in the centre, which matched with the mirrored walls all around the sides of the club where the tables were. It was a great optical illusion that gave the effect that the room was always packed, which in fairness it actually always was, and almost always full of good people. When folk stepped on to the dancefloor of The Phono it was like a festival of preening peacocks. We were flamboyant. We were all performers, the *patrones*, the bar staff, and the DJs too — what a place it was in Leeds legend.

The owners were also freaky-strange, two small guys, identical twins. They hardly ever smiled and weren't known for being friendly, nobody could get a good angle on them. But they liked me, they always let me in for free, along with whoever I might be with too. They mostly made their money off the students spending their grants rather than off us locals mostly on the dole, but the twins were smart — they knew that us locals were part of the décor, part of the club's attraction, like movie set extras. We all thought of ourselves as the real stars of the show anyway, but the twins actually knew we were. That's why some of us got the straight-in, free-entry treatment. They weren't friendly twins, but they weren't daft twins either.

The club was located underground, which was fitting — underground alternative music for underground alternative people. It was inside a modern-style type of shopping mall at the top end of town, easy to get to from where I lived, but also a pretty dangerous place to be come closing-time for us alternative types, because upstairs there was another club, a massive capacity space playing chart music and disco — a fucking Tiffany's chrome and carpet club, which catered for the flickheads who thought we were all puffs, soft wankers, and weird dickheads.

Well, some of us were puffs, and others were hetero fuck-machines but looked like puffs, some were hetero-puffs who'd fuck anything with a pulse, some were soft, and probably did like to have a wank, while some were right hard wanky bastards. Most of us were weird dickheads, even the girls. I didn't mind what they thought we were. I even called myself a freak, an idiot, a dum dum dickhead. We knew who we weren't. We weren't fucking flickheads — that's for sure.

*

The flickheads were a massive but loose group of mates. They had loads of tight-knit cliques inside a bigger mob, and they would always travel in packs. Almost all were football hooligans who wore trendy smart fashions — real casual stuff. They all had the same hairstyle, short at the back with a long fringe in a side parting that they had to keep flicking away from their eyes to see. Hence, "flickheads".

For them, a night out wasn't complete if it didn't involve knocking the fuck out of someone, usually five on one or eight on three — always numbers in their favour. Whereas we didn't want to end our night out fighting anyone, we wanted to end our night out fucking, or being fucked up on drugs.

Loads of the flickheads from the club upstairs were part of the Leeds United Service Crew, one of the country's top firms of footie thugs. I knew a few of their boys because I'd been in school with them since age three or four and right through till leaving at 16. We'd grown up together, played football and started going to Elland Road together.

103

As lads, we'd all gone to the games, starry-eyed fans, to marvel at King Billy, Sprake, Reaney, Cooper, Charlton, Hunter, Lorimer, Clarke, Jones, Giles and Gray, with Madeley and Bates as all-purpose subs — Revie's Team. We were just innocent fans at first, young kids just wanting to see the mighty Whites in the flesh. Then things started to change a few years later when we all got to be about 13 or 14.

One night, we all went down to Elland Road for a midweek league cup game, Leeds v Colchester, a 3rd round knockout game. Leeds were a top-division team with all international star players and Colchester played a couple or more leagues below us. We ran out 4–0 winners. Job's a good 'un. Let's get back to Whinmoor.

As we made our way, I could see a good-sized group of Leeds fans, older than us, up ahead. They were pointing towards us, so I pulled my scarf out of my jacket to make sure it was on full display, just to be safe, so everybody could see I was "Leeds Leeds Leeds". As we got closer, I realised they were looking past us and honing in on two men who were walking and talking as they made their way back towards the city centre too — all nice and friendly, pally joking kind of stuff. It was obvious they were mates. One had a Leeds hat on, and then I noticed the other had a Colchester scarf around his neck. "You daft twat," I couldn't help but think, "What're you fucking thinking?". They were having a good time, oblivious, so far as I could make out.

Keep in mind that Leeds had won 4–0 and Colchester were a tiny club compared to Leeds. So I'm thinking we should all be on our way back to Whinmoor nice and happy. But there was a feeling in the air — the sound of violence before violence actually happens.

I was right. All of a sudden, the Leeds crew — 20-strong or more — ran as one towards the hapless two. But rather than physically attack right off the bat, the mob pulled up just short and circled them. My mates, future *boys*, future *flickheads*, lads I'd grown up with since childhood, all ran over to join the circle. I stayed and stood where I was. I didn't want to be in the mob, so I kept back on the side of the road looking on, fearing the worst for the two fellas.

One of the two blokes shouted: "It's alright, lads, I'm Leeds, he's with me, he's my brother-in-law." He'd found the eye of the leader and thought his "I'm Leeds" plea would save the day. It should have…

The entire mass moved as one, following the leader who'd landed the first big crack. They collectively stomped the fuck out of the hapless two. Kids my age, my mates, were trying to get a boot in from the back row of the attack circle. Then, after about thirty seconds or so, which felt like minutes rather than seconds, the leader shouted, "Enough, they've had enough, lads," and everybody gave way.

I wanted to shout "Too right, it's enough, shouldn't have even started, we fucking won four-to-nowt, you daft twat" but I didn't. I kept my gob shut tight. The leader grabbed the battered Leeds fan, scruffed him up by his hair, his Leeds United hat well gone. The poor bugger's down on his knees, blood streaming down his face — not crying though. He pleads: "We're sorry, we're sorry, come on, leave it, let us go, I'm Leeds." The fella couldn't get to his mate, who'd taken the brunt of it and looked in a right state, laid out flat, not moving much or making a sound either — I thought the worst.

Then the leader says to the Leeds gadger: "Go on then, all right, it's over now." He then says to the mob "It's enough, lads" and makes out as if to be leaving. I feel a sense of relief as the circle starts to relax its stance, but it was a dirty trick. As quick as the leader had feigned to go, within a split second, he'd turned on his feet, a "Gerd Müller in the box" turn, and smacked the man full in the face again. It's another free, uncontested big shot. The crew are just as quick — they all jump at it for a second time. It's another eternal thirty-second kicking, maybe more this time.

I could see some coppers running towards the carry-on. I shouted as loud as I could, "Coppers are coming, coppers are coming."

Not that I wanted to warn the mob so they could save themselves from the cops — I shouted out because it was the only way I could see of trying to give the two victims some help in making the attack stop.

Even if it were just a few seconds, a few less boots, it was something. They scattered fast, out of there before the police were anywhere near them. The mob had pulled out and split away, split into loads of smaller packs, threes and fours, odds and sods and whatnots. The leader gave me a thumbs-up and a wink as he passed me: "Well done young 'un," he said as he walked right in front of me. He thought I'd done it for his benefit.

The mob were all walking towards town now, getting far away from the scene as quickly as they could. I lagged behind, I stayed on my toes, but at the same time I was rooted to where I was, just for a few seconds more. I didn't want to be part of it.

The two fellas were holding their heads and faces, both beaten up well enough, one trying to lift the other. Both were now moving at least. I wanted to help but didn't dare. On one hand, I didn't want the leader to look back and see me helping "the enemy". On the other hand, I didn't want the police to think I was part of the mob doing the kicking either. The best bet was to slink off towards the city centre. I finally managed to make my legs work and walked away from the scene of the beating.

I felt bad it had happened. I'd not been involved, and I couldn't do anything to stop it, well, not more than shout "The coppers are coming". Maybe in *The Hooligan's Rule Book*, these geezers were fair game, that fella was walking as bold as brass from the ground to town wearing the other team's colours. What the fuck was he thinking? Did he think Leeds was somewhere where the fans didn't give a shit and all and sundry had a free pass to walk through in their own colours? I don't know. I just knew that kicking these lads to bits, well, it wasn't for me.

Over the next few years, those lads from school went on to be a big part of the Service Crew, going to Elland Road matches just to see if they could have a scrap before the game in town, or after the game if they could ambush some poor cunts. But what they really loved were the away days, travelling all over Britain and Europe, fighting anybody who was up for it. They didn't care who got in front of them, big or small, tiny group or army, any and every fucker was gonna get it, didn't matter if they wanted it or not.

I still went to Elland Road. I'd meet those same mates in the big pool room of The Guildford pub before a game, but I'd always make sure I'd slope off to make my way to the ground on my own. I kept well out of the way of getting involved with the Service Crew. It was their thing, and mostly they were scrapping with other crews from other teams, so it was what it was. Nobody tried to pull me into it or slate me for not getting into it either. We all stayed mates, and I hoped none of them found themselves on the other side of a kicking.

*

Back at The Phono, I'd booked a show, where I met another lad, "Uncle". The Uncle nickname had stuck with him from school, I never found out the origins of it. Evo was mates with him and he introduced us. Uncle was from up Cookridge way, just a couple miles farther than my shit-sniffing job in Lawnswood, and near where I'd taken piano lessons as a kid.

As much as I always knew Evo was a rat-faced twat, a rat-faced twat who I adored, Uncle was somebody who you knew instantly you could count on. He just had this way about him that made you feel like he had your back like a trusted uncle — maybe that's where the name came from — rather than looking for a chance to stab you in it. That said, he could be a right naughty little bastard too.

107

Before the gig, we sat and drank some beers together. We got on right away and formed an instant friendship. Then, about thirty minutes before we were gonna play, he pulled out a bag with a couple of dope-cakes in it. He'd been playing Fanny Craddock, baking them earlier in the day: "Do you want one?" I didn't think twice and gobbled one down.

The Phono doesn't have a stage, you play on the same level as the crowd. But don't laugh, because years later The Clash also did a gig on exactly the same spot. And as the room is packed, it's a good feeling to be face-to-face with the audience.

I'm on guitar and vocals tonight, I set off with the opening chords of the opening song. The band falls in behind, it's sounding tight, then comes the guitar drop-down, a section where my guitar cuts out to give some space for my vocals to take over, the dynamics creating a sense of drama.

The cool groove is kicking along just fine — my brother is rocking the beat on the drums, the bass line is solid, and one of my sisters is on backing vocals too. So, the moment has come, I grab the mic and get ready to sing. That's when the dope cake hits like a hammer, knocking me fully off my feet. I'm laid out across the front of the non-stage at foot level. I need a moment, or three, before even thinking of getting back up again, but the show must go on. The crowd aren't sure if this is all part of the gig anyway. So I turn on my side, grab the mic and start singing into a sea of feet, rather than a sea of faces — to be honest the crowd doesn't seem to mind, they seem to like that I'm rolling around on the floor.

Something catches my eye through the waves of boots and legs. Focusing in, I can see Uncle laid out in the same position as me, but he's at the back of the crowded room while I'm at the front. Neither of us is quite in the fetal position, but it's close — we're both fucked on dope-cake. Uncle catches my eye with a massive manic grin on his face as he gives me a thumbs up across the mess of beer and fag-ends on the floor. I put my thumb back up to him, barely. He breaks into a fit of laughter and I can see him rolling about the floor. It sets me off too; I start wriggling about even more on the floor, laughing down the mic, my guitar thrashing around my body, banging on the floor around me and making a screeching racket, accidentally sounding like Thurston Moore from Sonic Youth. The crowd seems to really love it by now. It's like I'm having a fit, it's like something they might have expected from Iggy, Johnny, Vega or Fad Gadget. Everybody goes with it and the band just plays on. Near the end of the song, I bounce back up again and light up the guitar with a Thunders "sonic Chuck Berry" one-note wail: "It's on, baby!"

One way or another, the show develops into a great gig, I'm tripping out of my mind all the way through it, but everybody seems to love us, everybody does love us, including the brilliant Phono DJs, the great club staff and even the bloody twins too — but do you see what I mean about Uncle? He can be a right naughty bastard. It turns out that Uncle had made the dope-cakes using very strong Pakistan black hash, lots of it — and also "a secret ingredient", a handful of magic mushrooms!

After the gig Uncle comes back to 27 with me and Evo: "Tie it up, shoot it up, bang your head and throw it up, too much junkie business, too much junkie business." So then there were three.

We shot up all night, carrying on all through the next day, the next night too, a speed session where we talked, and talked, and talked. It could have been about anything; for sure, it was a lot about music. We were all equal fans of the same stuff.

I tell them that I really wanna make a proper band, a band of Punk-Rock'n'Rollers, real Punk-Rock'n'Rollers. It turns out Uncle is a drummer, and Evo is always talking about playing the bass.

It's a shame that Evo didn't have a musical bone in his body; even Sid Vicious sounded like a virtuoso next to him. It's a pity for Evo, because he looked fucking great in his own freaky rat-faced way, he would've looked ace up on a stage wrapped in a bass guitar… I did think about "Sid Vicious Mk II", but dropped that idea. I weren't no Malcolm M.

But no matter, the three of us started to hang out every day. Three are one. We think we're the drug version of The Three Musketeers — but we're more like The Three Stooges, not the band, but the old-time slapstick comedy idiots.

*

A guy I knew was an agent–manager and was connected in Europe. He met me down at another chaotic gig of ours and, strangely enough, offered us a tour of Holland. I didn't understand why anybody in Holland would want to book a band from Leeds who couldn't even get booked outside of Leeds in the UK, but apparently it was a trend. UK bands were perceived as popular and in demand in places like Holland, France and Spain. So after a few weeks shooting junk and cementing a friendship with Uncle and Evo, I found myself saying cheerio to them and setting off on that first tour of Holland, where I would do that first fateful gig in Schiedam, the one I told you about earlier — remember?

The tour was notable to me for revealing a few life-changing choices that I had to embrace:

One, I realised that the guys from school and Whinmoor were a tight-ass band but they were not true Punk-Rock'n'Rollers. That's not an insult or rudeness; they were major music lovers and good musicians. But given I was about to roll around in blood, puke, booze, and dirt, I needed a band who were just like me — or at least kinda like me. I wanted a band like The Heartbreakers, The Dolls, The Stooges, guys who would get into crazy shit just to see if they could get out the other side, adventurers, highwaymen who didn't fear the hangman. I wanted pirates and outlaw cowboys.

Two, I had met the super-sexy Bea — she asked me to return to Holland after the tour and move in with her at Hal's place. I wanted it, and Hal was cool with it even though he

110

had also had a stint living with her a couple of years earlier too. He didn't care, he just said, "Sure, come back quick. My house is your house."

Bea was gorgeous, she was also a soft-porn model, brilliant cook, and great in the sack. You might say she was a little off-beat and crazy too. Her invite was like the call of the wild, how could a young boy resist? This was the type of girl that could make a grown man cry.

Third, I liked *the life*. Now that I had tasted life on tour, I loved *the life*. I wanted more. It meant the drug taking was legitimate — in my world, all Punk-Rock'n'Rollers, the ones I loved at least, were Punk-Rock'n'Roll Junkies. This was it for me!

I knew what I had to do. I had to make a proper, real, Punk-Rock'n'Roll band. I was living it; my band had to live it too. But first, hold that thought. I was going to go live it up in Holland for a bit with Hal, Long Johnny, and Bea.

As soon as I got back from that first ever tour, I gave notice to leave my job at the Ministry of Agriculture, Fisheries and Food. The world was gonna have to survive without me, or despite me.

The hardest part was saying my goodbyes to Uncle and Evo. I told them I'd be gone for a minimum of two months up to a maximum of six months and that when I got back I was going hell for leather on creating my new "real band proper". Maybe they could look for somewhere we could all live together, maybe even think about starting up the new "real band proper" together if rat-faced Evo could pull his finger out of his ass and learn to play the bass by the time I returned?

With my severance pay sorted, I took the coach to Hull docks, the ferry to Rotterdam, and then rode a tram into Schiedam. Bea was waiting, knickers down as soon as I got back into town. Not only was she the fuck of the year, but she was also the cook of the year. We spent most of our time sucking on a bottle all around town, fucking whenever we

111

felt like it and eating well. Bea was making me feel like a god. Life was sweet.

The next three weeks were more paradise with Bea, sex, food, drink, sex, food, drink, sex, food. This was the life. "Non-stop erotic cabaret" — the sex sessions could go on all day and all night. The drinking sessions were the same, all day banging on the bottle, hitting up all the bars in Schiedam, or bouncing over to Rotterdam for kicks.

One afternoon, Bea took us to the Red Light Zone, where she paid for me to have sex with one of the prostitutes working down there. She picked out a cute Asian girl in one of the street window booths. Bea wanted to watch me fuck with somebody else while she got herself off with her fingers. After we'd finished, Bea paid more money to the Asian girl, this time to let us two fuck each other right there in her Red Lght room. I guessed it was some kind of role-play shit with Bea now taking on the role of the prostitute, maybe a reprise for her of times gone past, while the Asian girl was now role-reversed as kinda my girlfriend — this time it was her bringing herself off with her fingers in the same way that Bea had.

It was all quite the experience, especially given that I'd never been to a Red Light Zone before — I'd never been with a prostitute either. It was wild and wandering; this was all new stuff.

Then, one day, out of the blue, Bea says, "I'm going on holiday to Greece for a month with my boyfriend."

What? With your boyfriend? There was no making sense with this nutbag, I was just happy to have experienced her wildness. Whatever, so long, crazy Bea — it's been wild!

After Bea had pissed off to Greece, things took on a new twist — I was getting ready to go on a road trip to the south of Spain. I'd decided to freak out my long-lost dad with a surprise visit. I don't know why. It just came over me as something I wanted to do, even though I hadn't had contact with him for five years or more.

The idea was to hitch to his place down in Puerto Banus, where he apparently had his own piano bar these days. The plan was to hang out for a week and see what would come out of it — maybe something, maybe nothing. Then hitch back up to Schiedam, collect my stuff and get myself set to return to Leeds and start my new "proper real band".

And then, equally out of nowhere, I came into contact with the vision that was Dee.

It was the most amazing moment. The setting was miles removed from a typical scene of romance — no candlelit lighting or hazy looks across a seductive room, not that I'd ever done that kind of shite anyway. It was as normal as real life can be... kinda.

I came out of a small shop where I'd been looking for something sweet to satisfy the munchies. As I started to rip into my chocolate bar, I absent-mindedly looked up the street. I caught sight of a girl dressed in black about to step onto a tram taking her to Rotterdam. Call it a twist of fate, but our eyes met, and truthfully the world stood still. I was frozen in mid-chew, she was frozen in mid-step.

Hal came out of the shop. "Hey, what's up?" he shook me playfully.

"Who's that girl, mate?" I asked as he looked towards where I was fixated.

"I know her. Dee. She's totally fucked up in a bad situation — forget it, man."

She, Dee, held tight and didn't climb onto the tram immediately. Instead, she waited for everybody to pass, making herself the last to board. Finally, she climbed up — our eyes never left one another.

The tram set off and I finally broke my stance to run level with her window. I tried to tell her something; I hoped that I'd delivered my message so that she'd understood — waving hands and pointing fingers, I told her, "Meet me here tomorrow at the same time." It seemed to work in the movies after all. I'd acted without thinking, spontaneous, reacting to her, reacting to her departure. Dee smiled a beautiful smile, blew a sexy playful kiss to her excited stranger, made a little wave goodbye, gave a last backward glance, and then the tram was too far gone. A few moments later, she was out of sight.

Hal looked me in the eye: "If you think Bea was trouble, well, she's just trouble for kids. This girl, Dee, she comes ready bagged with real problems. She's tied into a drug dealer from Rotterdam. She's not kids' stuff, mate. Definitely not kids' stuff."

Regardless, I was at the bus stop the next day at the same time, and in the same place. She didn't turn up, and I thought that was that.

Back at Hal's local pub, the jukebox local, the scene of the triumphant gig that had started everything, me and Hal were loudly knocking back cold Heineken beers and Jack Daniels chasers, soon joined by a good crew from the local Schiedam Boys Gang, Long Johnny leading them of course.

The bar was full of Punk-Rock'n'Rollers and cute punkettes, the party was rockin'. The killer jukebox was on good form too, belting out tracks by Motörhead, The Stooges, Elvis, The Damned and loads of great selections from different people. All was well, then Hal's face dropped.

I looked at him, not sure if I should be concerned. "What's up, mate?" I said as he broke into a gigantic, ice-cold, blue-eyed smile. It was as good as Iggy's *Lust For Life* album cover smile. He laughed out loud, put his hand on my shoulder, paused, drank a beer in one giant gulp, and looked at me and said, "Dee, the dream, is right behind you."

He looked at me, looked over my shoulder, then back at me again with a face that said, "Fuck me, the shit's gonna hit the fan — but if it does, I'll be right here to help clean it up, if I can."

He wasn't messing about, it wasn't a joke. I turned around and Dee was right there. My inner voice did its best Iggy take: "Now we're gonna be face to face, and we'll lay right down in my favourite place."

She was beautiful, not in a Liz Taylor classic Cleopatra type of way, but more like Liz Taylor, "been through the mill but still holds a rare beauty", type of way. Dee's dark brown eyes were looking straight into mine as I blurted, "I have to leave on a road trip in a few days, I know this might sound weird, I know I don't know you, and you don't know me, but I love you."

WHAT?!

I looked intently at her: "I've been looking everywhere for you."

She broke into a big smile, I thought that we would fall into a passionate kiss. We both wanted to, I could feel it, but she didn't let it happen. She gave a signal, one finger placed across her gorgeous lips and said, "Come to the quiet corner and we can talk."

It was the first time I'd heard her voice. She spoke with a slow cool beat, it reminded me of how I'd heard Nico speak, in that severe "broken English" with a heavy, sedated accent. She sounded as sexy, as sultry, as she looked — it was just as I had imagined her voice might be — while I was sounding like Stan Laurel, probably.

Dee slinked off towards the table in the quiet corner, gorgeous, sleek, with a proper groove to her step.

"Hal, she's amazing," I said over my shoulder, so as not to lose sight of her.

"I know she is, everybody knows she is. Be careful, buddy," he countered as he slapped my back, nudging me forward towards her table in the quiet corner.

With a couple of cold beers and whisky chasers for both, I sat down with Dee — a little drink to reset the dial: "Let me try again. Hello, Dee…"

6. TIME SLIPS AWAY — BUT KEEP HOPE ALIVE

"Stay cool. I'm coming back for you."

I was trying to reassure Dee that my plan was for me and her to be together. I explained that I was going to Spain to catch up with my dad, and then I'd return to Holland to help her with paperwork and arrangements to get out of Rotterdam for good. Then, I'd return to Leeds to set up a place to live, and finally, I'd come back to Holland and chaperone her home to England.

"It's not true," she cried. "You're leaving me to die."

While Bea had been like a Punk-Rock'n'Roll fantasy girl, nothing but cartoon capers in La La Land, Dee was the Punk-Rock junkie reality.

She was 22, a young woman I suppose — but so far as I could make out, she was nowt but a kid herself really, same as me. Only, her story was harrowing, given that she'd been a heroin addict since age 16.

Dee had been abused throughout her entire childhood and pushed into prostitution before she'd even turned 17 — and by the time she was 20, her life had been taken over by a Rotterdam gangster; marked up as "property of". By the time I met Dee, she'd been on the methadone programme for a year already, and was desperately looking for a way out.

This wasn't kids' stuff, and she made no apology. She didn't need to; she was a victim, not a participant. It was a real thing to her; no glamour, no glitter, nothing much more than sadness day by day. Moments worth a smile were captured where she found them. In her eyes, I was her moment.

When I looked at Dee, it should have scared me straight; it didn't though. She was tragically beautiful; she had a proper real gritty story. It didn't scare me away; it attracted me more to her, kind of like how people back in Leeds were attracted to me, Evo and Uncle, especially when we looked

116

more dead than alive, and drug-fucked. The thing is, everything we three had been doing with drugs just felt like fun. It was fun. The basic reality of sticking a needle into a vein didn't register as being a cause for concern on any level. We revelled in being the Idiots, the Dum Dum Boys, the Dirtbox Junkies. It's as if my compass was broken, the point on the dial fucked.

So, like I said, looking at Dee should have made me shudder, seeing the reality of life in a drug-dependent world. It was right in front of me; I was face to face with her, a girl whose life had been so damaged, degraded, ruined and ruled by drugs and abuse. But instead of shaking, I defended my own want, the want to experience drug adventures into oblivion. The voice held tight to that thought too. "We're speed freaks and Dee's a smackhead — that's the big difference, buddy-boy." It was pretty brutal, but I agreed with myself.

I told her again, "Stay cool, I'm coming back for you." I meant it too, right there and then. I know I meant it at that moment in time. But if I'm honest about it today, years and years later, in retrospect, then maybe I was just seeing a twisted kind of trophy girl in her, my own private Nico? I'm not saying that's how I felt. I'm asking myself, is that what it was?

Dee was pathetic, which isn't to beat her down; I use the word in its purest form. She was a mess, pathetically ill-equipped to beat her situation. When she said "You're leaving me to die" it wasn't fake attention-seeking drama. She didn't trust that she had it in her to get her life together.

In the short space of time we spent together, just seven days, she entered my world for a lifetime. Dee saw in me the chance for something better, to leave her lost life behind and start afresh with me. It was no more than a bag full of days, but everything felt momentous.

Dee was desperate for a new life, a new country, a new world, a world played out to the backbeat of Punk-

Rock'n'Roll — my world. She saw me as I fancied myself to be seen — some kind of somebody.

She didn't look at me with eyes that saw somebody probably doomed to failure, one of God's Sad Boys. Oh no, she saw in me somebody with something, a hero to someone. She wanted to believe that maybe that someone was her. I was into it, even though she was on the slow road to leaving drugs behind, while I was running towards drugs as fast as I could. At least she wouldn't be owned; she would be in a better place than she was right now, free at last. I wouldn't ever clip her wings. She'd have a new life in the fun house. I wanted to give her that chance, I wanted to save Dee, I really did.

*

That first night in the bar we spoke together for hours, the party erupting around us, but we were oblivious to it — caught up only in our own company. I wanted to kiss her from the first moment, and keep kissing her in every moment. We huddled in the corner of the room; we could have been on a slow boat or in the middle of Times Square. It wouldn't have mattered, we were in a private bubble.

The conversation moved on from compliments and grand statements of desire to who she was and the essence of her situation — which was dire to hear out. She told it all, the reality of living behind a glass door, selling her body hour after hour, her life in chains with a drug-dealing Rotterdam gangster. The story had no romance; her years as a scag-head should have seen me push eject; it didn't. Her childhood of abuse made me sad and mad.

The want of a sweet embrace with this incredible, seductive, tragically beautiful woman was one of the strongest sensations I had ever felt so far in my young life. It was impossible to kiss those red lips and hold this slender woman in my arms — the room was filled with the eyes and ears of others. The danger for her was very real, and for me too, although I hadn't fully understood it yet.

118

Dee was another first, the first real drug-dependent person I had ever met in the flesh. Her reality was that she had a physical and mental addiction to heroin. It had led her to make money for drugs as a prostitute, it had led to her now living under the hammer of a proper real Gangster — not the Jimmy Cagney gangster of the movies, but a violent thug, a pimp-drug-dealer, lower level to a boss at the top of the food chain in his district.

He was no joke. She'd been at his disposal for the past two years, farmed out to associates as a gift, shared with other associates at private parties, fucked by all at his whim, but also kept close to home as his toy. She lived this life for the sake of a syringe full of smack.

During the past year, she had been trying to get through a methadone treatment program, looking to clean herself up. It's hard without day-to-day home support, so of course she had slipped off the treatment, climbed back on, slipped off again and so on. But she said, "I really want to make it this time."

I was risking myself, offering salvation to this Queen of the Street, but it didn't register as dangerous. I thought of it as romantic. To be truthful, I wasn't being cocky or tough, I just didn't truly think that anything bad would happen. People split from each other all the time; it wasn't like we were in the movies. Things would be alright. But I hadn't factored in that somebody truly believed they had ownership of another human being — and that they couldn't just let her walk away. Not because of any emotional tie, but simply down to what they considered property rights. They would have to give her permission to allow her to walk away — if they didn't give her the green light to go, then she'd have to stay put… or she'd have to run away.

At the end of the first night at the Jukebox Bar, Dee returned to Rotterdam. We had managed to sneak an emotional kiss; I had managed to hold her slender body. Long Johnny and Dutch Hal both spoke seriously with me, giving me fair warning.

"It's better if you don't go there, her man is serious. Things will not go well if he hears she is with somebody without consent or payment," Long Johnny warned.

Dee and I arranged our secret liaison. Hal continued to offer his basement room as my home even though I had offered to leave and find somewhere else. The basement room had simply been a venue for fantasy fucking with Bea, but now it was a private haven, a sanctuary for Dee and me.

The first time we lay down together, it felt like the first time I was making proper love. Despite the multiple one-night stands, the "sometime" girlfriends, and all the sex I'd had with the "non-relationship regular fuck" girls, nothing had felt this way before. It was another first, making love with Dee. Despite her life in the red light, her body farmed out like a toy, she said she felt the same. Maybe she spoke the truth, maybe it was just desperate words? Who knows what's real in moments of high emotion? At 18/19 years old, I wanted to hear and believe it was true.

For a handful of days, we continued in this fashion, becoming increasingly renegade to the reality of her situation. We were comrades in arms, Bonnie and Clyde, Frankie and Johnny — fuck the rest of the world.

We repeated the mantra, "It's all about us. It's all about us." We stayed in that room for days and nights, only leaving the bedroom to shower or take delivery of Chinese food, Jack Daniels, beer and hash. Dee drank her treatment, taking her methadone daily and on time. She was making her break for the border.

Even more importantly, she hadn't gone back to the Rotterdam Gangster, not even once. During pillow talk, we declared we'd be together. Then reality bit as a team of guys approached Hal's place. We had been found.

*

It was a Saturday, late morning, just before midday. Hard knocks slammed against the front door, as if with clubs or hammers, shouting out for "Dee", shouting even louder for "the English bastard", demanding we go out on the street and

120

face them. For all the bravado of romantic love and desire, when reality calls you out, most people will generally shit their pants.

"Fuck me, we could really get fucked here," the inner voice spoke up, sounding worried — and then it switched gears on me. "I bet you feel like Paris getting offered out by Achilles, don't you? But where's Hector? If only Hector was here, right? What are you gonna do, Paris? Go out and take a battering for the hand of Helen there?" It was goading me. "Calm down, pal," I told myself. "Don't fucking worry yourself, buddy. I'm going out, and by the way," I paused for effect, "Hector is here! And this Hector is harder than club-foot Achilles — and he's rolling with a few Trojans too."

I pulled my pants on and reached for my fighting boots, well my Dr Martens. Sometimes you just have to go full tilt. And then there's fate.

Fate is a fickle friend; it can work against you but can just as quickly work in your favour. On this day, fate came knocking twice. One knock was a sledgehammer from the Rotterdam Gangsters; the other, earlier knock, was Hector in the shape of Long Johnny — along with a collection of Trojan soldiers, the best of the worst from the Schiedam Street Gang. Thank the gods of football for delivering hard-core football fans, at least on this day.

Long Johnny and his boys wanted to take me to the football that day to see Feyenoord of Rotterdam versus bitter enemies Ajax of Amsterdam — football rivals, Dutch-style. It was a bit like breaking the chair over Long Johnny's back. I had no choice but to agree to go, come what may, even knowing they were fully tooled up with blades and Stanleys. They always carried knives — some so big that they looked more like swords. It was just part of their regular everyday attire. Everyone carried a weapon; mind you, they were all full-time criminals. And so, as fate had played it out, here they were, Long Johnny and his Schiedam Street Gang, already in Hal's backyard drinking vodka and wine, eating barbecued burgers and preparing their blades for the anticipated bloodbath ahead at the big game.

Dee and I heard the door banging and the shouting in the street from the Rotterdam Gangsters. At first, we felt the jolt of fear, but that fear was diluted with relief. We knew we had Long Johnny and his hardcore crew on our side and in our backyard. They were already hyped and ready for war because of the football clash that would come later — the Rotterdam Gangsters had no idea what was coming at them from the other side of the door that they were abusing.

From our basement bed, we heard the almost immediate charge of Long Johnny and his boys running from the backyard across the hallway above us, crashing into the street, attacking without pause. They were masters of extreme ultra-violence. Whoever had come calling aggressively at Hal's door was gonna pay a price. They didn't even ask who it was that they were now fucking over. We were saved.

I rushed upstairs to get involved and play my part, though it was more for show than any real desire for action. I didn't want to be physically involved in this kind of fighting, it was leagues above my temperament. If I'd had the constitution of "Ronaldo Raccoon", a guy I hadn't even met at this time in the tale, but a character who'd become a lifelong friend later on, then I'd have probably been out of the door even before Long Johnny. Ronaldo being one of those rare specimens in life with the courage of a bull and the stones of a lion. I could write a whole book on "The Adventures of 'Bad Lad' Ronaldo" — let's just say that it wouldn't read like Huckleberry Finn... maybe one day I will...but back to the moment. I weren't no Ronaldo Raccoon when it came to ultraviolence, but Long Johnny, Scar, and his boys definitely were. Hal stopped me at the doorway. "Don't be crazy, man. These guys live for this, they love it. They'll be more pissed off with you if you go out and get hurt. You're their guest in Schiedam."

None of the guys now fighting in the street were strangers to violence, I mean proper violence on a brutal scale. On the one hand, you have a crew of organised criminal gangster muscle, paid workers who deal in daily aggression. On the other hand, there's a vicious street gang that has grown up together and lived on the block together, facing daily battles of one kind or another together, a fighting unit their whole life. They are also a real football factory — The Feyenoord Ultras. Long Johnny and his boys have no respect for the food chain, this is their turf and their life. They fight regardless of reward, fearless and unwavering. They couldn't care less who the other guys are. Other kids from the neighbourhood run over to join in; there are soon three or four Street Boys for each one of the Gangster crew. It's ten minutes of madness. The intruders have no option but to run for it.

Let me tell you something, for those who don't know — ten minutes of fighting, and I mean hard fighting, is enough time to be scared of what you're witnessing, excited by it, sickened by it, and relieved when it's finally over. You go through a lot of different thoughts and emotions in a short period of time. It either leaves you shell-shocked, drained and freaked out, or hyped up on an adrenaline rush. I'll plead the 5th and not reveal how I felt other than the relief that Dee and I were still standing. The Gangster himself hadn't made the journey in person, it was just his paid muscle; there was lots of muscle to be paid in Rotterdam.

I asked Long Johnny if he thought things would escalate from here. He didn't even know who they'd been fighting with until Dee explained it. Long Johnny didn't care. "Fuck that fucker. Come on, let's go to the football," he said, passing me a joint. "Those Ajax bastards are waiting for us in Rotterdam. Viva Schiedam, Viva Feyenoord."

I was being carried along, not making decisions, just rolling with it. I had no choice about it really. Better to be in bed with Long Johnny than thrown in a canal for dead by the Rotterdam Gangsters. Dee was taken off to a neighbourhood house on Long Johnny's estate for safety. Nobody would be dumb enough to even dare to go in there without an invite. Even the police hardly ever ventured inside.

Some of the boys were told to hang out at Hal's and watch the game with him on TV, just in case anybody was too stupid to return — the Trojans were on guard. Two lads were sent to a bar in Rotterdam with a message to the guy who wanted to get at me and retrieve Dee, like emissaries sent ahead to either set terms of a truce or lay out the rules of engagement. It was more new stuff to me. I'd never been involved with anything like this before. School vs school, or estate vs estate, skirmishes as kids back on the Whinmoor, were one thing. But in truth, I'd only ever seen this level of violence in the movies. The only thing was that in this movie, I was one of the two leading roles.

*

I managed to front myself up pretty well at the football game, seemingly anxious for action with the enemy. However, I was secretly relieved when nothing went off, thanks to an incredible police presence. The atmosphere in the ground was on fire, but the fans were well separated, and the game passed without incident, either inside or outside the ground.

Long Johnny and his boys were happy enough though. I mean, they'd been involved in the annihilation of the Gangster crew earlier, so they were proper made up already. "Thanks for setting that up," they joked with me. At least some joked and others thought it was scripted for their benefit. These lads were proper basic, nothing mattered to them outside of crime for cash or battling. But at the same time they were also incredibly good-hearted and faithful. If they were with you, they were with you.

There was one of the lads who I liked a lot. He was covered from neck to knee in scar tissue from being burnt on a bonfire. He wasn't a big lad, small and skinny, pretty vacant rather than street-sharp — but he was fearless. They called him Scar, of course. I guess so far as he was concerned nobody could do worse to him than had already been done. His brother had thrown him on to a bonfire when he was

124

super-high on glue. He didn't even try to rescue him or put out the fire burning on his brother's body once he'd got himself off. The story went that he just laughed while watching him burn. He was now in jail for attempted murder, even though the burnt brother, Scar, forgave him and didn't want to bring any charges.

To him, it was nothing but an accident, and besides that, it hadn't killed him. Scar had been in the backyard when the Gangsters came banging on the door, and as small as he might be compared to the general tall Dutch lads, he was second out through the door behind Long Johnny, who was one of those guys who liked to lead from the front. From behind the window, I saw Scar cut at least two guys during the kickoff; he went at it like a man possessed. I liked him, he liked me. He was one scary little dude.

Back at Hal's, Long Johnny demanded that he and a few of his boys would stay the night. "We have a party," he said. So we did, just the boys, Long Johnny, Hal, and me, smoking and drinking until almost morning.

The next day, Scar went to collect Dee and then the four of us, Hal, Long Johnny, Dee, and me, sat down to work out what would come next. Dee offered herself up. "I will go back to him and make it good."

Long Johnny replied, "You are with this man now. Forget that prick. We can have a war if he wants it."

Dutch Hal asked, "What do you want to do?" looking at me. I tried to balance out what was going on. Dee saw me as salvation, and Long Johnny saw a chance for a war that could lead to who knows where. Maybe it would be profitable for him to take this guy out of the scene? Hal was basically a music lover, just a good guy who was into Punk and Rock'n'Roll bands, a fella who loved his friends, but now I'd brought all this shit to his doorstep.

I was the centre of the story. I was the catalyst of everything that was going on. There was real violence in play and I didn't like the sound of that drum beat. This was *Romeo and Juliet* playing out in real time.

125

"OK, this is what I think we need to do. Hal, you and I take that road trip to Spain, just as we've already planned. Long Johnny, you put the word out that 'the English' has left town and has gone for good. Maybe things will calm down if they think I've run away. But mate, can you look out for Dee, and keep an eye on her and let everyone know she's under your wing?

"Dee, you need to get your passport sorted out. If you need to go to your mum's in Den Haag to do that, then do that. But stay cool, I am coming back for you. Everything's gonna be cool beans — that's the plan. What do you all think?"

Dutch Hal spoke first. "Perfect, we'll go tomorrow as we planned — I'm in."

Long Johnny offered some assurance. "Don't worry, I'll look out for Dee. When you get back, we'll talk about everything again."

Dee was panicked, she wanted to come to Spain with me, but I explained, "Baby, you can't come on this trip, you haven't even got a passport — you need to get one so that you can come to Leeds with me after I get things worked out and set up. This is a good plan. If I stay here now, and we carry on as we are, people will get hurt — and probably hurt much more than they did yesterday. Maybe next time, one of Long Johnny's Boys will get stabbed, or worse than stabbed. This is the best plan."

Dee couldn't get past her own emotions. "If you leave me, you leave me to die."

I reassured her again and again, "Dee, stay cool — I'm coming back for you."

But she insisted, "It's not true, you're leaving me to die."

The final day and night passed very slowly — but at the same time, it was over and gone too soon.

While seconds dragged their heels as they turned into minutes, and minutes seemed to idle as if they believed they were hours, Dee and I were making love.

126

Actually, it was intense, raw, emotional, mind-blowing, goodbye sex — hard fucking, basic instinct kind of stuff. It was the most intense and passionate 24 hours I'd ever experienced; in fact the past seven days with Dee had been like nothing I'd ever lived through before.

In reality, Dee cried the whole time during that last 24 hours, she cried so much that it felt at times like we were emotionally drowning in a room of tears.

I hate to admit it, but throughout the entire drama of it all, I was actually tripping on the buzz.

Time slips away unless you grab it by the throat and own it — I don't want to sound uncaring, or insensitive to Dee's reality, but I had both hands wrapped around the neck of that soap opera. And even though the entire scene was dripping in danger, I loved the thrill of it all — I wrung every drop of blood, sweat and tears out of the moment.

By the time Hal and I were due to leave, I could say no more to Dee than I already had — there were no more words other than to bid our farewells.

*

Dutch Hal and I took a tram from Schiedam to Rotterdam, then a train to Amsterdam. Once there, we decided to go our separate ways — the plan was to meet up in Barcelona at a famous rock bar designated by Hal, down in the Ramblas.

I made it to Brussels quite easily, then got a great ride to Paris from an incredibly kind old hippy couple who gave me enough money to get a train to Barcelona, and to look after myself for a few days.

Once in Barcelona, I headed straight to the Ramblas area and surprisingly easily found my way to the designated bar. With money in my pocket, I started drinking, had a little hash and bought a little powder.

As the night was taking over, and with no sign of Hal, I decided to enjoy the moment and wandered further into the neighbourhood, where the atmosphere seemed to increase in tension. Then, out of nowhere, an African girl approached me

127

and took hold of my arm. "Hello baby, come for a party with me."

She was ebony, small and slender but obviously physical; her tight pants showed off strong thighs and a healthy muscled ass. She had a tiny, fatless waist and a face that was spotless with not a blemish on it. She had real black-black skin, gorgeous hair in braids pulled up into a nest on top of her head, magnetic lips, a killer smile and big brown eyes. She had my attention, but my focus was still on Dee.

"Look, love, I'm up for hanging out but not up for anything else. Do you want to show me around Barcelona? I'll pay, but let's just have a laugh."

She looked at me, at first not totally understanding, "No sex? Don't you want to suck and fuck?" She looked confused.

"Well yeah, but… I just wanna hang out."

"OK, vamos, but only an hour, I have to make my money."

So off we went, she took me even deeper into the underside of the Ramblas. We were having a really cool time, hitting backstreet bars that were full of other hookers, druggies, musos and street people; it was like a community of associates in the underground. I snorted my way through the gear I'd picked up earlier. She didn't indulge, but she smoked up the hash with me and, in the end, hung out with me for nearly three hours.

I couldn't pronounce her name, so I christened her Paul. Don't ask me why I gave her a guy's name; we were just messing about, and she thought it was funny. I asked about her young life.

Paul was from Nigeria, had a daughter still back there living with her mother, named Hope, already four years older since the last time she had seen her. The story Paul told me was tragic, maybe even more tragic than Dee's.

She had been trafficked in a group of twenty across to Spain, starting from her village in the south of Nigeria but getting underway for real from Lagos. They were driven by bus through to the Western Sahara, and from there they were half driven and half walked across the desert itself, walking in the cold by night and sleeping under the shade of a tent by scorching day.

She told me they lost four on that leg of the journey, left there for the sand, no ceremony, no real acknowledgement of lost life, just angry traffickers pissed off at the missing cargo. Once across, they then went on by vans through Algeria and Morocco; four more fled from the caravan once near the north. At the Mediterranean Sea, they were loaded onto a fast Scorpio boat that flew across the sea in the dead of the pitch-black night, with no lights other than the shoreline behind and beyond. They were told to hold tight to a fixed rope hand-rail — if you went over then you were gone to the sea, because this boat wasn't stopping for nobody. She had feared the worst in the boat. She had only stayed aboard thanks to a very big guy, a co-traveller, who held her down tight when she almost lost control of the bounce as the boat skipped hard over waves, crashing onwards at speed. On landing, the two male passengers were loaded into one car and driven off to... *to somewhere*. All the girls were split into groups of twos, threes and fours, and assigned destinations. Paul and another girl were selected for Madrid.

Her understanding before the journey started was that she was going to be a cleaner-cum-nanny-cum-housekeeper for a rich Nigerian family living in Europe. She climbed into the van and slept on the mattress in the back without cause for concern, happy that the journey through to the Spanish capital would take her to a better place.

The van arrived in Madrid, nearing morning but still dark, Paul and the other girl were led to a house and each assigned a room. She slept the entire day, then after a good dinner, she slept more, on and off, through the night, half excited and half curious about the new life about to start. She was looking forward to being assigned to the wealthy Nigerian family to begin work, earn money to live, pay her debt, and still have more than enough to send back to her mum and her kid, Hope, back home.

129

Paul told me she was in a state of shock when told what her new job entailed, pleaded that there must be a mistake, begged to let her be the service maid to the house at least. I could see how beautiful she was, and for sure the men and women who had her in their hands could see it too — they were never gonna waste such potential earnings to let her cook and clean instead.

I was surprised that she said there was no violence involved, no physical brutality used to make her compliant, and that it was not a male-only chain of control. The house was controlled by two older adult women, and two adult men. They explained that she was alone in Madrid, with a debt, she had no way home without their help, her only option was to work hard, respect her oath and not to let down her family.

She was told it would "only" take five years to pay off her debt. It was only sex — like shaking hands, dancing for money — and she would be fed, get clothes, a TV, a bed to sleep in, a room of her own, access to an electric washing machine, a toilet and shower. They said the time would fly past, she would be fine, she would be happy and have no troubles. They told her that the alternative would only lead to detention in a Spanish jail as an illegal, and then deportation back home — with debt still owed.

It was a heartbreaking story, and at that time, in the early '80s, such stories were not commonly known in the UK, at least not in Leeds they weren't. Or maybe this stuff was known but I hadn't bothered to hear it. It wasn't something that was on my radar in any shape or form — years later the lid of this scandal was blown off, and the practice of trafficking was the subject of films, documentaries, news headlines and international outrage.

She only left the house twice in the first six months, working 12 hours a day and servicing between five and ten clients a day, sometimes less on a slow day and occasionally even more on a holiday weekend.

After two years, Paul had serviced more men than she could remember or count. She offered up a calculation: If she averaged 5 men x 5 days = 25 men a week x 40 weeks, that equalled 1,000 men a year. So 2,000 men. Just let that sink in.

Paul believed in God and that God would protect her, so one day, she packed her bag, walked out of the door, and left Madrid for Barcelona. There was no dramatic escape, nobody chased after her. No one was sent to bring her back. She just walked out and walked away — she would be a partner in her own destiny.

Once in Barcelona, she needed to work, but the only work she now knew was as a hooker. With no proper papers or passport, she couldn't get an official job — so she took to the streets of the Ramblas, just as so many girls before her through the ages have, and just as many more in the future will.

I have never had, then or now, any desire to be a campaigner, to change the way of the world. Still, I promised myself I would always treat anybody who was a prostitute as a person first and foremost, I would remember to be aware and understand that they all have a backstory, and I would always treat them respectfully.

During the four years that Paul had been in Spain, she had actually made decent money. As hard and as bad as the work was, it paid well, even in the madhouse of Madrid after all the deductions they took.

Paul sent money back home every month, and by now she'd sent enough cash back that her mother had been able to buy a small plot of land. Their plan was to build a simplistic little house for them all to live in — just a simple bare concrete and tin house, a bungalow with two bedrooms, a living room–kitchen, a toilet with shower, and a garden running all the way around to grow vegetables, have some chickens, and a goat.

Paul believed that it would take her another year, two at the most, and by then she would have sent enough money back to build that home — she kept the meaning of her daughter's name, Hope, alive inside her.

Finally, we parted ways with a big kiss, a proper kiss in a tiny street inside a dark doorway. A kiss like that is something prostitutes rarely do, as I found out later in life. She must have thought she'd give me a small gift as she took her hand and rubbed the front of my pants. It felt good, but I placed her hand around my shoulder. I dropped most of my cash on her, thinking I'd not need much to get from Barcelona to Puerto Banus. It was worth the money for a lifetime memory — a night on the tiles with Paul.

I wonder what happened to Paul — did she build her small family home in Nigeria? If so, what did she do next, did she marry, did she stay in the game one way or another, did she make it through without trouble? I have thought of her often.

7 ON THE ROAD, JACK...

I headed towards the highway with my thumb out, ready to catch the next buzz. I was on the road, Jack, even though I was just about out of money again as I'd given most of the money I had to Paul last night, but I wasn't bothered — I felt as if Jah would provide.

I'd heard a Rasta once say it back in Leeds down at a Sunday afternoon Reggae Bar called The Strega, and I liked its vague, yet certain, promise. I was rolling with it.

It was morning rush hour, and after a very short time, a car pulled over and a guy wound his window down. "How much?" he asked — he thought I was walking the line and looking for business. "Fuck you, dude. Get the fuck on your way."

This happened three more times in the next hour. "What the fuck's going on here?" I asked myself as I looked to see if I was on somebody's trick spot. I don't think I was.

Another car stopped. "Where are you heading to?" he asked. This time it was a single guy, smartly dressed, office worker type, a regular fella. "Valencia direction," I looked at him in hope. "No problem. I'm not going there, but I can take you to a better place to try for a lift." OK, he didn't speak English, nor Yorkshire, nor Leeds. It was a broken Spanish effort of English. I understood him. Or so I thought…

We drove for about fifteen minutes more or less in silence other than the usual introductions. Then he said, "I help you, you help me." He looked at me with a raised eyebrow. "What?" I asked, but I already knew the answer.

"I can take you to the train station further down the road, buy a ticket to Valencia, give you some money. I help you, you help me, OK?" I looked out of the window, trying to collect my thoughts. By now, the effects of the night before were starting to make an appearance. I thought I had escaped the comedown, but I could tell it wouldn't be long before I was heading towards a delayed hangover. I didn't fancy another hour or more trying to get a ride, and I remembered

133

my newly released love and respect for prostitutes, those wonderful and brave street warriors.

"Fuck it, what do you want?" I looked at him with manic, yet vacant, eyes. It should've been a look that would make anybody think twice about pushing an agenda, but this guy didn't take a second to pause. "I suck you, you suck me," he said bluntly.

It was a shock, it was weird because he looked so normal, like a stand-up fellow. It struck me as pretty freaky and even made me think that maybe he was a psycho killer rather than just a deviant.

Well, I thought to myself, maybe him sucking me off wouldn't be so bad. I could just close my eyes and imagine it's Paul, or Dee or Bea. But then I thought, I'm not up for sucking his junk off. I decided I'd wing it for a bit, play it out and see where things went. I was almost broke and needed cash — maybe this was how Jah worked?

"OK, we can work something out, but where? And how much money are you offering?"

I looked him straight in the eye, still with the manic-vacant glare.

Well, now I'd started with that look, I had to keep it up. I was trying to make myself look as ugly and unappealing as possible, trying to push my broken nose forward from my face, if that's even possible. I didn't really understand that looks played no part in his interest. I mean, he didn't want a boyfriend, he just wanted to get off.

He didn't answer, he just took the next exit off the highway, which gave me a shiver. Then, after a few more minutes, we were heading up to the hills. He was already starting to rub himself over his pants while driving. He looked over at me, smiling. He was happy. "We'll have a good time." I shook my head and giggled, the kind of giggle that nervous people make, a little subdued.

I didn't like how it sounded, so I exaggerated it into something more abstract, like The Joker might sound. "What the fuck is this nutty chuckling?" I said to myself. "You're

134

fucking nervous." Trust the voice to get involved. It started singing "Hey babe, take a walk on the wild side, say hey, sugar".

I must've been pretty nervous because I blurted out, "Stop playing with your dick, let's make a deal first. How much cash?" I thought I sounded like Malcolm McLaren, a confident deal-maker who was taking control, but he just kind of grunted. "No problem, don't worry, I have good cash," he said, still driving away from the highway and up to the hills, still rubbing his prick through his pants. Again, I just giggled. It was a kind of "What the fuck is this shit I'm in now?" type of giggle.

Before I knew it, he pulled off the road into a giant lay-by, like a parking layover for truckers, and drove to the furthest point from the road, up towards the brush and trees that framed the zone, still pulling at himself. I could feel butterflies as I was registering bit by bit, inside my head, that he was massaging himself ever closer toward an erection. "This shit is real, man. Am I about to become a prostitute, a rent boy?" I was looking to find the thrill of it all, stalling for time, trying to find something positive in the experience that was happening.

I raised my voice like I was getting pissed off. "Give me the fucking money first, pal." I looked at him, a hard, violent look this time, eyes now bulging, but he still didn't seem that fazed.

He pulled a wad of cash out of his pocket and started to peel off a good few notes for me. "Here, take the money, now suck my cock." He started undoing his belt buckle as I put my money away: was this now an unbreakable contract?

My head was spinning, I was mapping out a bunch of scenarios as to how this was gonna play out, when suddenly it seemed like slow motion took hold of the scene. By now, I was almost betting myself that I could do it, arguing things like, "Surely people like Jim Morrison, Stooges-era Iggy Pop, or Wayne County/Jayne County had done worse? If they could do it, then surely I could do it too?"

He reached over, making his move towards my belt. "Ya pays ya money, ya takes ya choice, ya know." The little bastard voice in my head was taking the piss out of me. "Ha, you dumb fucking wanker," the voice slapped the back of my head. "What you gonna do, Punk, make his day?" That voice was a brutal fucker.

I instinctively lifted my arm up and blocked his move, pushing him back.

"OK, you do me first," he said matter-of- factly. "No," I replied, in one deliberate, crystal clear, firm word.

His demeanour changed in an instant, and he looked at me, not knowing if he should start a commotion.

"No?" He repeated the word back to me, then paused for a split second before trying another gambit. "OK, you can fuck me if you want." His voice now belligerent, he was getting desperate to get what he'd pay for. I went back at him even stronger, "No! No Fucking! No Fucking Nothing!" I was cold about it and he started to protest, he was flustered, no doubt wondering why things were going south. I made my move, opened the door and got out of the car, not really sure what my intention was, if I'd run away or not, but run to where? I was up in the hills a few miles away from Barcelona. All I knew was that I had to move away from him and get out into an open space, just in case we were going to get into a row. He got out his side too.

"What's this shit? I paid you, what's this fucking shit?" He raised his voice, angry now, and started as if to make a move around the car towards me. I raised my voice louder than his, "Stay over there, pal! if you come over here I'll give you a proper fucking — now fuck off!"

I raised my fists up, taking a boxer's stance. I couldn't really say what was going through his head by now, but it was obvious to me what I was gonna do — I was gonna keep the cash and he was gonna get to fuck, or get totally fucked, maybe I'd even rob the rest of his cash if he pushed his luck. I was pretty sure I could beat him in a fight.

136

He kept moving around the car, ignoring my advice, and blabbering loudly in Spanish while I was shouting even louder in English, gibberish in both directions. By now we were facing one another, it was on!

I landed a good and hard hit, right smack in the middle of his face as I charged through him. He dropped to his knees on impact. I'd got lucky and broken his nose with my first punch. "Fuck him up, fuck him up, go on fuck him up," the voice was pushing me on.

I pulled up, pivoted and spun back around, took a split second to set myself, then gave him a second smack, another completely free and unprotected hit — it was like the one the leader gave that fellow Leeds fan after the midweek Colchester cup game on the way back to Leeds city centre from Elland Road all those years ago. The action stopped as quickly as it had started.

I was hepped up, but I was also relieved that it was over. I wasn't really a fighter, didn't ever really get into scraps either, this was a case of needs must. And then it got even better as I heard the voice of a fella shouting in Spanish from across the far side of the lay-by. It was an older trucker:

"Nino, nino, muy peligroso aquí, pervertidos — vamos." I got the picture right away: the trucker knew that men would pick up young vulnerable guys from the highway, and no doubt girls too, and bring them to this trucker's lay-by for sex. He didn't see me as a rent boy, he saw me as I was — a victim. I ran across to him as if escaping the clutches of a monster, quickly climbing into the cabin and locking the door as if in a state of distress and panic while he climbed in and started up the engine. Not all heroes wear capes.

He drove me back down to the highway, where, as hoped and predicted, Jah provided (as I knew he somehow would). The old fella took me all the way to Valencia, where he was picking up a load for his truck. He gave me three big bottles to rehydrate, and he also let me bed down on the bunk behind the seats on the ride down the east coast so I could sleep off the hangover that had now arrived in spades, waking me up as we hit Valencia. As he dropped me off, he gave me a big bocadillo sandwich from his snap bag and we said our goodbyes. "Mira, muchas pervertidos, es muy peligroso, cuidate, buena suerte English, adiós." I didn't speak Spanish back then, but it was a warning, advice to keep my distance from perverts and danger. He'd told me to be careful, and wished me good luck, "English", and goodbye. He'd been a good old boy to me. But that's proper truckers for you, men's men, good men.

*

I'd made it to Valencia and had money in my pocket again. I'm not sure if I could claim to be a highwayman, but I decided I'd call myself one anyway. I'd earned the legend in my book. There'd even been a touch of the oldest profession about what had happened too, but the main thing was that I'd got through the experience intact.

The next day I took the train all the way to Malaga, and from Malaga, I took a bus across to San Pedro and walked the final part to the rich man's paradise of Puerto Banus.

The hunt was on to find my dad.

*

Puerto Banus was still a rich man's paradise of yachts, gorgeous cars, super-looking women, expensive stores, great restaurants, bars, and piano bars, and now there were even some discos. When I'd last been here, six or seven years earlier, the only late-night entertainment places were the piano bars. There were loads of them in and around Marbella and Puerto Banus, but the two most popular — with the biggest spenders from the stars of sport and British TV — were Joy's Piano Bar and Crystals.

The piano player's job wasn't easy, they had to have a giant repertoire of songs so they could take requests from anybody who tipped for one. They'd sometimes have the same song requested multiple times in a row. And let's face it, if a known gangster with a reputation for rage asks you to play and sing "My Way" five times in a row and drops a few big bills on you to do it, it's hard to say no, even if you want

138

to. The piano man would play something like eight hours a night, maybe five, six, or even seven nights a week, and their glass was always full with invited drinks from customers who insisted you join them in a special toast. It is a very hard and tiring job without the reward they truly desire. Yes, they earn money, yes, the crowd tells them they are the best, but what they really want is a shot at being a star. These piano bar entertainers really are the epitome of God's Sad Boys. They're super-talented and reach a certain level of success, but their destiny is never to attain the success they really want. They end up as near-on junkies if not proper rattlers, and most of them finish as shaking, liver-damaged alcoholics. It's pretty brutal. Let's raise a toast to the dead men on horses.

I hadn't seen or heard from my dad for maybe six years, and that included the important teenage years, from 13/14 through to 18/19, moments when you're making big decisions, moments when you're supposed to be learning to drive, when you're leaving school and joining the workforce, experimenting with girls, booze, drugs, making choices, choosing which fork in the road to take.

I don't really know why I was even thinking about stopping by. I felt like I hated him for the way he'd treated my mother, not forgetting he'd basically abandoned the family. Even so, deep down inside, now a little older, I didn't really begrudge him his personal search for what he was looking for — fame, respect, and acknowledgement from his peers. He'd always been like a man possessed in his pursuit of success, he wanted his name in lights, he wanted stardom. Now I was in The Port, looking to get face to face with him, I wondered what was driving me?

Maybe it was just curiosity that had brought me here, looking for understanding, maybe it was a deeper need, a want for closure? Or I could've been just looking for drama.

I wandered up and down all the streets looking for clues. Maybe a poster with his name on it would lead me to him, something like *Live Tonight, The Number One Piano Bar*

Entertainer in Puerto Banus. Or maybe we'd walk straight into each by chance?

I put my head inside a couple of venue doors, maybe somebody would know him personally. But the staff gently bounced me back out before I could even ask the question. "Not in here, kid, try the rock club in the street behind."

They didn't like my clothes — but more than that, they thought they were doing me a favour by giving me directions to a place that was more fitting for me, as four or five different people directed me to the rock club. But I wasn't here to go to a rock club. By about midnight, I gave it up and decided to go back to San Pedro. I felt half relieved it had been a bust.

The next day I decided to check out of my room. My plan was to hang out at the hotel pool for the day, go to The Port late afternoon or early evening and have a final sweep about the place before spending the last of my highwayman cash on a night out at the rock club. Then I'd head straight to the highway with my thumb after the club closed. It'd already be the early hours of the morning. I'd wait for the dawn sun and begin the long hitch back. I was excited, wondering what might happen this time.

Plan in action, I landed back at The Port by 8pm, more or less at the time I'd hoped for, and I figured I'd locate the rock club now and get my bearings before my visit later. It was in the very back street, away from the port side, overlooking rough ground where cars parked on the outside of the Banus bubble. It wasn't street level either, it was up a flight of stairs, the first corner place in a little narrow precinct street. Judging from the posters on the wall, they played good music here. I name-checked lots of bands that I liked well enough, so I was happy with the idea of coming back later.

Instead of turning back down the stairway I'd walked up, I decided to walk on and exit through the other end of the block. That would bring me out at the far end of The Port, nearer to a little bar I'd hung out in the day before, so off I went.

Boom! Somebody works in mysterious ways, because, to my complete amazement, there was another music venue on the other end of the block to the rock club and it had his name in lights over the door: Lloyd's Piano Bar.

What fucking witchcraft is this? You've gotta be fucking kidding me!

I'd found him, but I was so shocked that I ran straight past the door and jumped down the stairs at the end of the passage three at a time — my nerves were on edge. I kept going, and before I knew it, the small bar from yesterday was right in front of me. I'd duck in for a beer and a neat double Jack, hoping he wouldn't be sat at the bar.

I guessed things must have been going OK. He'd made it to some level of success after all. It wasn't fame, he wasn't a household name, but it seemed like he got somewhere at least.

"Don't judge a book by its cover, kiddo," the voice offered doubt, "there's bound to be a story behind it." Sometimes it made sense.

After an hour of drinks and contemplation in the little bar, I made my way back up to Lloyd's Piano Bar and rang the bell… nothing happened. I rang it again, and then a third time — nothing. Then, just as I was about to turn away and go, thinking I'd try again later in the evening, I heard somebody call out.

I didn't catch what they actually said, but it was probably something like, "Oye, ¿qué pasa?" I looked back and saw this bad-tempered, angry-looking man standing outside the gateway to the stairs that ran up a floor next to the bar.

"Who's that? What do you want?" This time he spoke in English. The voice was hard, ill-mannered, part defensive, more aggressive at the same time, confrontational. I was about twenty yards away, maybe a little more. He looked bloated, not fat or big-boned, but bloated like an overindulged pig. The body didn't seem to fit right on the thin, spindly legs. His face was almost lost of definition as if it had been sunk into inflated, pumped-out cheeks and

141

swollen eye sockets. Even the ears looked odd. The entire head/face area was almost a continuation of a tree trunk neck, like no neck really existed — just a gorged pulp on top of a blown-up body with hidden eyeballs screened by steel-rimmed glasses and a mop of badly combed-over, thick, style-less hair on top. The arms were the only parts that actually looked like they were right, muscular Popeye-style forearms and large hands.

"Don't you know me?" I smiled. We both stood our ground, like a scene from a gunfight at the OK Corral. Eventually, "Is that you?" He said it with a tone that suggested he was properly pissed off, maybe I'd interrupted something important. He walked towards me. Eventually, he arrived right up to my face, like to study if it really was his son, out of the blue, after so many years. "What are you doing here?" he asked.

"Just passing by," I deadpanned. "Thought I'd say hello."

The reunion with my old fella was a disaster on one level and a triumphant success on another. He put me up in his place, a small three-bedroom apartment above the bar that he shared with his wife, the same one he'd left us for. I didn't hold it against her, I never had. It wasn't her fault, she was just one of the elements that had guided his judgement, and to be honest, she was a pretty cool woman.

As for him, I couldn't stand him from the first minute I saw him, and I was happy to see he had let himself go so much. There were no big hugs, no back-slapping, no tears of happy emotion, no joy at being reunited. He was the anti-climax in vivid Technicolour.

We nervously kind of tip-toed around each other for a couple of days and nights. I'd sleep in late, and by the time I got up, he'd have already escaped on business for the day. When he'd get back at around 8pm, we'd all three have dinner in the apartment together. Then he'd go to bed early at night, as he was catching up on sleep while the bar was closed for repairs. When we did talk, we'd both be careful not to stray too close to the topic of why he'd fucked off and abandoned us without a backward glance, no money and no contact. Sure, I let him know that despite everything, my siblings and I were doing just fine. It was a strange couple or three days, each not sure of how to put a foot firmly in front of the other without tripping the other one up.

I went down to his club with him on the third night; it was reopening after a lost week. And I have to say that despite looking like a bloated Quasimodo without the hump, he could still do it when sitting at a piano. And the piano bar seemed to be doing OK for him, even if the days of the piano bar scene had moved out of vogue by now, even in Puerto Banus.

A couple of days later, we were a lot more loose with each other. He was more relaxed, dropping his guard by the hour, taking it upon himself to believe it was good faith on my part that had brought me to Southern Spain to see him, and to restart a relationship with him too.

We eventually decided to spend an entire day and evening together — we'd have a proper drink and get to know each other. Well, the first reveal on our voyage of discovery was that he was obviously a cokehead when on the pop; he couldn't keep it under wraps now he was on a large one. It came up, and we found ourselves having a good sniff from his bag of Charlie. I wasn't used to coke. I'd done a little bit back in Leeds with Evo and Uncle and also with Long Johnny and Hal in Schiedam, but generally, I couldn't afford it. It seemed just like an expensive version of speed to me anyway. But we got right at it, and it turned out that I didn't mind it at all — so long as it was in front of me, I was happy to sniff it up. I didn't think it was as good as a dig of speed, but, well, you know, any port in a storm.

That day we hit lots of bars in Marbella, San Pedro, and The Port, drinking and sniffing Charlie along the way. Then by midnight, we were in his piano bar. It was packed, like a throwback to better days. All the local movers and shakers were there, as well as some celebrities. He was well happy.

143

He played the piano and sang songs for nearly six hours that night, from midnight opening through to 6am closing. He was on form, still really good at his craft, even if he looked a mess. He still knew how to go about his work, talking to the crowd over the microphone and introducing his long-lost son. We even did a couple of duets together, Fats Domino's classic "Blueberry Hill" and Gene Vincent's killer "Be Bop A Lula".

Everybody was smiling, cheering wildly as each song ended. I can see their sentimental eyes even today. "Family is the most important thing in life, don't forget that, the two of you," some washed-up old British comedian said to us earnestly after the second song we sang together. I'll not say who it was by name, but what his TV audience back home in the UK didn't know was that he was a pissed-up cokehead inside Lloyd's Piano Bar in Spain. He was a big star then and is still a household name today. Who am I to shit on his parade, right?

After the bar had shut, my old man and me were walking his dog, both out of it in a drunken, coked-up but coming-down vibe, mumbling and pontificating.

All was going OK until he started talking about why he had left the family. I knew eventually we'd get to this, the apex, the crescendo, the high noon moment at dawn's early light. And so he started off with his version of reality, the bottom line being, in his mind, that it was all my mum's fault.

How? All she'd done was hold the fort back home while he had worked away on the road. She'd brought up the kids day by day, night after night, clothed and fed us, helped us through school days, pushed us to practise playing the guitar and the piano — and kicking a football. When ill, she nursed us better and scolded us when out of line. Parenting, as simple as that, and waiting for the time when we would all make the break for the border and move our lives to the south of Spain and the sun. She hadn't abandoned him. She didn't have a new partner set up like him. She'd been the one left behind holding the babies. Then he starts up with, "She's not innocent — she's had you all fooled all these years that I'm the bad guy, but it's her who's always been off with other blokes."

He kept on, accusing her of all kinds. His rhetoric got on my nerves, while at the same time, it just confirmed what I already thought of him, that he was a sad, deluded tosspot. Finally, I cracked.

"Look, mate, just stop making things up already. There's no need to be making excuses; it happened, you had your reasons, and you wanted to follow a dream — it is what it is, and it was what it was. Time has passed, and I'm not even mad about it anymore. I understand the call of the wild, really I do. But don't make shit up, don't slag Mum off just to bury your own sense of guilt. There's no need for it, there's nothing to gain from it. Face the facts and embrace the reality that you were a shithouse."

I thought what I'd said was pretty reasonable, a way to put it to bed — but maybe he wasn't hearing right. "Now it comes out, does it?" he says. "You've just come here to stir everything up and create problems for me, problems I don't need or want. Well, you can fuck off."

I wasn't angry, I wasn't vexed — I'd wanted him to get to the point where he'd tell me to my face "Fuck off".

I had the high ground. I would have the high ground forevermore. I'd made the effort to track down my missing dad. I hadn't started the conversation on why he'd left us all behind, he had. I hadn't even reacted badly when he had been so hateful, hurtful and unkind in his comments about my mum. All I did was simply point out that there was no need for it, that it achieved nothing. But his own guilt and bad-mindedness ruled his words. He'd revealed himself to be unworthy of benefit. I'd let him run his mouth tonight. Just this one time, he could yap and yap, dig his own hole and bury himself in it.

I turned away from him. It wasn't a power play, it was just an instinctive momentary move to break the vibe, to cool the fire down. It didn't work though, because as I turned back

145

towards him — bang! — he smacked me a good one right on the side of my head, a full fist on the end of those Popeye arms, a free shot carrying a lot of bloated weight behind it. It knocked me on my ass. It was a cheap, cuntish shot, yet he was still spitting piss with anger. "You can fuck off back to where you came from, go on, fuck off, grab your stuff and fuck off."

He had his fists up, ready for a fight — but I wasn't. "Put your mitts down, you daft bugger. It's almost tomorrow already. I'll come back to the flat, grab a few hours of kip, and when I wake up I'll get on my way — fair enough?"

I'd said it firmly, but calmly, I was leaving him in a position to feel victorious. "Come on, then," he said, now dropping his fists. "Let's away back to the flat, I'll make a bit of something to eat — and tomorrow's another day."

So that's what we did. Off we went, walking in near silence, apart from the sound of me whistling (instead of singing) the words to the old song, "The party's over, now it's time to say goodbye". I knew that my none too subtle message wouldn't be wasted on him. Eventually, he says, "I never stopped loving you, none of you, not even your mother." I should've felt the wet tears of sorrow rolling down my cheeks, but I didn't. I didn't feel anything for him, I just simply said, "Sure, fella, no doubt." I said it again, "No doubt, no doubt." As we continued our walk back, now in complete silence, I knew what my next move would be. I had no doubt what it would be.

*

Around midday, I was ready to go. He'd made me a bacon sarnie, a hot coffee, and also packed me a Spanish ham bocadillo sandwich for the journey. Then he slipped me a small roll of cash, about a hundred quid in Spanish notes, as he walked me to the bus stop that would take me to Marbella. We were still pretty much in silence. The hangover of the day and night before was vexing us both. As the bus came, he stepped forward to embrace me, but I held my hand up to halt his movement. "Best not," I said. "I'll always have you in my heart, son," he was playing out the epilogue. "Aye, I know, I know you'll not forget me. And who knows what'll happen in the future? The world could turn on its head in the next minute." I left him to ponder on that thought as I boarded the bus and shot him a mischievous smile. He stood there on the hard shoulder. I walked to the back seat, pushed open the full sliding window on the right-hand side and leaned out.

The bus started off, and he started to wave with a look of love in his eye. As the bus was pulling out onto the highway, I shouted back, "You'll not forget me, will you?" He looked up sincerely. "No, son," he called back.

"I know you won't," I shouted with a laugh in my voice, "look at this!" I held up a wad of more than two thousand quid in Spanish notes, and waved it about in the air.

The bus moved at the perfect pace, hitting the highway as my voice carried toward him in the slipstream. The penny dropped, finally registering on him that I must have slipped into his desk, broken the lock of his money box and swiped his petty cash away. His arms raised, he tried to scuttle forward after the bus, after me, but his skinny legs couldn't carry the bloated blob above them with any kind of proper speed. "Adios, fucker!" I shouted at him, with a tinge of aggression now, while still waving the wad of cash. "Fuck you later, Pater," now bellowing at the top of my voice, my head and body leaning right out of the bus, two grand gripped in my hand, and his other hundred quid snug in my pocket.

By now, the bus was well away. He stood there shaking his fist while making slashing motions across his throat with his thumb. I flipped him the one-fingered bird, let it morph into a two-fingered "Kes", and just laughed at him until I slipped back inside and settled into my seat. I did think about tossing the sandwich he'd made up for me out of the window, like a final "fuck you" for him to catch on to, but I ditched that idea quick enough. I was gonna savour and enjoy that bit of snap en route to Malaga.

What had been the point of the journey? Well, let's just say it was an itch of curiosity that needed scratching.

One thing for sure was clear: I hadn't come across the dad who had been a hero to me as a kid — all I'd found was the loser who'd left me as a young teen. I wasn't surprised he was an arsehole though; his talent should have delivered more for him. I mean, not that life in southern Spain wasn't a decent reward, but it was scant consolation for him. He wanted to be a TV star like his clients were. He wanted fame, money and adulation. He saw himself as the star on a *Royal Variety* TV special. He envisioned a life where he would make guest appearances on Saturday night peak-hour talk shows. He was one of God's Sad Boys alright; for him, it was a bitter taste, he was a bitter man, the epitome of the angry man behind the comedy mask. Unfortunately for him, and for me — in fact for all of us — he wasn't a hero, he was just another might-have-been.

For the record: I hadn't set out to steal his money, I didn't make the journey with any intention to rob a paltry 2,000 quid from him — even if it was a fair bundle back then. In reality, the situation simply played itself out, circumstances dealt the cards and I felt compelled to take the stash. You could say it was compensation, and if you did call it that, then he'd got off light — two grand was cheaper than five years of child support.

I'd given him a fair go at showing me something, something better than he inevitably showed himself to be. My search for him was a fool's errand, but it'd been a riot every step of the way. The journey itself had been worth the effort. The people and things that'd happened were memorable, the good and the bad. It was enough for me.

Once in Marbella, I abandoned the idea of hitching. I didn't want to risk it with such a wad of cash. So I took a coach to Malaga, scoffing the Old Duffer's sarnie in comfort rather than on the side of the road, and then bought a train ticket to Paris, where I stayed a night in a hotel — just around the Charles de Gaulle Station area. I wanted to go out on the lash in Paris, but I didn't trust leaving my cash in the hotel and I didn't want to be out on the street with it either. So I just ordered room service and sat on the balcony, enjoying the simple pleasure of that, before sleeping heavily. I'd do Paris well enough in the future. I'd sleep in a dead man's bed, I'd fuck with an Amazonian Beauty (OK, she might not have been a native of Brazil, but she looked like the stereotypical Amazon Queen, and that was close enough for Rock'n'Roll), I'd jump over the giant rocket fireworks that are fired down the streets on Bastille Day, in Bastille; I'd host a House music party on a boat sailing through the city on the River Seine, I'd play a Punk-Rock'n'Roll show at the legendary Gibus Club, and I'd also be wined and dined in a penthouse looking on to the Eiffel Tower by the guy who created the Village People. I'd do Paris, but not tonight.

The next day, I took another train that went through Belgium and on to Rotterdam, where I jumped a tram to Schiedam, and Hal's place.

As it turned out, Hal had returned early from Amsterdam. He'd had another night out in the cafe bars of the Red Light area, and then he'd gone home to Schiedam. He told me Dee had gone to Den Haag a couple of days after I'd left on the trip. She'd left even before he had got back from Amsterdam, and there'd been no sign of her return since. Could she have gone back to the other fella's place in Rotterdam? Hal told me that Long Johnny hadn't heard about it if she had, neither had Scar.

That night, I met up with Long Johnny and Scar. She had left a message with Scar for me. It wasn't melodramatic or poetic, she'd told him simply to "tell him goodbye". Nothing more. She had released me from my improbable fantasy.

The Killing Joke Smile, it'd all been in vain, doomed to nothing, but man, the thrill of it all. It was over and done; it was what it was. I'd had a crazy time on my Dutch–Spanish adventure. I'd been thrill-seeking, and I'd appreciated it all: I'll say it again, the good, the bad — and the ugly of it. I'd had a bag full of experiences that I treasure still today.

The next morning, I told Hal I'd be leaving that evening, heading back to Leeds. Dee was now out of sight; Bea was a headcase. I was off home. I like to think that Dee meeting me had given her the push she'd needed to get herself well enough to start a new kind of life. I don't know if she did. What I do know is that when I had been with her, it felt like I was in the middle of a tragic dramatic love story, a movie, and I never forgot her.

As Roland S. Howard put it so well: "I keep her photograph against my heart because in my life she's played a starring part." But now, I was ready to return home. First I dropped some cash on Hal, given that he had covered almost everything while I'd been in his apartment — and not forgetting that I'd brought chaos to his front door: a little bit of gratitude cash was the least I could do. I then paid the cost of my trip back to Leeds, and even after those expenses, as well as the cost of getting from Puerto Banus to Rotterdam, I still had a pretty good stash of money left over from robbing my old fella to rent a place with Uncle and Evo in Hyde Park and Headingley, LS6, Leeds.

Leeds was calling me, putting together a proper Punk-Rock'n'Roll band was calling me, my dream of getting into the music business "proper" was still calling me. I returned to Leeds with adventures to tell.

8. THE DEAD VAYNES — IN THE BEGINNING

"Hey, want a bang?"

Uncle held up a syringe, offering it like a pistol in a game of Russian Roulette, already loaded and ready for a dig of methamphetamine. Methamphet, also known as speed, used to be hard shit to take, a dirty concoction about as low as it gets — but not anymore.

Now it was like magic nectar to us. "Course I do." It'd been a rhetorical question really, and there wasn't even any need to respond with words. At that stage in the game the answer was always yes. I grabbed it from him, and with a gleam in my eye, I went about my business while regaling the room with a rendition of "Motörhead" by Motörhead, sinking the meth into my vein, while singing the words: "I should be tired, but all I am is wired, ain't felt this good for an hour." Then, bang on cue, as I pulled the needle back out, the money line: "Motörhead, remember me now, Motörhead, alright, yeah yeah yeah yeah."

We all fall about pissing ourselves. Uncle gets up and puts on the same Motörhead album it's from, *Motörhead*, cranking it up high. We all started playing along, Uncle on "Philthy Animal" Taylor air drums, Cyrus on Lemmy air bass, me on "Fast" Eddie Clarke air guitar. Evo, Skum, Dil and CJ, well, all of us, shout along to the words: "Motörhead, remember me now, Motörhead, alright." The whole room is speeding their tits off at the same time, all talking a million miles an hour, talking shit, shit and more shit. No one gives a shit. We're having the time of our lives.

Who are these people?

Let me introduce them. You met Uncle and Evo already — you might remember that we'd planned to all move in together on my return to Leeds from Holland and Spain?

Well, it didn't quite work out that way.

Uncle and I both kept to the plan, and we ended up moving into a house where two other lads, Foxy and Tenni, already lived.

They'd had the house since before I even left for Holland, sharing it with two nameless students. In fact, we all used to hang out there from time to time because it had a cool cellar that Tenni had set up as a music room, and he'd given us an open invitation to go down and jam whenever we felt like it.

By December 1983, the two nameless students had turned their keys in. They couldn't hack the fact that Foxy and Tenni had some pretty strung out mates that used to trot in at will, make a racket in the cellar for a few hours, raid and empty the fridge, and then just fuck off again — all this, regardless of if either Foxy or Tenni were even in at the time or not. So, the students gone, they needed two people for the spare rooms.

Uncle had actually moved in while I was away, but he'd also reserved the room next door to his for me.

Evo, well he was supposed to take a small converted room on the top floor, the attic — but, that would've meant he had to pay rent and also his share of the bills. So he opted to just float in and out, mostly in, but come and go as he pleased and pay nowt!

He were a cheeky cunt, but we didn't mind — Evo was Evo, a rat, a low-down dog, he was like a pet who'd wag his tail and do tricks, bringing you treats, bringing you moments of joy. But if you left a joint unguarded on a table, he'd be away with it. I guess we were soft on him, we let him live like the famously incorrigible Riley — what a life.

Cyrus Murphy — what a fantastic name, what a fantastic guy. He was a beast of a fella, a rough and tumble type with a heart of gold. He was a Punk, a Rocker, a Big Bike Lover, an Irishman and a Proper Leeds Lad. Everybody loved Cyrus. RIP.

I had some great times with Cyrus when he lived in Leeds, and some mad times later when he lived in London too. He was the very first bass player for The Dead Vaynes, and was a perfect fit for the band, apart from the fact that he could hardly play the bass at all. But he was a trier, one of God's Sad Boys — as limited as he was, he was still massively better than Evo the Rat.

Cyrus was the type of fella that would give it his best shot, whatever he was doing, be it riding a bike, having a scrap, drinking on a bender; he'd always put full commitment behind it. He had bags of enthusiasm and was brilliant company, and for all those qualities alone he was welcome in the band. He was the kind of guy who'd get his hands dirty, get some skin in the game and give it a go, whereas Evo — who wanted to be the bass player — would talk a good game, and looked good in his own way, but… well, he was the type who preferred to keep his hands clean. Which was ironically impossible in his case, because he had dirty hands of a different kind — sticky fingers. He'd rob anything off anyone, friends, family, complete strangers, it was all fair game to him, and without any apology about it either.

Another feather in the Cyrus cap was that he was a big, BIG drinker, as well as loving the drugs too. Any drug would do for Cy, it wasn't long before he had a tie around his muscles and a gun stuck in his arm. He'd shovel down anything that was in front of him, often doing everything at the same time, polishing them all off together in one swoop. I once saw him drop eight tabs of acid in one sitting, and at the same time he cranked up two grams of methamphet and also smoked a block of dope — he didn't care, so long as it "gave him a buzz".

Skum… Now here's a kid who changed his name by deed poll to Dave Skum Vanian. He loved The Damned, whose singer is called Dave Vanian, so he had to have it, and that's what he did. I have no idea where, or why, he also got the idea to take on the name "Skum" — but he did, and not to do things by half measures, he had it tattooed inside his bottom lip too.

He didn't have many other tattoos back then, but over the years he finally ended up with his entire body inked, and also got some white tattoos on his face as well.

Skum was a funny lad — I mean funny ha-ha — and he's still hilarious today. But, despite the fact that he's a skinny lad, he was always the first in line to stand up for one-and-all if a scrap was gonna kick off.

Small as he was, he also worked security at loads of the early Punk gigs, back when those gigs could turn into a Skins v Punks riot at the drop of a hat. For all that, he wasn't a troublemaker himself. He has a unique Skum Moral Code, whereby he'll stick up for whoever needs a helping hand, even if he doesn't know who he's sticking up for. It could be for his best mates or for complete strangers, it made no odds — in Skum World, right was right, and the rest was bollocks.

He always put me in mind of a cartoon, and I don't say that disrespectfully at all. The fact is that if he didn't exist you'd have to make him up, and truth be told, by the time he was covered completely in tats, he actually looked like he was a made-up, multicoloured, walking, talking, human, cartoon drawing come to life. Dave Skum Vanian was a proper Punk. Then, as time went on, he suddenly got bang into Big Motorbikes, just like Cyrus was into them. Those two ended up as really big mates; well, in truth, we were all really big mates, we all hung out together, but the bike thing cemented it for those two.

Just an aside: I can honestly say we all loved the bones off of one another. we were a crew and we all shared a special bond. Maybe the bond that bound us was the drugs — actually it was — but it was also much more than that.

However, when it came to shooting speed, we were all equally insatiable, we were always looking at ways to get the best hit possible from a dig.

We'd try various veins around our body; hands, feet and groins were often hit as an alternative to our arms — but Skum went further than anyone.

154

He once shot up in his actual dick. "It's the biggest vein in your body," he told me. "Gets you fucked up quicker, give it a try." He was a funny bugger and always had me laughing. Then, to top his dick trick, he announced one day, "I'm gonna shoot up both sides of my neck at the same time," and got Cyrus and Evo to both do it for him, regardless of the consequences. It nearly OD'd him on the spot.

Next up, Dil — the world's forgotten boy, the original Dead Vaynes guitarist. He was supposed to be my Straight James Williamson while I would be his Iggy Pop, my Johnny Thunders while I would be his David Johanson, my Cheetah Chrome while I would be his Stiv Bators. And it started off just like that. We were tight, brothers in arms. The adventures we were gonna have together would become the stuff of legend. The music we were gonna make was gonna rival anybody. We loved each other's company. It wasn't the same as me and Evo, who I loved but knew was a rat-dog, or even me and Uncle, who I loved more and who was my best mate. But me and Dil were gunslingers. It was a musical connection, a special chemistry that came as naturally as breathing. It wasn't to be, though.

Sad to say, what should have been ours never came to be. He lost his mind, or found himself, it was one or the other. I looked around one day and he was gone. He'd joined a religious cult and just disappeared into them. From being the coolest Punk-Rock'n'Roller one day, to being a Bible-Bashing Holy-Roller the next, he just fucked off, and what made it worse is that it happened just three weeks before we were supposed to record our debut album!

CJ — I'll get to her in a second, but it's safe to say that me, Uncle, Evo, Dil, Cyrus, Skum, and CJ were almost always around one another, day and night, night and day.

There were other cool folk that were also around almost as much, including other girls too.

There was Flo, who I always thought had a little "something something" friendship with Dil, but I'm not sure. Then there was Franky, Uncle's long-term girlfriend. They'd been together since school. She was a tiny skinny lass with a mothering nature. But still, she loved the junk as much as the rest of us — in fact Franky was part of the tight-knit day and night crew. Her and I were so tight that we'd kid each other that we were brother and sister. There were lots of other cool guys and girls who were major characters in our scene; peeps like Fisherman Moore, Ronaldo Raccoon, Slater, the Brothers Rush, and loads more, but let's talk about CJ.

Ever since I'd been back from Holland a few months earlier, we'd been together. While Bea had been a cartoon caper, and Dee a vivid love story that was a blend of fact and fantasy, CJ was the real deal. She was like my Siamese twin, definitely my muse. Almost everything I wrote was inspired by just being around her. We were like Bill & Liddy, Frankie & Johnny, Bonnie & Clyde, Sid & Nancy. In my eyes, CJ was not only beautiful, but she was the coolest cat in the city.

I hadn't wanted a girlfriend, nor did CJ want a boyfriend. In fact, we didn't officially announce that we were a couple. We just were. Everyone knew we clicked together in a special way. We almost always ended up in each other's beds, even if we went out separately with no plans to meet. Eventually, we'd crash in on each other. It could be at any time of the night or day. One was always welcomed by the other. The thing is, we just didn't get on each other's nerves, ever.

She was super-good-looking, sharp, really funny, never clingy, up for a laugh, always trashed or sleeping one off. A proper Punk-Rock'n'Roller. A hardcore druggy, she was my Siamese twin.

CJ was just like a female version of me, except she didn't play a guitar, didn't sing songs, she wasn't found stripping off on stage or glassing herself with a pint pot during a gig. I did all that stuff, and she loved me for it. She loved me for it because she knew I didn't do that kind of stuff just for show. I did it because it just happened. I didn't constrain myself. I was me, however that manifested itself. I loved her because she loved me, for being me. We connected in every which

156

way, mentally and physically, with what we liked and didn't like; it was a rare love.

*

I was signed on within a week of returning from my adventures in Holland and Spain — the dole and housing benefit cheque double whammy.

It was great. Uncle and me would sign on and cash our money right away, close to the dole office in the Post Office opposite the amazing Leeds Indoor Market and just a spit away from The Duck & Drake Pub. Cheque-cashing day was brilliant. We'd suddenly find ourselves with a decent amount of money in our hands, on top of our drug dealing cash. We'd go straight out on the piss, straight from the cashier's till to the barman's register: happy fucking days.

Now living in Glebe Ave, we set up our equipment in the cellar and got ready to plug in and play. I gathered the crew around me and made it clear what music I wanted to make and what kind of songs I was gonna write. They could get on the Punk-Rock'n'Roll train or find another wagon to hitch up to with no bad feeling. I outlined my ambition and told them I'd fucked about long enough. I was 20 years old and hadn't done anything near what I wanted to do, but with The Dead Vaynes, that was all gonna change. "I don't want us to fall out about it later. Are you up for it, or is it not for you? If it's not for you, no problem. We'll kiss and say goodbye as far as the band goes. But if you're up for The Dead Vaynes, then let's fucking have it!" Uncle, Cyrus, and Dil were bang on for it.

As I'm making my call to arms speech, Tenni sets up his big Marshall amp and cab.

"What are you doing, Tenni?" I look at him. "Setting up for a jam." I look at Uncle, who just holds out a spliff to me. "We're not jamming, Tenni, we're starting up a band." Tenni chuckles while tuning up: "I know, but as it's your first session, maybe a jam's a good way to start. I don't wanna be in a band, I'm too busy with work and that, but we can have a jam today, can't we?"

157

Dil and Cyrus started laughing, then Uncle, then me, then Tenni. "Fuck it, it's not a bad idea that, Tenni, yeah, let's have a jam today." We spent the next fifteen minutes all tuning up with each other until it seemed like we were in tune. If we weren't, then it wasn't by more than a gnat's pubic hair, and everybody in a band knows that's close enough for Rock'n'Roll. I called order.

"OK, that's close enough, listen up. I've got two songs that'll be easy for us to do as a jam; they're both 12-bars in the key of A, one's slow, and the other's the same chords but just speeded up with different words, OK?" Everybody nodded. I didn't know if they knew what I was on about.

"All you gotta do is follow me for direction on when to take the volume up, take it down, who's hitting a solo, where the chorus is for anyone who fancies getting involved on backing vocals — all that stuff, you know, the dynamics." They just nodded. We were all stoned already. I just thought, well, we'll just have to suck it and see, let's hope for the best.

"We'll do the faster one first. This is for CJ and the rest of the girls, it's called 'Dead Vayne Woman'; it's simple as fuck, ready?" All together: "Ready," and off we went:

Dead Vayne Woman
You're a Dead Vayne Woman
Dead Vayne Woman
You're a Dead Vayne Woman
Ooh, Aah,
Ooh-oh-oh-oh-oh
Dead Vayne Woman
You've got a Dead Vayne Woman
Dead Vayne Woman
You've got a Dead Vayne Woman
Ooh, Aah,
Ooh-oh-oh-oh-oh

Repeat all
Solos at will

158

Call and return vocal lines
Jam till fin…

There it was, a 12-bar Rock'n'Roller in the key of A, the absolute best key of them all for guitar solos played with a Punk vibe and attitude, Punk-Rock'n'Roll, the words so simplistic but effective enough for a fun all-in-it-together carry-on.

It wasn't a classic, well it was in its own way, but it would never be anything more than a soundcheck song, or maybe even a warm-up rehearsal song. It didn't matter what it would eventually be — it was "our song", a Dead Vaynes song. We were starting something right off the bat. I was chuffed with the subtle, not so subtle, wordplay between "You're a Dead Vain Woman" (cool as fuck) versus "You've got a Dead Vein Woman" (as in a queen of the junkie scene).

It was also a cute little example of why I inserted the *Y* to make a camouflaged word for a catch-all name. Dead Vayne meaning, Dead Vain with a Dead Vein, or maybe we should've just called ourselves Cool As Fuck! But the name The Dead Vaynes, well, it just worked.

We were all happy, exhilarated and laughing, cracking cans open and raising a toast to the beginning of The Dead Vaynes. We'd had a proper blast, a 25-minute blowout on a brand new song, birthed to the world from a cellar in Glebe Ave, Leeds. We'd begun feeling each other out in terms of musical chemistry. We were starting our band. We had Johnny Thunders in our sights, not to shoot him down, no, not at all. We'd be shooting from the hip right alongside him one day.

I didn't know in that first session, after that original song, that we'd be playing on the same stage as Thunders within six months, before I was even 21. I couldn't have predicted the future, where all the things that happened with Johnny and me would've happened. I dreamed it, wanted it and said I was sure of it, but in reality, it was a million miles away at that moment in time. Even if it was less than six months away in reality — it was all unknown right there and then.

Tenni turned out to be an amazing guitarist. It wasn't the style I would let into this band, but for fuck's sake, he could play. He could do all that heavy-rock band crazy million-note solo stuff. He played that Eddie Van Halen style like a motherfucker, which, seeing as we were just jamming, I told him, "Play, play, play."

If he'd have been more like "Fast" Eddie Clarke, or Larry Wallis, or even Captain Sensible from The Damned, then maybe — but The Dead Vaynes' style was more Thunders/Heartbreakers, Cheetah Chrome/Dead Boys, Wayne Kramer/MC5, Ron Asheton/Stooges, Straight James Williamson/Stooges–Iggy Pop and Dave Parsons/Sham 69; me and Dil had that stuff locked in tight between us.

"Next up." I called order again, immediately establishing that I would be leading this band. They were all cool with it, they just wanted to play. "This one is in a Punk-Blues pace. It's basically a slower version of the same 12-bar we just did, but this one's called 'Jesus Loved To Sing The Blues'. Ready to roll?" Of course they were:

Jesus Loved To Sing The Blues
Mary Was Staccato
Joe You Were A Public Fool
Judas Was A Liar
Oh Jesus Loved To
Sing Those God Damned Blues
Mary, Mary Magdalena
I Wonder If He Ever Knew
The Guy That Was Your Stoning Saviour
The One They Called King Jew
Oh Jesus Loved To
Sing Those God Damned Blues.

Straight off the bat, song two is the same as the first. It'd never amount to more than an encore song, not even first or second encore in fact, but it would be a good one for a soundcheck. The main thing is it was another one of *our*

160

songs, and it showed me that the basic ingredients were there. Just like "Dead Vayne Woman" had lasted 25 minutes, so too had "Jesus Loved To Sing The Blues". It gave me a chance to hear Dil on both songs. He was the real fucking deal.

Of course, Tenni could play the guitar the same as millions of others who sounded impressive, riffing million-note guitar solos, but Dil could *play* the guitar. He could play it the way only a handful of guitarists can play. You could hear the route of Dil's playing. It came down the pike from Chuck Berry, through Johnny Thunders and landed on him. Whereas Tenni, his route probably started from Dick Dale, then through to Eddie Van Halen, and he simply mimicked them. No offence to Dick Dale, Eddie Van Halen, or Tenni, but do you get the difference? In Dil, I heard the Punk-Rock'n'Roll greats, not just Chuck and Johnny, but killers like Link Wray too. I adored the sound of Dil.

We finished that first session as The Dead Vaynes with a 30-minute version of "Louie Louie", a song that fits anywhere in a band's repertoire. It's a bona fide classic, covered by everyone from Thunders to The Stooges, Sid Vicious to The Dead Vaynes. We'd been in the cellar for two hours and had done three songs, two originals and one classic cover. We were gonna be great — did I tell you we were called The Dead Vaynes?

"OK, that's enough for today, let's go have a dig" — Cyrus, Dil, me, or Uncle could have said it, anyone except Tenni. He didn't shoot drugs at that moment in time. He'd have a sniff and loved a smoke, but he was not shooting *yet*. He didn't say much either, Tenni, but his story morphed into something mental.

None of us knew how it happened, but one way or another, after a while, Tenni eventually became a massive drug dealer. Not like Uncle and me serving up gram after gram all over the Leeds 6 map — that was pretty low-key, even if it was a lot of grams. But Tenni got into selling big weights of speed and hash. He got himself connected in Manchester and

161

London and moved out of the kids' club and into the men's room as a serious player across Leeds and all over Yorkshire.

Of course, one day he got busted, holding a fair cop of gear too. He was looking at a decent jail sentence of between seven and 15 years, best and worst case scenario. But he didn't fancy jail at all, even though he was a proper hard nut when he needed to be. So he absconded to Holland, where he got a new ID and kept his head down. He also worked as a tour manager for Johnny Thunders and The Dead Vaynes, whichever of the bands was touring in that country. Finally, some years later, he'd had enough of living on a fake ID and set about cutting a deal to return home and face the music. He found a good lawyer via a guy who went on to become the manager of the gigantic Leeds band The Kaiser Chiefs, and pleaded along the lines of absconding because he feared for his life after threats from a hardcore organised criminal gang.

I think he ended up doing his time in a low-category prison, something like three years, maybe it was even an open prison. He paid a big fine, did some community service work and had to go and give talks about how "crime doesn't pay — drugs don't work" in homes for young offenders and council estate high schools. After a while, he got bound over to keep the peace and eventually rejoined the normal world. All of that started from living with me and Uncle and getting into speed. Forks in the road, eh? Fate and chance, you never know what's coming down the line, so you better make sure you walk it, day by day.

*

Things were going good. Uncle and myself were never short of money or drugs. We spent our days crisscrossing Hyde Park, Leeds LS6, calling in on between ten and twenty different shared houses a day, a gram here, four grams there, a lump of dope to another, and on and on. We'd have a spliff or a quick line with most of the student or muso customers. By the time we got back to Glebe in the early evening we'd be buzzing nicely already, and then we'd get down to the

162

proper drugging business with the closest of our crew. As The Clash sang, it was "drug-stabbing time".

It went like this almost every day and every night, constantly speeding our bollocks off.

If we weren't selling gear in LS6, we'd be practising the songs I was writing in the cellar. But usually, it was selling in the week and practising on the weekends. The neighbours would bang on the door and cause holy hell when we played during the week. As I wrote in the Dead Vaynes song "Midnight Man", they'd scream red violence, threaten to have us beaten up by well-connected families or threaten to call the police. But even so, depending on if we were freaky-head fucked or full of spit and piss, we'd deal with them depending on our mental state. Nothing was set, it wasn't fixed. We did what we wanted whenever we fancied. The only thing that was fixed was *fixing up* and signing on for cheque-cashing day, once every two weeks.

By now, I'd taught the band the two songs I'd written back at 27 Leicester Grove, "Tonight" and "You Lost Your Respect". But Tenni kept insisting on sitting in on the sessions, and his style didn't fit those two — and those two were the direction I wanted to go. So we only practised them when Tenni wasn't there, and he always seemed to be there, which was starting to peeve me. I mean, Tenni wasn't in the band, so I wasn't playing the music I really wanted to because we could only play the music I really wanted to when Tenni wasn't there. To make it worse, I started writing songs with his guitar style in mind. They were good songs too, but not what I wanted the band to sound like, so I was getting frustrated.

I booked a studio session, deciding we'd record these Tenni-leaning tracks, but after that I was gonna put my foot down and tell him to back off. It went great; the very first recording session was a riot, as it took us as long to load the booze into the studio as it did the amps and instruments.

In that session, I was on guitar-vox, Dil lead guitar, Cyrus bass, Uncle drums, and Tenni lead guitar. We also had Skum, with a girl he was knocking about with called Dawn, as well as another of the close, crew Flat Top Tom (RIP) all on backing vocals. Skum, Dawn and Tom weren't supposed to be doing anything apart from hanging out, but I decided to get them involved — I always liked to involve everybody, even if I wanted to get rid of Tenni.

Flat Top Tom was a couple of years younger than us, a nice lad who loved bands like The Meteors and Theatre of Hate. He hadn't been around us long, but he was already cracking gear and wigging out like a pro. He did well for himself a few years later though, I mean many years later. He ended up in Leicester, owning and running a fantastic live venue called The Princess Charlotte, which became one of those must-play venues on the live circuit. He ran it for years, and then, years later, he found himself living in the south of Spain near Alicante. So, a happy ending for Tom, with a colourful journey along the way until his tragic passing due to cancer. He has the honour of being on the first-ever Dead Vaynes studio session. I'm sure he took that proudly to the grave.

The songs we did were "Suicide", "Dead Vaynes Rock That Rock'n'Roll", "Get Back To You", "Dead Vayne Woman" and "You've Been Crying Over Me". Well, the booze flowed, the drugs got smoked, the speed got shot and the session went amazingly well. Proper power from start to finish.

Cyrus was so happy to be on the recording; he'd played solid enough, if not spectacularly. Uncle was like a cross between Paul Cook from The Sex Pistols and Rat Scabies from The Damned, with a good touch of Jerry Nolan from The Heartbreakers too. Dil was like the son of Johnny Thunders and Steve Jones from The Pistols, and Tenni just rocked out a million-note solo every time I gave him the nod.

I underpinned the entire body of the songs with tight-ass rhythm, barked my way through all the lead vocals and directed the band through the session. Skum, Dawn, and Tom had a blast with the singalong choruses. I couldn't tell you much about "Suicide" and "Dead Vaynes Rock That Rock'n'Roll" these days. They sounded great at the time, but they never made it past that session. They were like a present to Tenni, so I could tell him he had to stop coming to the practice sessions.

You're already aware of "Dead Vayne Woman", and the other two were "Get Back To You", a throwaway three-chord trick in the key of G that we played live for a while before dropping, and "You've Been Crying Over Me", which became one of the lost Dead Vaynes classics. It was the first song I'd written for CJ…

"You've Been Crying Over Me":

Since you've been gone
I've been so alone
Tears falling down on my pillow
I see you walking by
With another guy
And I know it's not the way we used to
Together baby you and I
Oh, come on, come on, honey, we could try
'Cause you've been crying over me
I said you, you've been crying, I can see
I said you, you've been crying over me
I know you have
I told you I was your Romeo
And you were my Juliet
It doesn't matter what you want
'Cause what you've got is what you've get
There's no use playing hooky from the school
Oh, and you're getting along
And you're having fun
But deep down, you know
It won't last forever
So come on now and lay down by my side
Keep me warm, and I'll keep you safe at night

Yeah, I will give you shelter from the storm
'Cause you've been crying over me
I said you, you've been crying, I can see
I said you, you've been crying over me
I know you have.

It was a Rock'n'Roll love song in the key of C. The chord sequences, the tempo, the words — I was proud of it as a fully finished and rounded song. It lasted from then till today for the closest of the crew that made it through. I say it's a lost song because apart from that first ever live recording and playing it live at the first handful of shows, it has never been recorded and hasn't been played live since 1984 as part of a full band performance.

So that was it; we were up and off and now we had something to play: we could now think about gigs. The only problem was that Tenni wouldn't take the hint that he had to stop coming into the cellar, and unfortunately I knew we needed a better bassist than Cyrus. As much as I loved him, he would never be a bass player who could learn an entire set. He didn't know an A note from a B note, didn't know how to make bass lines or keep a rock-solid one-note hard rhythm. But Cyrus, being Cyrus, understood completely. He knew he wasn't good enough and wouldn't get better. He agreed to leave, and our relationship remained exactly the same. He was our friend and also a fan of the band; being on the first ever recording, which sounded great, was enough for him. The thrill of that would last him a lifetime.

I had to sit Tenni down and talk it out with him: if he wasn't gonna do the right thing then I had no choice but to make everything clear. I pointed out that I was writing songs with his sound in mind, which wasn't the sound I wanted for The Dead Vaynes going forward.

Unfortunately, it didn't go well. He didn't get where I was coming from and before long he got proper moody about it. The next thing that happened was the vibe inside Glebe Ave went to shit, and that put us on pause for a while, just as we

166

were getting ahead, getting something going. I decided to move back into the heart of Hyde Park, just around the corner from The Royal Park pub, which was like ground zero for the entire area. I thought that if I was away from Glebe I could orchestrate the band better without having to deal with a daily uncomfortable situation with a mate who I liked but whose guitar style I didn't want in my band.

I got super-lucky and moved into a tiny basement flat, with kitchen and small hall area, on Brudenell View. There wasn't a bathroom but that didn't bother me. I could hardly remember the last time I'd had a bath or shower anyway, and the toilet was a floor up outside my entry door, which was a drag, but it was what it was. The entire space was maybe ten square yards, but I was the sole key holder and my little window, which peeked out at street-foot-level, was just fine for me. Even better was that CJ moved into a shared house right opposite, only she had the top floor attic room, which was perfect. We were like a Punk-Rock'n'Roll Romeo & Juliet, me down below the street, literally living at gutter level in squalor, and she locked up in the attic, head in the clouds, so to speak. It appealed to the twisted romantic in me, and in her — Gutter-Glitter; we'd found a new way to be together, to see one another, on Brudenell View.

Cyrus was now out by mutual consent, and Tenni was sidelined even though he'd never officially been in; I set about replacing Cy and adding a second guitarist.

I didn't want a normal guitarist; I wanted somebody who knew how to make a guitar sound sonic, with controlled-uncontrolled noise and feedback. I was looking at a Thurston Moore type of technician, which was kind of strange because I wasn't a fan of his band, Sonic Youth, or Thurston Moore as a guitarist either, but I wanted a "something something" *other* sound.

As for Thurston, I saw him in concert years later while living in NYC. He was on a double-header with the legendary Suicide at a tiny underground venue in the arty meatpacking district on the West Side of Lower Manhattan.

167

At this time — let's settle on 2004 — I was fully involved in the House music scene, running the world's number one House music label, Subliminal Records, in Weehawken, New Jersey, as the Label Head, Business & Legal Affairs Director.

I'd only heard about the Suicide show on the actual day of the event and tried to rope in a couple of people from the record label to come with me. But despite my efforts to educate them — Suicide were one of the pioneers of electronic music! — I had no takers, even after telling them my Soft Cell story: how Suicide influenced Soft Cell, how Soft Cell influenced others, etc. These guys didn't even know who Soft Cell were. It was a lost battle and a wasted effort.

"Fuck it — philistines," I said to myself, with Jam and Bravado listening in, "I'll go on my own — there's bound to be good people there."

So off I went, straight from Weehawken to Manhattan, and found my way to the small downstairs venue — maybe a capacity of a hundred — and I did meet a good guy.

Michael Imperioli is an actor. He was standing in the corner of the bar on his own. Fate and chance landed him right next to me — we were both trying to get the bartender's attention to buy a beer. I recognised him straight away from a handful of films I'd seen him in, roles like Bobby from *The Basketball Diaries*, where he loses his hair and dies of leukaemia, setting Leonardo DiCaprio's Jim off on his descent into drugs and prostitution. I knew that film because I was into Jim Carroll — I'd read and loved *The Basketball Diaries* book, and I really loved his big song "People Who Died", which was a battle cry for most of us back in the junkie days of The Dead Vaynes in Leeds 6, 1984.

I recognised him even more for his memorable cameo role as Spider in *Goodfellas*, where he gets shot in the foot by Joe Pesci's mad character Tommy: "Dance, Spider, dance, you mutt." And then he gets shot dead after telling Pesci's crazy Tommy to go fuck himself.

But more than those films, I recognised him straight away from his role as Christopher in *The Sopranos*, which was the uncontested biggest show on American HBO cable TV when I stood side by side with him at that bar. He wasn't just a cast member flitting in and out of the show — he was one of the principal characters, the assassin nephew to the lead character Tony Soprano himself. Christopher had already bumped off something like seven people by then — he'd go on to do nine in total before getting killed himself by his own Uncle Tony for being a degenerate junkie who'd fucked up.

So, yeah, I knew who he was right away. But for some reason, I decided I'd pretend I hadn't a clue.

Now, before I go on, let me just clarify that Thurston Moore was absolutely self-indulgent, arty-punk, non-Punk shite! As bad as I'd always known he was going to be. His performance was just him, his guitar, a microphone, and about fifty different effects pedals all connected on a table in front of him. He'd play a noise and let it run through the multiple pedals. He did the same with the microphone — bark a noise and let it ride through the pedals. So basically, he made these noises and then played the effects pedals, manipulating the sound into a cacophony of absolute bat-shit bollocks.

I looked around the room. The hipsters were nodding their heads and pulling approving faces of ecstasy like they were having an epiphany, a religious awakening.

"Oh, fuck off," I said to myself, but out loud.

I stuck it out for about twenty minutes and then escaped to the bar.

"What do you think of Thurston Moore?" I asked the guy standing next to me at the bar, who was also trying to buy a beer.

It was Michael Imperioli.

"Well, I'm not sure I get it. I'm only here to see Suicide."

I liked that answer. He'd politely said, "Shit, let's get Suicide on already."

I expanded on it a little.

"I couldn't take anymore, had to get out — it was doing my head in."

169

We started laughing. The bartender got to our side of the bar.

"Buy you a beer? Heineken OK?"

"Sure, I've got next."

And so we started to talk.

I have no idea why I decided I wouldn't let on that I knew who he was, but once I started, there was no turning back.

He went first.

"You live in the city? Work here?"

A usual, regular question. I let him know I lived in the Lower East Side but worked in Weehawken running a record Label, which piqued his interest. It turned out his big passion was music. Well, I should have guessed that, seeing as he was here on his own, same as me, at a Suicide gig in a tiny dive bar venue. But it still came as a surprise.

Even more surprising was that he made music himself — he was a musician. So I gave him my business card and suggested he contact me to arrange for me to hear some of his stuff. He was well made up, proper excited.

Then I asked him where he lived and what he did for a living.

That gave him the chance to confess.

"I'm an actor."

Now, right then, I could have said, "Yeah, you're Michael Imperioli, I've seen you in *The Basketball Diaries*, *Goodfellas* and *The Sopranos* — it's a pleasure to meet you."

But I didn't.

"An actor? Wow. What kind of work do you do — theatre, film?"

He could have said, "I'm Christopher from *The Sopranos*. I've been in films with De Niro, Pesci, DiCaprio..."

But instead, he said:

"I've done a couple of things. Theatre. Some TV."

Real vague. Not coming fully clean. Like he wanted me to recognise him rather than have to tell me outright.

So that's how you wanna play it, Christopher...

"Theatre? That must be hard. Anything in movies, TV?"

He looked a little taken aback. I mean, his face was on billboards all over the city. He had a unique look — slicked-back hair, a strong nose — a good-looking guy who appeared exactly the same in person as he did on screen. He had to be used to people recognising him at first glance.

"Yeah, a few supporting roles in some movies, and I'm on a TV show that's running right now on cable."

I kept it going. "I don't have cable, I don't watch much TV." It was basically like saying "TV is for people with no life". But I added, "My girlfriend has it. What show are you in?"

He hesitated, unsure if I was genuinely clueless or just being a prick. "I'm in *The Sopranos*."

That was the moment. The fork in the road.

"I've heard of that, but I don't think I've seen it. Sounds great. Is it a big role, or are you just, like, an extra? Small supporting role?"

He should have smacked me in the mouth right then.

"I'm one of the lead roles. It's a really big show. Syndicated across America, plays all over the world. It's been running for a few seasons already."

Now he was running out of goodwill. I ordered a couple more beers.

"I'll try to catch it at my girlfriend's, see if I can spot you in it."

Easily one of the dumbest things anyone could have said to him. He had a face you couldn't miss — exactly the same on screen as he was standing right in front of me.

I pushed on. "I know a guy in the movies. He got a Best Supporting Actor nomination at the Oscars but didn't win."

He looked at me — somewhere between crestfallen, ready to swing a punch, or wondering if there was a hidden camera filming this prank.

"Oh yeah?" He said it just like Christopher. "Who's your actor friend?"

I knew I was about to impress him. "Joaquin Phoenix."

He wasn't really a friend. I'd met him a few times at my local bar on the Eastside, BarOnA. He was good mates with a friend of mine from Leeds who had made it big in America and was with Joaquin's sister, Summer Phoenix. She'd even come to a party I once threw at the Chelsea Hotel.

"Anyway, it's been good talking to you. Suicide are about to come on. Good luck with the acting, and give me a call if you ever want to get some music to me for the record label... Michael."

I winked. We both started laughing.

"You motherfucker. Fuggedaboutit."

He was a good sport. We clinked bottles and laughed some more.

"When Suicide start playing, you better be dancing. Dance, Spider, dance, you mutt! Don't fuck it up, or I'll shoot you in the foot. See you inside."

We clasped hands, pulled in for that cool, street-style American man-hug, and I headed off into the small live room to find a good spot for the gig. Suicide finally started playing about thirty minutes after walking on stage, but the wait was worth it. They were everything they should have been — and all the better because it was such a tiny dive bar venue.

I never saw Michael Imperioli again. And he never called me about his music. His loss. Subliminal was the most influential label in dance music — who knows what could have happened?

Oh well. Next!

Back to my life… I recruited Martin as the "sonic noises" second guitarist. He was a lovely fellow who liked to dress in women's clothes, not in a gay way, more in a flamboyant way. He just liked women's clothes. It was freaky, his guitar style was freaky. I brought him in on a suck-it-and-see basis. Maybe it'd work out, maybe not. As for replacing Cyrus, well, Cyrus found the replacement for us. It was a giant biker-looking guy who lived in a shed with his beast of a self-made motorbike. I never knew his real name. I only ever knew him by the name he christened himself with, "Smelly". It was a

172

perfect name for him. He was dirtier than anyone I knew. He wore the same leather pants 24/7, never washed, ever, not even pits and bollocks. Even I made sure I did those. He had a denim cutoff jacket that he wore over his other leather biker jacket, with the legend written in studs "I AM NASTY" as a headline on his back. Despite his image and look, which was always angry with an undercurrent of violence ready to break out, he wasn't a druggie and he wasn't a big boozer. But once he joined The Dead Vaynes, he started getting on the speed, and before long, he was shooting up just the same as everyone else. He was a good bassist, though. Sometimes he even used a knife instead of a plectrum to pluck the strings.

After rehearsing for a while together, maybe a couple of months, the lineup of me, Uncle, Dil, Smelly and Martin was ready to play live. The big news that broke, news that sent the entire city mad with anticipation — but nowhere more excited than us in Hyde Park Leeds LS6 — was that I had begged Ian Dewhirst from The Warehouse booking department to let us, The Dead Vaynes, play a gig there as the official support band to the one and only Johnny Thunders. It wasn't just Johnny either — his band would feature fellow ex-Dolls and Heartbreaker, drummer Jerry Nolan, and another Heartbreaker, bassist Billy Rath. The date was set for August 28th, 1984. It was a dream come true for me and the band and everyone in the crew who was part of us. This was going to be a major night for us all. Fork-junction, fate and chance.

9. DTK — LAMF

Everyone around the LS6 scene was super-psyched — Johnny Thunders was coming to Leeds. Not just Leeds but The Warehouse. There wasn't anybody in our area who wasn't a fan of Thunders or wasn't buzzing about the gig as soon as it was announced. We all loved him. He'd played in Leeds only three times before.

The first was as far back as 1973, with the legendary New York Dolls themselves. One or two people I knew had even been old enough to witness that fabled show — not me. I would have just turned ten years old and was singing along to David Bowie's "Laughing Gnome" at the time.

But one point to make in regard to that Leeds show by The New York Dolls...

At some point during the day on November 24th, 1973, Johnny Thunders was walking in the streets of Leeds. I know this because it is part of Rock'n'Roll folklore and history, that when The Dolls appeared on the legendary late-night cutting-edge music program *The Old Grey Whistle Test* a few days later, the band mimed their way through a blistering performance of their classic song "Jet Boy" — and the everlasting memory of that appearance is the brattish, raw energy, of a young Johnny Thunders swinging about a white, pearl-finish, Vox Teardrop electric guitar.

With his leather jacket, that shock of wild black hair, and the cool as fuck Teardrop, it's an image that's often referred to as "The Dog's Bollocks". It may have even been the unplanned bastard "Birth Of Punk-Rock'n'Roll". The connection to Leeds? That guitar was bought in the city on the afternoon of November 24th, 1973 by Johnny Thunders for just £25, according to the rumours, from the second hand store Big Deal, to use as a prop-guitar for their upcoming *Old Grey Whistle Test* appearance. It puts Thunders firmly in bed with Leeds, and it puts Leeds right in the mix when it comes to the History of Punk, and Punk-Rock'n'Roll.

174

The second time he rode into town was on the infamous Anarchy Tour in 1976, the first ever UK Punk tour, along with The Sex Pistols, The Clash and The Damned. Although it might've been an ill-fated Punk tour with most of the shows cancelled, the Leeds gig survived. In fact, it was the very first show on the tour to go ahead and feature all four bands. A few more people we knew had attended that iconic night too. Unfortunately, not me. I was discovering Punk, but I was only 13 years old. It's funny to hear some people, who would have been a similar age to myself, claim they were there — but they weren't.

The last time Johnny had played Leeds was a year later in 1977, as part of the promotion cycle surrounding one of the greatest Punk-Rock'n'Roll albums of all time, The Heartbreakers' *L.A.M.F.* That visit went into folklore because The Heartbreakers all ended up getting their fingerprints taken at a Leeds cop shop. It's a weird story involving possibly-maybe hitmen, possibly-maybe secret agents sent to protect them from assassination, possibly-maybe a promotion stunt, possibly-maybe one big hoax. You'll have to read about it in a book by one of The Heartbreakers.

But those prints made it on to the back cover of the *L.A.M.F.* album itself, which linked The Heartbreakers and Johnny Thunders to Leeds for eternity, which we all appreciated and saw as a badge of honour and pride. More people in the scene had been at that show, but again, not me. I was still too young at 14 then, plus I was into The Stooges until my moment of discovery when The Dead Boys were delivered into my life, and it was a little while longer before the penny dropped with Thunders.

So, three shows in 11 years, the last one seven years ago. You could say that this was a major event for supporters of a certain sound and lifestyle. And we, The Dead Vaynes, were right in the eye of the storm. We weren't just going to be making up numbers either, Leeds was ready for him, I was ready for him. But the main question I wanted answering was: is Leeds ready for The Dead Vaynes?

*

We were already infamous across the city — on one hand, that was due to my own limited but explosive history of local gigs over the previous couple of years, and for having had a record out with my previous band that had made a small dent in the scene.

On the other hand, we had also made quite a noise around town with our Dead Vaynes *Lion Studios Session Tape*, which had been passed about all over the place and caused a massive stir in the local scene. That tape had been copied and played to death in all the shared houses where me and Uncle served up our drugs across LS6.

The other thing was that we had a general vibe around the band, created via Chinese Whispers, based on wild tales of debauchery that swirled about everywhere. "Oh yeah, The Dead Vaynes, that's that crazy band of junkies, right?" Our name was already well known before anybody had ever seen us play.

In the lead-up to the show, Smelly decided he wanted to stay up speeding for an entire week before stage time. The night of the gig was set for Tuesday, August 28th, 1984 and Smelly began his quest seven days earlier — he drove me nuts cribbing gear off me to keep him awake and buzzing.

Now, I wouldn't recommend anybody trying this, but Smelly was attempting a seven-day stay-awake marathon, which is a really dangerous challenge to undertake. I should say "don't try this at home, kids". Lack of sleep like that can damage you massively. I don't know if it will kill you, maybe it could? I don't know. What I do know is that you're going to hallucinate and lose all perception of reality. What I also know is that Smelly was fucking up my vibe by the sixth day. He'd parked himself outside my "gutter window" on Brudenell View, begging for more speed one minute, then begging to be taken to hospital the next, whimpering, then shouting, crying then laughing — as I said, don't try this at home, kids!

176

The thing is that his tolerance wasn't anywhere near the super-levels of tolerance that me, Uncle, Dil, Evo or CJ had — and even we wouldn't pull seven days and seven nights straight. He could hardly tell by now if he was awake or asleep or what was real and what wasn't. He was fucked. But I didn't feel sorry for him. I hadn't told him to go on a crazy bender. It was his idea.

Eventually, I couldn't deal with it any longer. Despite him being an ogre, a bad-tempered "fight everyone" nutter, something flipped inside my head, probably because it felt like he was about to piss on my Thunders–Vaynes dream gig with his dumb show of oneupmanship. I lost myself in the moment and screamed at him, "Fuck off, get the fuck away from my window." I paused for his reaction, but he was just staring at me with dead eyes. I stopped shouting, now speaking in a calm voice. "Look, Smelly, if you don't fuck off then I'm gonna have to sack you from the band, I mean it fella, I'll sack you right fucking now and go get Cyrus to play the gig tomorrow. What you gonna do?" I knew I was gambling, Smelly was an ogre, remember, but I decided to go out and confront him on the street. I got lucky and won.

I caught sight of him at the bottom of the road trying to kick cars as they drove by, but at least he seemed to be going in the right direction towards his hovel shed. From my point of view, it was infinitely better than him beating the shit out of me outside of my street-level gutter flat… "Clarke, one-nil". Result!

Finally, the day arrived, and there we were, sitting about with our gear stacked up and ready at the side of the stage. We couldn't take it on to the stage because Thunders' stuff was set up there, and we were waiting for him to show up and do his soundcheck first. Somebody told us it was protocol. To be honest, for this gig, I'd have waited as long as it took without a sigh of complaint.

In reality, we'd been hanging out for about an hour, not sure what we were supposed to be doing apart from waiting. Then all of a sudden we sensed something was happening. A

177

feeling kind of rose in the room; there was movement from the club staffers and the sound and light crew started bobbing about like they were busy. The game was afoot, and in walked "The King of Punk-Rock'n'Roll" — Johnny had entered the building. The Heartbreakers — Johnny Thunders, Jerry Nolan, and Billy Rath — were here in the flesh, minus Walter Lure, who strangely enough (even though he sang loads of the songs, and played loads of the guitar leads with The Heartbreakers) I didn't really care about. Well, actually, it's not that I didn't care about Walter, but, for reasons unknown even to myself, I just never felt any sense of connection to him, despite his crucial role in the band, his playing, his vocals, his foil to Johnny's onstage persona. I can't say why, but I just didn't ever really care about Walter Lure — sacrilege to fans of The Heartbreakers, I know, but it is what it is. The main three to me were here, in the same room as me — I was the proverbial pig in shit.

Now, you know when you want something, you dream of it, you crave it, you're certain of it, and then when you see it, touch it, get in front of it, it's a let-down. You wish you'd have left it aside, safe from any chance of anti-climax, from being ruined forevermore. Well, this wasn't anything like that.

This was everything and more. Charisma dripped off him. It was tangible. You could reach out into the air and grab a palmful of magic, hold it to your nose and breathe it in. He was hypnotic. Nobody in the room could take their eyes off Johnny. He was effortless, naturally dominating the atmosphere around him. I'd never been around anybody like him before, not even when I'd talked to Iggy inside these very same walls. I've never met anybody since who had that sense of "This Is A Star" about their very presence.

Maybe the only other time I felt it was when I almost bowled David Bowie over in a street in London years later. It weren't anything really, to be honest you could class it as a "nothing happening" moment — I turned around and accidentally bumped face-to-face into David Bowie. We both excused ourselves and moved on — of course, it probably never even registered with the great man, but I felt like I had been touched by God. And I have to admit that both Liam and Noel Gallagher also have that *thing* about them, especially Liam, which I'd feel a sense of, years later, at the pub near our future mutual offices in Marylebone. But even Bowie and the Gallaghers didn't match up to Johnny.

He was so mesmerising that I can't even remember seeing him walk. It's like he was here, then there, like he'd levitated across the room. I couldn't say what he was wearing either. All I know is that he just looked super-cool. The first striking thing about Thunders is his hair, a big thick black shock of hair. They call it a bird's nest in the press sometimes. It looks best when it's combed back at the sides like an overgrown DA from the fifties. Let's just say, that as far as hair goes, Johnny's was miles better than Stewart Granger's, better than James Dean's, and even on par with Elvis!

The next thing you notice is his nose. It's not a cute button Hollywood nose, it's a real, multiple-broken street nose. Not massively big, but maybe just slightly too big for his face. If it were a hat, it'd be a "look at me" Fedora, or if an actor, then it'd be a Dean Martin-sized Hollywood star of a nose, rather than a too-cute Straw Boater, or a Jerry Lewis "I'm famous too" nose. It told me this guy's been in a few scraps, win or lose, he don't mind getting involved.

We kept sitting where we were, not wanting to make fools of ourselves or get in the way. Johnny and his crew had a chat with the sound guy. It was about five minutes of mumbling, head-nodding, pointing and whatever. Then, as quick as they'd come in they were gone again. Johnny, Jerry, Billy and a couple of others in his crew turned around and left. Nobody had said a word to us. We didn't know if they were supposed to say a word to us actually — I'd never been a support to anybody up until now, so I didn't really know all the protocol stuff. I didn't know if things were always like this between a famous headliner and support or if we'd just been stiffed. Then his tour manager came over to us. Unbelievable luck — Jah providing again? — it turns out

179

that this guy knows Uncle, he was a Leeds fella from up Horsforth way, same as Uncle, and now he was Thunders' guy. "Alright, Uncle, listen, Johnny's not doing a soundcheck. He's been travelling all day and needs some rest, so we need you to do a backline check for us. That means you can use the drum kit but with your snare drum. You can use the bass amp and cab too, but you need your guitar amps. I also want to set his mic to reverb the way Johnny likes it. Is that OK?"

I jumped straight in with the answer. "Sure, no problem. Set the bass and drums through the desk however you want. We'll go with it too, however you want it — no worries." I was just gibbering, saying whatever I thought he wanted to hear.

It really was like a dream coming true. We plug in and do a version of "Louie Louie" as a Johnny mic test, and for the overall soundcheck, since Thunders usually does his own version of that classic song. Being truthful, we sound phenomenal!

The club's tech crew tells us we sound great. They also let us know it's going to be packed early doors — a sold-out house is on the cards. Thunders' tour manager thanks us for setting up the sound, says we're fantastic and that we're going to smash it come showtime. In three hours, we'll be in the eye of the storm. I know we're all a little nervous but also massively confident. "Get to fuck, The Dead Vaynes are here."

The needle goes in, blood, push, one gram of methamphetamine drains into the vein, and Uncle and Dil both shoot up too. Johnny walks in just as we're digging away and speaks to us for the first time. "Hey, what's that you're cooking up?" I'm already preparing a dig for Smelly by now. He's been drinking brandy, and flagging; I want him sharp. We're going to hit the stage in the next 15 minutes. It lightens his mood no end to know he's about to get things fixed.

"Methamphetamine," I say, looking at Johnny. "Do you wanna hit?" Jerry and Billy have already followed him into the small dressing room that we're all sharing and their attention is on The Dead Vaynes too. Johnny looks at them, saying, "It's methamphetamine." All three pull a "fuck me" face. Johnny looks back at me. "You guys are crazy shooting that stuff, that shit'll kill you. Are you crazy?" I'm rushing because I've just banged a gram, Dil and Uncle too. "We all do this stuff in Leeds." The three of them are watching as I gun up Smelly. Johnny speaks to me again: "OK, have a good show you guys. Are you sure you're OK to play on that stuff?"

It's rhetorical, I think, before he departs saying, "Make sure to stay around to see our show too. Let's hang together after, alright?"

The three Heartbreakers leave us to it. They're being ushered up to the VIP area upstairs. Well, fuck me, Johnny just told us we're crazy, just encouraged us to have a good show, told us to make sure we see him play and wants to hang out after. For me, the gutter just got sprinkled with some glitter — it's perfect.

The Dead Vaynes hit the Warehouse stage — our first gig and the room is full. Loads of people have come out to see us, not just Johnny but The Dead Vaynes too — like I say, we weren't there just to make up numbers. It's a cracker of a show, the crowd seems to love everything we do, though nobody knows many of the songs, except maybe "You've Been Crying Over Me", and "Get Back To You", songs that have survived from the *Lion Studios Session Tape* that has been copied and shared all over the city ever since it was recorded. Another song we played from that tape session is the first song we ever did together in the Glebe Ave cellar, "Dead Vayne Woman", which I get everyone in the room to sing along with. We also do "You've Lost Your Respect" and "Tonight", which I'd written back at 27 Leicester Grove.

Basically, everything we play sounds killer and goes over really well. The best of the lot though is one I wrote up just a few weeks earlier called "Midnight Gun". It's a proper bollock burner, get-to-fuck, Punk-Rock'n'Roll killer. It'll

181

become our anthem, and it'll last for decades in the hearts of
our closest fans.

"Midnight Gun":

This is the Midnight Gun,
And I'm packing silver bullets baby,
Bang Bang!

The house is shaking, my nerves are breaking
Madness is taking control again
You be a general or even a colonel
'Cos now I'm talking and nobody's listening
If you really want to care about it
Listen baby, you can take my place
Baby, baby, you know I'm not crazy
We both know who's right again

Baby, I'm the Midnight Boy
Baby, I'm the Midnight Gun

Do you feel alright in the dead of night
Do you knock on wood because you look so good
But did you realise, you know, that I'm the guy
Who died a million times last night
I'm a Dead Vayne Boy
And I will fall for you
Yes, I will fall down for you
If you call me, I will
Be a running fool for you

Don't You Hide
Don't You Lie
Wanna Know The Truth
Who's Who!

182

I'm The Boy, I'm The Boy, I'm The Boy, Baby I'm The Midnight Gun — You Better Believe It!

It was a triumphant debut gig, the band made a mark that night. It kick-started everything that would follow on over the next seven years. This is how an eyewitness wrote it up:

The Dead Vaynes Live at The Leeds Warehouse, 28th August 1984
The Night I Found The Dead Vaynes — Flash Tightpocket Review

"These fine fellows first came to my attention at the Leeds Warehouse in 1984, when, in one of their earliest shows, if not even their actual debut show, they supported a Waldo-less, Johnny Thunders & the Heartbreakers. 'Twas indeed an epiphany for your genial host, for they were raw beyond belief, they had a stage presence like none other & a certain 'je ne sais quoi'; that indefinable quality which set them apart from the other unworthy pretenders. With their eyes as wide as the finest bone china dinner plates, they were indeed, wired beyond belief. A heady brew & righteous stuff indeed. I attended the aforementioned show with a good friend of mine & we must have looked like Beavis & Butthead as we stood like statues, eyes & mouths agog & salivating as we absorbed this delightful, aural & visual onslaught. Later in the evening, my pal plucked up the courage to attempt a chat with one of them. (I can't remember which one). Hey fellas, great show, where do you come from? quoth he, FUCK KNOWS came his response. Your host was on his neck with hysterical laughter."

As for Johnny Thunders, he — along with Jerry Nolan and Billy Rath — was sensational, delivering everything I'd hoped of him.

From the moment he stepped on to the stage he was in attack mode; "Countdown Love" was followed by "Personality Crisis", a one-two punch from his Heartbreakers and Dolls back catalogue. I was straight in the moshpit with the rest of the disciples before the opening song had even reached its first chorus. Any thoughts of "playing it cool" — given that I was one of the evening's *stars* — were rightly abandoned, and soon enough he hit us with an unofficial LS6 anthem, "Too Much Junkie Business". Well, that was it — arms, legs, bodies, all a mess of mayhem, the entire room losing its collective mind.

This was the first time that I'd seen Thunders live on stage with my own eyes, in the flesh; "The Boy Looked At Johnny — and it was the best moment of his entire life up until that point."

I knew that there was nobody else in the room that could see him the way I could see him. And even though he was from New York City and I was from Leeds, there were commonalities that seemed to me beyond doubt. I could hear, I could see, Johnny Thunders.

That night at The Warehouse has passed into fable and legend in the city of Leeds — Johnny was triumphant and The Dead Vaynes made their glorious debut. People say they were there, even if they never were, and those who were there wear their attendance as a badge of honour — even to this day.

We did hang with Johnny, Jerry and Billy after their set, drank some drinks and chatted like old pals. We made a connection and they said we should've done the whole tour with them — sadly, too late to get all the promoters on board for that this time, but they told us they would call us up the next time they were touring the UK, and we took them at their word.

After about 30 minutes The Heartbreakers left, and me, Uncle, Dil, CJ, Evo, Flo, Franky, Flat Top Tom, Cyrus and Skum all headed back to LS6 and got wired for the next 24 hours; we thought we should celebrate — The Dead Vaynes were in The Game!

*

A couple of weeks later, after the Johnny Thunders gig, I was setting up more shows and writing more songs, but before going back into rehearsal mode I knew I had to sack Smelly.

I don't mind saying I was shitting myself — Smelly was a big bugger and moody as fuck. I didn't know if it'd end up in a fight. I'd liked the idea of him, a big biker-looking monster, but the reality of it had left me less than content.

When I got to his shed, only five minutes away from my gutter, I banged on the door and was met with, "Fuck off, I'm sleeping." I pushed on, "Smelly, it's me, open up. I want to talk to you." It was quiet, and then I heard something like a bottle smash on the other side of the shed door. I jumped back, nearly shit my pants and almost ran. It went quiet again, then I heard him say, "Look, don't be pissed off, but I'm leaving the band, no hard feelings, OK? It's been a laugh, but I don't want to get hooked on speed like you idiots."

I couldn't believe my luck; he'd told me he was leaving himself. I could've jumped somersaults. "Oh mate, what, you're leaving, why? Are you sure?" I prayed he wasn't gonna let me talk him around. "No, I'm done, you're speed-freaks, I don't wanna be one, no hard feelings, sorry to bail on you. Here, I've got this for you as well." I picked up a wedge of notes he'd pushed under the door. I gave myself a chest-thumping Leeds Salute; he'd paid me what he owed me for all the speed during his marathon week. "OK, fella, I understand. Go back to sleep, see you around sometime." I half waited for the answer, but truthfully, I was already on my way counting my cash so that I couldn't hear any possible last-minute change of heart.

Smelly disappeared soon after and drove off on his motorbike heading south. Years later, word reached us that he had made his way to Australia and became a pilot flying a crop sprayer, which made me happy to hear. It felt as if that was probably the best job and lifestyle he could ever have;

185

flying a plane, living out in the middle of nowhere, happy with himself while hating on the rest of the world.

I brought in a gorgeous-looking lad called Toddy to take over bass duties — all the girls liked Toddy, a cheerful and friendly guy that made him the polar opposite of Smelly. The Dead Vaynes did a few more shows which all went really well, and Toddy really was a good bass player and a great guy.

But then, one of my good mates, Harry, the bass player from Abrasive Wheels — remember, I mentioned them earlier — well, he left the Wheels and let me know he'd be up for joining The Dead Vaynes if an opening came up.

Harry'd been hanging around LS6 and getting into the gear more and more over the last few months, shooting up methamphetamine, and now he wanted a more Punk-Rock'n'Roll band to play in, rather than the straight-up Punk style that Abrasive Wheels were. I couldn't resist it. Harry looked and acted just like me, Uncle and Dil. Toddy took it well, he wasn't mad about it. He knew Harry and me had been mates since way back from Whinmoor and Crossgates as teenagers, so he stepped aside without freak-out or fanfare.

Toddy went on to do good things; he played in some good bands, achieved some success, toured and made records, but his best was to come later when he opened up a live music venue in Leeds called The Cockpit, which was a big success and played host to hundreds of famous bands during the time he owned it.

Eventually, everything became too much for Martin; he handed in his resignation soon after Toddy had been relieved of his duties. In some ways I was sad about it, mainly because he was always such a nice lad to be around and massively creative, but we both knew the end of the line had come for him so far as The Dead Vaynes — he was cut from a slightly different cloth.

Martin wished us well, we did the same, and now we were four. If I'm honest about it, then this lineup should have been the one to stay together and take on the world. We looked the dog's bollocks. Me, Uncle, Dil and Harry just fit together in every which way; we were all caning the gear, all played Punk-Rock'n'Roll as our first love, and all had the same style and vibe about us. When we walked down the street or into a bar or on to a stage, we looked amazing and gave off an aura that was right up there with The Heartbreakers or The Dead Boys or The Stooges. It was effortless, it was natural, no pancake makeup or clownish costumes — we were the real fucking deal and we sounded better than any other version of us that had previously been. No disrespect to any past members, but Harry on bass, Dil on lead guitar, Uncle on drums and me on second guitar and vocals, it was just right, and everybody around our neighbourhood seemed to love us for it. We were as authentic as the actual Punk-Rock'n'Roll stars that we all loved. We were "Down To Kill — Like A Mother Fucker". What we needed now was to make our own classic album, something to sit alongside the likes of *L.A.M.F.* or *Young, Loud and Snotty*.

By now, time had ticked through to March 1985 and opportunity was just about to knock.

10. GET TOTALLY FUCKED OR GET TO FUCK

Goth music had become the dominant sound across the UK and The Sisters of Mercy could probably lay claim to being the most influential band in Britain, maybe even Europe by now — they led the movement from Leeds to the world, along with fellow Leeds LS6 Goth bands Red Lorry Yellow Lorry and The March Violets.

They were all major players through the early and mid-80s, headline bands at home and abroad. LS6 bands were doing well; we were all proud of them.

The Sisters were without doubt the Dark Lords, the men in black with shades onstage and big-brimmed hats, outlaws of the badlands. Surrounded by smoke, dry ice and strobe lights, they were a real experience live, sometimes incredible and sometimes not so much, depending on the consumption beforehand. They had grown as a band; their sound, image, intensity and emotion all amplified.

Red Lorry Yellow Lorry were the respected "proper" band, all thunder and hurricane, a whirlwind of edgy and aggressive beats and guitars — of course, they were also surrounded by smoke, dry ice and strobes. Everybody had a little love for the Lorries; they weren't faking, they were real, with great songs living under the emotional barrage of guitar sound. You had to put some effort into liking this band; they weren't for kids, they were just simply a great band in the studio or on the stage — they were intense.

Then there were The March Violets, who were like the scene's strange and weird agent provocateurs. They had female and male *dual* lead vocalists and were harder to define than the other two; they had something to say, but it wasn't always said in a straightforward manner. They had poetry and a sense of theatre about them, not in a soft-smooth flowery way; they weren't hippies, it was more in a demented carnival puppeteer confrontational way. Likewise, they too

188

were surrounded by smoke, dry ice and strobes. It was a Goth thing. Si Denbigh, the male vocalist, was a bear of a man, the master of ceremonies who could put fear into a room just with his sheer presence and force of nature. As a live band, they were a trip.

These three paved the way for so many bands in their slipstream, and not just the bands that had a Goth musical style. They shone a light on the Leeds scene.

Those three brought fresh attention to Leeds, just as The Gang of Four, The Mekons and Delta Five had done before them, and as The Three Johns did too. Any band from Leeds that had the national music press featuring and reviewing them was good for everyone in the city, especially LS6. Every John Peel show that a Leeds band did drew attention up north towards us. It didn't matter that a band like The Gang of Four sounded so different, with their scratchy attacking guitar making for an attention-demanding Punk-Funk-Fucked-Disco-Noise or that The Mekons were so uniquely eclectic. The main thing was that they brought attention to the city.

Bands like The Wedding Present, Age of Chance, Cud, Salvation, Rose of Avalanche, Hollowmen, Hang The Dance and loads of others did well from the connection of sounds and a focused lens on Leeds. But for The Dead Vaynes, not so much, although we were connected with a lot of bands as friends, mainly because we all drank at either The Royal Park during the day or up at The Faversham at night. Musically we were off-kilter with almost everyone else; we didn't have a common musicality with the Leeds scene. We were a Punk-Rock'n'Roll band.

A lot of the action took place at The Fav, a massive pub located behind Leeds Uni, and just up the road from Hyde Park, LS6. It attracted a proper mixed bag, but there were rarely any trouble in the place because it was run by a cool family who knew their patrons. More than that, they employed "Big Tom". He was a brilliant fella, an ex-sailor who happened to be a massive music fan, who acted as the security, or more like the go-between, between the bar and its customers, somebody who spoke the same music language as the bands that hung out there, and the music lovers who drank there too. Tom was key to The Fav's success. Sometimes, often-times, there'd be over 500 folk packed in there and just Tom as the gatekeeper and controller — he did a fantastic job in a very important Leeds meeting place.

So many great bands used to hang out there; every corner or strategic table would be home to a band. We all knew one another, but for us, even though we did a couple of shows with the likes of Red Lorry Yellow Lorry, Salvation and Rose of Avalanche, we were always set apart. I don't mean that we were better; we were a different sound, maybe an old-fashioned sound, which meant we were not part of any trend or movement.

In my mind, the bands we needed to be playing with were Johnny Thunders, The Dead Boys or The Gun Club — that was our scene. But they were already on the map, American gutter-glitter Punk-Rock'n'Roll stars, while we were lost in Goth City, LS6 — an authentic Punk-Rock'n'Roll band trying to be seen above the smoke, dry ice and strobes of all the bands around us.

I knew that we needed to get some material released, something to justify doing proper shows and give us a reason to get on to good tour supports. We could accept being the mavericks in our city, we just had to find a way to get our music released and stake our claim, even if we were swimming against the musical tide.

*

It happened one night out of the blue. Si Denbigh from The March Violets decided he was leaving his band to start a new act, The Batfish Boys, and wanted to establish his record label, Batfish Inc., via a P&D deal with Red Rhino.

During a chat over a few drinks up at The Fav, he offered me the chance to release an album by The Dead Vaynes on his new label. There would be no fannying about with singles either; we'd come straight out of the traps with an album,

190

which was pretty genius thinking by Si. Think about it: if you release a single or an album, both are 12" pieces of vinyl with a record sleeve, but an album is much more of a statement. It's also the same cost to manufacture but three or four times more to buy. That's the business of the music business. The real economics of releasing a record were of little interest to me then, but a few years later they would be all-consuming. I would nickel and dime the micro costs of every element that went into manufacturing a product, gross costs versus gross return and net profit. But that kind of thinking wasn't for now, that stuff would only cross my mind once I'd finally managed to become part of the business of the music business. Soon enough you'll see how I got from that careers advice chat at John Smeaton School to an office on Broadway, Manhattan, NYC and beyond. But for now, Si offered a way to release some music. All he asked were two or three questions to make sure we were on the same page. "First, do you have enough songs for an album? Second, I'll cover manufacturing and marketing costs, but you have to pay for the recording studio yourself. Have you the cash to cover the studio? If not, can you raise enough cash to cover it? Because I'm ready to go ahead with it right away. Lastly, have you got a full working band right now?"

Did I have an album's worth of songs? No. To be clear, I did have a lot of songs, but I knew they all had to be rounded out and given arrangements before they could be considered ready for a record. Most of them had only been played live and those versions could be short or long depending on how I felt at the time. So I had to get into the songs and give them structure.

Did I have a few grand to record the album of songs? No, but come on, man, I was a drug dealer! I just had to sell enough drugs fast enough to get the cash needed while at the same time avoiding doing so many drugs myself that I'd eat deep into the profit and the studio budget — that would leave us back at square one again. The name of the game was to try and keep focused.

191

Did I have a full band? No, not anymore.

Around Easter 1985, Dil disappeared. I spent a couple of weeks trying to find him, following the trail, making sense of the clues but it was no good, he'd gone. Then one day the news came over that he'd gone on a trip up a mountain to find himself, as part of a religious cult experience — a weird kind of intense sect with its messiah-style leader. I had visions of Charlie Manson.

I tried to track him down again, but they were a secretive bunch and I couldn't find him. But even if I had, I wouldn't have got in his way, I would have only tried to give him another point of view and a reason why he should stay with the band, standing side by side with me, rather than walk behind some religious "Charlie" leader — I would have respected his choice to live as he wanted to, I just wanted the chance to make a case. I wasn't happy about it, but I wasn't hateful towards Dil. I loved the bones off him. I was sad that we wouldn't do great things together. We weren't going to be David Johansen & Johnny Thunders, Mick & Keith, Iggy & Straight James, Stiv & Cheetah Chrome. But in my mind, the door would always be open for him to come home.

I recently found out that the reason he left was down to being ill with paranoid psychosis, which we had all been experiencing to varying degrees. Still, it seems his was much further developed than anyone knew. He even thought I was attacking him when in fact I loved him.

That resonated with me because back at that same time, I was probably at the height of my methamphetamine shooting gallery lifestyle — a speed-freaking baby, talking to myself almost uncontrollably at the time. Two voices, as well as my own would squabble over every single decision I made, from getting out of bed to getting into bed, as well as everything that happened in between — keep in mind that it could be days between each action of getting in and getting out of bed. My paranoid psychosis was obviously as developed as his own, but neither of us had fessed up to it.

Writing or arranging a song was a massive challenge, as I'd argue with one voice, Jam, causing me to self-doubt and question everything — which was sometimes, well most times, for the best if I'm being honest with myself. Then, the other voice, Bravado, was full of beans, confident like Muhammad Ali, cocky like the Artful Dodger, a bragger, a can-do kind of voice that was equally as important to the process of getting the songs fixed and finished.

The old saying "suffer for your art" is a common refrain. Well, being stuck in between Jam and Bravado, fighting to hear yourself above the noise that they'd make, was inevitably less than fun — psychosis can knock anybody off-kilter, sending them running up a hill in search of salvation or digging deep-deep into a dark pit of darkness.

People think it's easy to knock out an album, that the songs and arrangements maybe just write themselves. In truth, it isn't easy, it's no walk in the park.

I was fighting day and night with me, myself & I, debating, dissecting, dictating and giving myself a proper headache to get an album's worth of songs in shape for a proper recording studio session that would deliver an LP worth releasing.

These multiple voices aren't unique to me, everybody has them; they're sometimes referred to as "The Angel and Devil on My Shoulder", and while most people don't pay them much attention, for me, being a speed freak, they came over with crystal-clear clarity. I'd embrace them, as I knew their benefits, but controlling them became a balancing act that in turn became exhausting. And when you're exhausted you start to become ill, physically and mentally, because it's a lot of baggage to carry around with you, day by day, hour by hour, minute by minute, even second by second.

It upset me to hear that Dil had faced the dreaded psychosis alone, not knowing that he could have come to me or CJ — if he had done so, I would have sympathised and related to his madness completely as well. All these years later, I found out that one of the reasons he had left to join a

193

religious group was because he felt alone in the Punk-Rock'n'Roll band — it was heartbreaking and emotional to hear.

As strange as his disappearance was, it turned out that he stayed in that cult and in the hands of God his entire life. His work in the sect had him going out to Africa on missionary goodwill visits, and somewhere along the way he fathered a child and learned how to become a champion competition surfer. The chances of the Dil I knew wearing a pair of swimming trunks were remote, but to become a champion surfer was pure fantasy. Another strange thing that happened to him was that he became a member of the Leeds United Service Crew, a full-on, home-and-away, hardcore member of the pack.

This was bizarre as he never showed even a passing interest in football in all the time anybody from our old crew knew him. Yet now, Dil's an expert on all things Leeds United and the Service Crew, even having a Service Crew tattoo on his forearm in praise and recognition of his part in the crew of football-fighting hooligans. It's freaky stuff; Dil was mischievous but not a fighting man, at least he wasn't back when we were in each other's pockets. But keep in mind that at some point, Dil was in a very bad car accident, damaged his skull and went into a coma. When he returned from the brink, new Dil wasn't taking shit from anybody. I believe he is officially termed as socially handicapped, unfit for normal work, living in assisted accommodation and seemingly existing right now in his own private Dil World, making strangely funny, social media videos and occasionally getting in trouble with the police for the chaos he sometimes causes around the village he lives in.

I wish he had stayed in the band and come on the journey with me. But back to the time and place, the result was that Dil was gone and I was devastated to lose him. All our plans seemed to be ripped to pieces.

How do I replace a guy who I believe to be irreplaceable? But it was what it was. You have to keep on moving. Jah will provide. Something'll come up. So what, whatever.

So I decided to blag, and raised a glass with Si.

"Yeah, fuck yeah, not a problem," I said. "I've got an album ready to record yesterday, and the studio budget, how much is it? Fuck it, don't even tell me, don't even worry about it. I'm killing it with the gear, so let's just do it, set the studio up, and as far as the full band question goes, of course I've got a full band, The Fucking Dead Vaynes, me, Uncle, Harry, and Dil. We're ready, born ready."

We celebrated into the night.

*

Within the next two or three weeks, Si had been as good as his word. He'd been serious after all and booked us to spend some time at a cool studio, The Slaughterhouse, where loads of famed bands recorded their albums. It was also in the birthplace of Captain Jean Luc Picard from *Star Trek*, AKA Patrick Stewart, and to finish off the trifecta of greatness, it's where the Dead Vaynes album *G.T.F.* came into the world.

From everything I'd mapped out, I selected eight songs as ready to roll: "You Lost Your Respect", "She Bit My Arms She Blew My Brains", "Tonight", "Motor City Baby", "Midnight Gun", "Television Man", "Christmas Time for The Wide Eyed Faces" and "Cry Me An Angel". They were a great collection together, but in retrospect, I should have swapped out "Cry Me An Angel" for another song I wrote called "Rock'n'Roll Christ". Looking back it was clear that the band weren't really ready to take on a more developed song like "Cry Me An Angel", which was a complex affair compared to the others. "Angel" was one that needed a smart producer, it should have been saved for the next album and developed even more and given a chance to become epic, especially given that "Rock'n'Roll Christ" was more in keeping with the raw power of the rest of the album in both style and vibe. But, it is what it is, and maybe it's just a personal preference.

The main thing was that I believed we had an album that would sit on a shelf, head held high, next to The Heartbreakers' *L.A.M.F.* and The Dead Boys' *Young, Loud and Snotty*. That was my goal from when I was 14 years old, and now at 21, I felt I'd done it. If longevity and influence is a measurement of success, rather than commercial pop numbers, then it sits in sync with those two benchmark albums that were my personal barometers.

The last song I wrote for the album was "Christmas Time for The Wide Eyed Faces". I wrote it right before the recording session. Dil is even referenced; see if you can spot him.

"Christmas Time for the Wide Eyed Faces":

In a combat zone, the feeling is scary,
A holiday camp, locked in by a see-through wall.
There's talk on the street, we're gonna meet our maker,
And nobody knows if he'll send us up or let us fall.
The black sheep's got a car, heading out to the sunset,
And a friend got a dog, she walks it in the park.
There's a place we all go, where everything's so-so,
Well, I guess it's okay, but then there's nowhere else at all.
There's an eye in the sky looking over the city,
A man in disguise, with a spy in his hand.
Bright light in a window, of a house on the hillside,
And a car passes by, every hour of every night.
Baby's going down to a miscalculation,
And Tracey's locked up on a long-term holiday.
A good boy lost his way, got a new occupation,
Now he's stoned on a hillside, he gave his guitar away.
It's always Christmas in my house,
With those wide-eyed faces at my door.
They look so pretty with those hungry faces,
But I just can't feed them no more.
Crazy baby, I hope you've got what it takes,
After all you've said and done before.
All your pleasure, all your pain,

196

You're looking for something,
But I ain't got it anymore.
There's a cloud in the sky, a real big black one,
And it's chasing my sunshine away.
We're just hanging out, on a government vacation,
And I'm having a ball every day.
It's always Christmas in my house,
With those wide-eyed faces at my door.
They look so pretty with those hungry faces,
But I just can't feed them no more.
I can't take it, baby, no, I can't take it,
It ain't Christmas time anymore,
All the sunshine's gone.

"Christmas Time" was a song about LS6, selling drugs, the effects of drugs, police surveillance, friends busted, losing grip and walking away. At its heart, it was about me and the entire crew around our scene in Leeds, a picture of life in LS6 told from my own drug dealing viewpoint. And as a drug dealer, I was almost always available, always on call for pick-up or delivery. I was open for business 24/7, day and night; you wanted to cop, you knew where Santa with his snow white powder was — "it's always Christmas in my house with those wide-eyed faces at the door".

I was planning on bringing the curtain down on that drug dealing part of my life, but that final call would have to wait a bit. I had to get the cash together to finance recording the album first.

I put some work in, kept my eye on the prize, and pretty quickly I had the album written and mapped out. I also had a plan on how to move enough gear, fast, to get the financing for the studio sorted too. Now all I needed was to find a guitarist.

*

I wrote down a list of possible Dil replacements. It needed to be somebody from nearby, Leeds-based and, even better, LS6-based. I didn't want to nick somebody out of another band. I didn't mind if it were somebody already intent on leaving a band; that would be their decision, but I wanted clean hands.

Nobody that I'd put on the list felt right. Something would disqualify them on closer scrutiny, but one night at The Fav I saw a guitarist I knew from a band I used to see play at The Staging Post back in Whinmoor a few years earlier.

He was about four or five years older than me, but that would've only made him mid-twenties anyway, like Joe Strummer was older than the others in The Clash, so the age thing didn't throw a spanner in the works.

I saw this guitarist across the pub and remembered how his style had put me in mind of being a cross between Frank Infante from Blondie and Straight James Williamson from Iggy & The Stooges. He had a look about him that was a cross between them both — so that was a good start. I knew he was a good musician — better than any of the remaining Dead Vaynes actually. That was the only thing that gave me a brief moment of pause; it was either gonna be a problem, or it'd make us all raise our game.

His band was tight, good players with good songs; they were called Shake Appeal, which was the name of a Stooges track on the *Raw Power* album, even if his band were closer to Blondie or The Pretenders than all-out *Raw Power*-sounding — I thought a conversation was worth having.

I introduced myself, even though he knew me already and I knew him. To be clear, we knew each other only by sight and reputation.

It turned out that the soon-to-be-christened Prince Michael De Vayne had some incredible positives about him. 1: He was disbanding Shake Appeal so he could explore new horizons. 2: He was the only person I'd ever met who had seen Johnny Thunders four times in Leeds — '72 with The New York Dolls, '76 with The Heartbreakers on The Anarchy Tour, '77 headlining as The Heartbreakers, and he was also at the '84 Thunders/Dead Vaynes Warehouse show. It turned out that Thunders was his favourite guitarist, along with

Straight James Williamson from The Stooges, but better yet... he thought The Dead Vaynes were the best Punk-Rock'n'Roll band around. He was a fan.

"Dil's gone off to find God. Do you wanna join the band?"

He almost fell off his chair. "Are you serious? Is this a joke?"

"No, I'm serious. I've even got your name. How do you like the sound of Prince Michael De Vayne?"

He stopped laughing. "I fucking love it."

Mick wasn't the kind of person to swear much at all, while I'd use swear words all the time, every sentence would feature swearing, words themselves would be punctu-fucking-ated. But not Mick. If he said, "I fucking love it," then you knew he abso-fucking-lutely fucking loved the fuck out of it.

Before sealing the deal, I told him a couple of things that he needed to consider before saying yes:

"We're recording our debut album in three weeks. It's only eight songs. Can you learn them that quickly?"

He nodded. "Hell yeah, no problem."

"We have to pay for the studio time. Batfish will pay for the manufacturing and promotion and sort the release out, but we've got to raise money for the recording session. So, if you're going to join, then you have to chip in. That means that you, Sir Harry, and Uncle will have to either put in £750 each, or you each have to take fifty wraps of speed from me and sell them at £15 a pop, and you've got to do it within the next three weeks. So, which is it going to be? £750 cash, or do you pick up the gear tomorrow, like Harry and Uncle? We can even have a song-learning session if you choose to sell the gear."

The idea of knocking gear out, even if it was to front studio costs to record an album, was a "Say that again?" moment for him. He hadn't expected me to put the offer of joining the band to him in that way, with those conditions — AND — it turned out that his day job was as a nurse for the NHS, so a conflict of vocations right there. But something

199

inside him knew what time it was. The Dead Vaynes was like a gang — if you're in, you're all in. And within five minutes, he agreed, saying he'd be able to knock that amount of gear out to his crew of mates and associates, no problem.

Bottom line, Mick was in — but I had another demand of him:

"Where do you live? Any chance of moving over to Leeds 6?"

It was a rhetorical question. He had to move into the area. Luckily, it was something he was already working on. The sooner he could find a place in the neighbourhood, the better for me and him.

The last point that I needed to be clear about, and be sure he understood, I put like this:

"Listen, I don't know what you know or what you've heard, but we're speed-shooting junk fiends. Sometimes one person or another can flip out, lose their shit, lose their mind. If they do, they do. It is what it is, but at this moment in time, that's where we are. We're all fine with who we are. It's not a rule that you walk this way too. You can be 'Straight Prince Vayne' for all I care, but you need to be aware that we're not fucking about when it comes to jacking shit up our arms. We're at it every single day, usually a minimum of three grams, often four, sometimes five grams or even more. I'm talking about marathon sessions. Look, Mick, I'm just giving you a fair and upfront warning. We're a band, we're good people, but we're speed junkies. We're more or less always on speed. Can you deal with that?"

He looked at me, unsure what he was going to say — but then said calm as fuck…

"Got any gear now? I'd love a line before going down The Phono."

Boom! Oh yes, he was going to be a perfect fit. We went to the toilets and I chopped him out the biggest, thickest, line he'd ever seen up until that moment in his life. It was a whole gram chopped in two. I nosed up my half, he got through half of his half and asked if he could put the rest back in the wrap

200

to do later at The Phono. I pushed him aside and snorted it myself:

"I've got two more grams on me. We've got enough for The Phono. Remember, fella, one of our mottos is G.T.F. - 'Get Totally Fucked' or 'Get to Fuck.' It's the way we roll."

We both started laughing. I liked the sound of it, "G.T.F.". I'd just made it up on the spot. I carried on:

"That's going to be the name of the album, like Johnny's *D.T.K.* and *L.A.M.F.* Our album's going to be called *G.T.F.* and people can wonder what the fuck it means."

He loved it.

"Come on Prince Michael, time for you to meet Uncle and Sir Harry. Now we have a 'Prince' and a 'Sir,' from the gutter to the glitter, Punk-Rock'n'Roll killers. I'm packing silver bullets baby, bang bang."

He was the happiest man in the world right at that moment and he turned out to be one of the secret ingredients that made The Dead Vaynes sound so special. From the moment he joined the band Mick 'Prince Michael De Vayne' became the only other constant band member as others came and went — Mick was my musical partner in crime.

The album was recorded and released by mid-June 1985 — THE DEAD VAYNES, *G.T.F.*

*

Band life was as good as it gets. I remember when we played at the Royal Park Music Festival, our already growing wild bunch reputation guaranteed that our room was packed tight. People were hanging off the walls, standing on chairs and tables up to the bar. People had even scaled the outside of the building, climbing up the walls to push their heads through the smaller windows at the top to catch a glimpse. It was bedlam, a good enthusiastic bedlam.

The Dead Vaynes were brilliant that day, a memorable moment in the history of the LS6 scene that is still spoken about today — it made it to folklore: "Were you there when the room turned into a riot?", "Did you see the singer get glassed during the set?", "Did you see the singer glass himself during the guitar solo?", "Were you there?", "I was there, I remember it like yesterday", and so on. If all the people who claimed they were there were actually there, then the venue and room would've had to have been ten times bigger than it was. All I know is that I was there and our whole crew was there. It was an amazing day, in an amazing pub, in an amazing area — LS6 Allstars in full effect.

"But Reality Bites, Babe." Even though there were many highs, many crazy good times, that's not the whole reality. For every yin there is the yang, every high comes with its low. The higher the high, the lower the low — that's a fact of life. And the truest fact was that I had caned so much gear up my arm that I had damaged myself and damaged my head in a brutal manner.

It wasn't just the time of my life, it was also a living nightmare of a life. The world was screaming at me from every direction as I'd developed a severe case of paranoid psychosis, a really acute case, to the point where anything I laid my eyes on, anything I heard said, be it on the TV, radio or in regular life that was going on around me, was screaming at me: "You Are A Cunt." This is what Dil had gone through.

Eventually, it got to the point where every waking moment I'd be under attack, and even when I managed to fall asleep, my dreams attacked me — visions of monsters, tiny ogres with sharp knives, or giant spiders, wasps and hornets that wanted to cover and sting my entire body. All manner of things seemed intent on wanting to do me harm. I couldn't even tell if I was awake or asleep some of the time. Not one thing made any sense, yet everything was crystal-meth clear. It was nearly impossible to handle and I thought about ending it all, sometimes constantly. Every coherent thought I could manage would focus on the notion to "just make it stop".

I didn't know it at the time, but once the paranoid psychosis got its grip on me, it would take two full years to come back from it — the first year almost unbearable, the second year putting my head back together one block at a time.

I was fried, fucked up beyond all self-recognition. The only person who knew how bad I'd got it was CJ — I made her promise that no matter how bad I became, to never let anybody section me into a nut-house, for fear that once in, I'd never get out again. She promised and faithfully kept everything to herself.

But I knew I had to do something about it. Things had become almost uncontrollable; I could barely function for days and weeks at a time, the non-stop voices of Jam and Bravado were fighting each other constantly, both pulling at me in every which way, on every single issue, sending me insane.

Eventually, and in a moment of rare clarity, I decided, again, that my salvation would be to concentrate solely on the band — and that I needed to stop shooting up methamphetamine drugs. Much easier said than done.

The problem with being a speed junkie is that it's hard to get things done. In band life, just writing a song, or arranging a studio session, attending rehearsals, sorting out a gig, or actually playing a gig, is an obstacle course of pontification and drama. In real life it's no better either; deciding whether to get out of bed, get dressed, and step out of the house is a minefield of decisions and choices, each one debated in circles. Choosing the day to start coming off junk — well that's a trip.

Things take longer to do when you're locked in on junk, not to mention that there's always another speed session breaking out around you to get on board with too… "Rock'n'Roll Train, Here It Comes Again."

It's a contradiction of time as well. Things appear to go slow, days melt together, day and night don't differ other than the street lights being turned on or off, but at the same time, life keeps chugging along. As the old saying goes, time waits for no one, and before long six months have passed and then a year is gone. The bottom line is that you're lost in the drugs, on the merry-go-round where everything is in a spin.

The options become: keep spinning, enjoy being dizzy and sick; or lean forward, tumble into the river and drown; or jump off a high building, take the hard knock, get back up off the floor and try not to do it again.

Coping with psychosis wasn't easy. I'd try to deal with it using two different techniques.

Option Fast: run faster than the paranoia, shooting gram after gram, four or five grams a day, one big bang after another. More speed was the medicine, and no sleep till collapse, head moving so fast that there was no rest-stop for the nags to take hold. This technique works fine if you have the strength to keep it up and enough gear to keep it going, which I did because my body was stubbornly able to take massive doses and I was also a street dealer who was moving a decent amount of weight. But outpacing paranoia is not for kids, and it taxes you personally; my skin turned grey for a while, my face looked like a skeleton and my body was like a stick — and the comedown, after a few days of speeding like that, is brutal!

Option Slow: to beat back the psychosis, the plan was to slow everything down, not with dope or hash — that would freak me out completely by now, one drag and I'd be hallucinating for hours. So my slow-down medicine was alcohol, bottles of whisky, vodka and wine, whatever was at hand, while also drinking beer as if it was water. The slowdown technique typically meant waking up from a pill-induced sleep in the afternoon. As soon as the reality of being awake becomes clear, just start pouring and steadfastly go about sipping the whisky chasers to complement the bottles of beer, or hit the vodka to go with the bottles of wine.

The Slowdown is cool beans until the time comes around that the works cross your scrambled thought process again, the works cut through the noise; you remember the rush that you know comes from shooting up speed and you say out loud even, "Well, I've been cool for a few days, my head's calm, fuck it, let's crack one up."

At the end of the day, the reality was, despite or because of my drug issues and the paranoid psychosis the drugs had caused, I'd written a collection of songs and arranged them into recordable tracks. Those compositions were caught on vinyl and released to the public. I was now a tiny part of Punk-Rock'n'Roll History, and as tiny as it may be, it's still there, it can't be undone. I'd achieved something tangible, so even if the drugs made me hurt, I don't ever regret it.

Between the Fast/Slow techniques, I survived the darkest, hardest, days and cherished the brightest, unbelievable times. But, much more than that, I left a scratch along the track.

I didn't know back in 1985 that people from a certain niche social scene would still play and reference that *G.T.F.* album decades later and consider it a classic of its kind.

In between outpacing it with overkill amounts of speed or wrong-footing it with copious amounts of booze, the paranoid psychosis would have me in its grip, awake or asleep. It felt never-ending at times and all the while I'd tough it out, cope with it, hide it, do what I was there to do — play a tour, do a gig, whatever — while trapped in a living hell of confusion, not understanding anything being said around me, as well as hallucinating without warning.

Nobody said it was going to be easy to throw the works away, but, as luck would have it, I got busted by the drug squad. It turned out to be the kick in the ass I needed to stop shooting up.

*

I never officially split up with CJ — the truth is that we were only considered boyfriend and girlfriend for a short while. And even though everybody always associated us as being together, like Sid and Nancy, the fabled Franky and Johnny, or the bad-land crazies Bonnie and Clyde, we had officially not been a boyfriend-and-girlfriend pairing for a much longer period than we had ever been one. Sometimes we'd be together, sometimes not.

205

It all changed when I stumbled across a beautiful English-Jamaican girl, Lucinda. As soon as I saw her, I knew that if we were to hook up together, she would give me another way of getting through the day. She was slamming — a red-hot beauty, brown-skinned, black-haired with flawless skin. Soon enough I started something up with her.

Lucinda was just what the doctor ordered. She was straight for a start, completely drug-free, did nothing at all and hardly drank a drop of drink either. We met by chance at The Royal Park one night, a complete accident, thanks to her friend, a punkette who wanted to be around the LS6 band scene.

Unusually for The Royal, Lucinda was a native of the LS6 area, not a student or musician who'd moved in from some other place. She was one of the few who'd lived there her whole life. She was a bona fide LS6 native, and the natives generally avoided the scuzzy Royal Park.

Having recently turned 18, she and her punkette girlfriend had started coming into The Royal, where they set about looking for 18-year-old-young-woman kicks.

Lucinda was a sight to behold, a fully developed woman with the body of a vamp. She didn't fit in here; she was clean-cut, innocent, extremely beautiful, young and healthy — the polar opposite of me. But at least there wasn't much of an age difference, given I was only 21. She was quiet, didn't smile much and would have melted into the background, invisible apart from her supermodel looks and that killer figure, which she'd innocently showed off to full effect in her full-body, skintight, black catsuit.

She had the attention of every werewolf in the yard and didn't even know it. Wide-eyed, innocent and curious, she wanted to taste the scene that was going on in her childhood streets, eager to experience things, eager to grow. And so Lucinda and her punkette mate left the paternal safety of their family homes and moved into a back-to-back rental house, just five minutes from The Royal, hell-bent on personal discovery.

With her, I felt cleaner than I had in years just by being in her presence, and when I say cleaner, I mean cleaner in every way. Her innocence had a surprisingly big attraction for me. I wanted to be innocent too — I was gone, feeling kind of giddy about Lucinda.

Lucinda didn't know much about me; she wasn't a Punk-Rock'n'Roller but she did know by now that I was somebody in the LS6 music scene. She also knew she was interested: the curious cat wanting satisfaction. I didn't need convincing about her. She arrived at the perfect time and lit a fuse. It would be a relationship based purely on animal sexual attraction, Beauty and the Beast. We started going steady for a few weeks, I calmed down a lot on the gear, never shooting up when she was around — and I wanted her around, in my bed, a lot.

Drinking days became the norm, drugs put aside as I passed the time sipping whisky and sucking on bottles of beer. My attention was equally focused on the gorgeous girl; we'd fuck like it was our last day on earth, hardly bothering to leave the big double bed for days at a time. Things began to even out for my head, pussy power beating back the psychosis. There are worse ways to self-medicate. She was falling in love, I was definitely in lust. All was going well.

After a month of this bliss, I was set to go on tour to Holland for a three-week stint. This made her nervous, it made me nervous too, but not for the same reasons. She had to face up to the fact that her fella was in a proper Punk-Rock'n'Roll band, a touring band, a working band, who went out on the road to promote its name and legend. We had an audience; we could fill a venue. The reality of this rocked her world a little, unbalanced her harmony, and she confessed that she was scared that I'd be out on tour, sleeping with girls, forgetting about her, and on my return I'd probably leave her behind. She didn't want that; she was committed already. I told her it would be impossible to forget her, that she was the most beautiful girl in the world.

207

She was good for me and I wanted to keep on keeping on with her once I got back. I wanted to cool her nerves and give her a sign, something to hold on to while I would be gone on the tour. So, about a week before the tour began, fate played its part. After a few early doors beers, I came out of The Royal Park and saw a small dog running on the field just opposite. I decided to make a play for the stray dog.

He was a little black mongrel with a docked tail and a small white mark between the front legs on his chest. He was about two or three years old, not a pup, well-fed it seemed, but I told myself he was just another discarded dog left on the streets. I saw him, he saw me, I beckoned him over and he bolted right up. I hugged him, gave him a rub, what we call "a love", and held him to me for a few minutes before letting him go free.

I started on my way back to the flat, which was only about five minutes away, just up the hill. The dog must have felt good with me because he decided on his own, without any more encouragement from me, to walk alongside.

I didn't call him, not even once, he just stayed by me and walked perfectly in my stride — I didn't try to shoo him away, that much I'll admit to.

I stayed silent for the whole trip back up the road, not wanting to influence the dog's decision to stay or bolt. When I arrived home, I opened the front door of the building and he scampered right in, he properly tore up the stairs in front of me, racing up to my top-floor flat where he sat patiently outside the correct apartment door waiting for me to arrive. It was as if he knew exactly where he was going, where he wanted to be and who he wanted to be with. I opened the door, and he ran in, jumping right on to the bed where Lucinda was just waking up. Her face lit up and her smile filled the room — remember, Lucinda didn't smile very often but when she did, she really did smile.

"Who's this little boy? Who's this beautiful baby?" she asked. I hadn't seen her as animated as this in the entire month I'd known her.

"This is James Bullseye Vayne, Esq. He's my dog. Will you look after him while I'm on tour?"

I was smitten by the little fella from the get-go; he seemed special. It was like we were destined to be partners. I also didn't know at that very moment that we would be joined at the hip together for so long — 15 years. I wasn't looking to be tied down to responsibility by either human or animal. It's one of the reasons CJ and I had always worked out so well; she expected nothing of me that I didn't want to give, and I expected nothing of her in the same way. We were both happy for each other's absolute freedom. But when it came to James Bullseye, I had no choice. We were hooked up, like it or not, we were in for the long ride.

Wherever I lived during the next 15 years, the dog came too, eventually moving to London with me but not quite making it to New York. By then, he was 17 or 18 years old and entering his final weeks and days; he wasn't healthy enough to change countries. But we'd had a good innings together — the end of his life, our union, was very sad but also very tender and beautiful.

"You see, Lucinda, if I didn't plan on staying with you when I come back, would I give you my dog to take care of? This dog means the world to me."

"I didn't even know you had a dog. Where did he come from?"

She was confused by the new arrival, but he would do whatever I told him to do — sit, sleep, stand, walk, run — whatever I directed, he would obediently follow, as if I'd trained him since being a pup. She may have been confused but she didn't question that the dog was mine. It seemed legit.

My beautiful girl pulled me back to bed, the dog curled up on a chair as directed and Lucinda fucked my brains out.

209

11. BUSTED, NOW GET BUSY

The tour of Holland was a Rock'n'Roll train wreck. I mean, the gigs were all great — good venues like The Melkweg in Amsterdam and Parkzicht in Rotterdam. There were lots of great shows, full houses and enthusiastic audiences. And the band played incredible.

But, of course, we had suffered another change in the lineup. Bassist Sir Harry had decided to leave the band to become an art student in Scotland about ten days before the tour started. As luck would have it, Craig Adams, the bassist from The Sisters Of Mercy, was at a loose end waiting to launch his new band The Mission — which worked out good for The Dead Vaynes as Mick roped Craig in for the tour.

Mick taught Craig the songs over a couple of sessions, then we had a couple of rehearsals together as a band and he made us sound better than we'd ever sounded before. His big, solid, growling bass sound nailed the rhythm to the ground, we were anchored so tight by Craig that we had room to develop the live sound of the songs into places we'd never gone before as a band — we sounded proper.

Harry had done us a favour by opting to chase his dream — a dream that eventually led to him becoming the Dean of the entire University Art Faculty where he still resides so successfully today.

Anyway, that was the good news. But on the negative side, well, where do I start?

I know where; I robbed a podgy gay guy on the overnight ferry from Hull to the Hook of Holland — hear me out before judging me. He was asking for it; I don't apologise for it. He was a sick fuck. Here's what happened...

We'd set ourselves up in the corner of the main room, just to the side of the horseshoe bar, as the ferry pulled out of Hull Docks. We were all happy to be on our way to Holland. I can't remember how many hours at sea we would be, maybe 11 or 12 in total? The timing meant that we would sleep wherever we could before arriving at our destination in the morning.

Taking stock of our surroundings, it seemed that the only passengers on board were us, The Dead Vaynes, and what seemed to be the entire cadet division of the Dutch Army — hundreds of them, all dressed in full camouflage kit. Other than those two contrasting parties, The Dead Vaynes v The Young Dutch Army, there was nobody else on the ship — well, almost nobody else.

We heard him before we saw him — an older guy, maybe mid-50s, well overweight, super-flamboyant, loud and camp. As he made his grand entrance we quickly realised that he had also spotted us — our black leathers and rags probably being a welcome contrast to the green army fatigues. He was making a beeline through the tables of cadets toward the area we had bagged for ourselves — our ground zero.

We were all very welcoming when he first joined us. His camp persona was fun; he was a funny guy. Gay or straight, he knew how to tell a comic story and all was happy in the camp — especially when he bought a bottle of brandy, a bottle of whisky and a 24-bottle tray of Dutch beer for the table. We were well chuffed as we weren't rich ourselves, in fact we were brassic, and it meant the tour was underway even before getting to the first gig.

None of us drank brandy or wanted brandy, so he sucked on that. We shared the beers and whisky between us and he even bought another tray of 24 — we were all having a good laugh for a few hours. At some point in the proceedings, with the brandy making its mark, he started telling us about "having a young guy", some kid aged 17, who he had set up in a sex flat in Amsterdam for his weekend pleasure. I didn't like what I was hearing and didn't want to know about it, it didn't sound right. I knew a lad who had been abused by an older man; he'd tried to commit suicide several times and then ended up inside for various petty crimes. Basically, his life had turned left when it should have gone right, all due to an older adult getting their kicks from the abuse of a younger

211

non-adult, who had been underage when their arrangement had started. So, now he was drunk and loose and telling his story; there's no need for me to go into details, as he did, but it's safe to say that he'd said more than enough for me to mark his card. I left the table as he opened his second bottle of brandy.

In my opinion, this sounded like exploitation, sexploitation and abuse rather than mutual fun. Maybe I was wrong and the kid, not much younger than me, was a willing player in the scene. Then again, I'd have to believe that a 16/17 year old non-adult has the wherewithal to even make such a life choice — and I didn't believe that for a second. I don't know for sure, but it was enough of a reason for me — my interpretation of his tale was that this fuck-pig was a nasty, manipulating cunt, so he was gonna pay. Gay, straight, man on boy, man on girl, woman on boy, woman on girl, that wasn't the issue — it was the adult on non-adult, sexploitation, that gnarled at me.

Later on as the ship sailed through the night, everybody was sleeping or passed out, curled up and snoring here, there and everywhere. Not me though; I'd been waiting patiently. The big bugger was passed out on a bank of seating on the other side of the bar from where ground zero was, brandy-fucked and out cold. "Go on, sort this bastard out," Jam and Bravado were, for once, in unison. Me, myself & I were in agreement as I wiped the twat out of everything he had on him — £200 in UK notes and about the same value again in Dutch guilders. Back then, that was quite a sum of cash. "Fuck him and feed him beans!" The last I saw of him was as we were driving off the ferry — I could see him remonstrating with one of the sailors, obviously complaining that he'd been robbed in the night.

So, we were on our way and it didn't take long before we found our digs. Johnny Thunders' manager/tour manager, the guy I'd met at The Warehouse gig via Uncle, was called Mick Webb — he had set this entire tour up, and had us stay in a wooden chalet located in the middle of a forested holiday camp for the duration of the tour.

With my stolen wads of cash, I had the driver take us to a big supermarket to fill the fridge and cupboards with booze and snacks. Mick and Craig were confused and surprised when I volunteered to pay the massive bill on my own — not at the act of kindness itself, that didn't surprise them at all, but they knew I didn't have the kind of money to hand over 200 guilders at the counter because we'd all been talking about needing our per diems as soon as the first gig was done. Once back at the chalet, I told them that I'd robbed the gay guy on the ferry and told them why. We all agreed it was justified, a case of older taking advantage of younger — it wasn't gonna be tolerated on our watch. Mick and I clanked our bottles together and gave a toast, "Let's Ride." We both loved John Wayne, we thought ourselves to be outlaw cowboys.

The first night was also the first gig. We were pretty pissed by the time we got to the venue, me more than the others as I'd been hammering the Jack Daniels. Then once at the venue, we demolished the drinks rider. By soundcheck, I was laid out on the stage and refusing to pick up the microphone — not being belligerent, just too drunk to focus. Not a very professional look, I'll grant you that.

The venue owner wanted to cancel the gig, but our tour manager, the on-the-run Tenni from Glebe Avenue, convinced the venue owner to talk to Mick Webb on the telephone. As I said, Mick Webb was responsible for the tour overall, but better still, he was known to the owner as the manager/tour manager of Johnny Thunders, so he had quite the pull. Mick Webb got on the phone. Tenni reported back that the chat went something like this.

"Is the singer off his head at soundcheck? Look, don't worry, he always gets like that — it's his thing. But I'll guarantee you he performs better at the gig if he's fucked up before the gig. Just keep feeding him with booze, all of them in fact, and you'll have an unbelievable night. You'd need to

213

worry about him if he was sober at soundcheck; if he's lively now, then he's shit for the gig — boring as fuck. Put some more beers and another bottle or two in the dressing room and it'll all be fantastic. He's like a dancing bear or a clapping seal, but instead of burning his feet or throwing him fish, just wet his beak, or powder it if you can."

Well, it worked. The gig wasn't cancelled, more booze showed up, a big crowd came out and we put on a fantastic performance as I came back from the dead to give the room a proper show. We played for two hours, all told, including three encores. Then after the gig, loads of punters stayed behind to hang out with us as we led them through a bizarre medley of Leeds United football songs — random, I know! The venue owner was well made up as they drank his bar dry too.

On the ride back to our chalet I passed out against the van's passenger door, and I mean dead out. As we arrived home, someone leaned over and across me to release the door lock. In doing so, they accidentally sent me free falling six feet from the van seat to the hard ground below, my deadweight body landing in a ditch in the pitch-black forest.

I must have been laid in the ditch for a while, maybe an hour or so, until Uncle noticed I wasn't in my bunk and raised the alarm. Nobody else had got out of the van on my side, and in the pitch-black, they didn't even know that there was a ditch drop at the place they'd parked the van. They told me later that I was out cold, so two of them had dragged me along the ground, grabbing my wrists and pulling me by my hands and arms, my feet trailing behind in the dirt, until they got me inside, dumped me on my bunk, fully dressed, still in my leather jacket, and threw a blanket nonchalantly on top.

When I came around the next day, I not only had a hangover from hell but I was in real physical agony. It turned out that I'd broken my collarbone in two places, the bone trying to burst out through the skin. It was a horrible sight. Mick Webb showed up that morning, thank God he did, and it was him that decided to take me to the hospital for a diagnosis. The news wasn't good, it was a terrible double break and the doctor's advice was to abandon the tour. But that was the last thing I wanted, so we figured out a game-plan of how to save the tour.

After chatting it through with the doctor, the bottom line was revolutionary — we decided to gaffer tape my arm, held inside my leather jacket, up against my chest like a sling. The doctor prescribed some tablets that he jokingly described as "like horse tranquiliser pills" which, all these years later, was most likely ketamine or something like it. So that was that — we decided to carry on and complete the tour for as long as I could manage it.

Abandoning the tour was never going to be an option for me, especially once I was pilled up and strapped up. I'd be OK, even if I was in pain, almost delirious half the time. I knew I'd find it in me to crack on and complete the tour — and I did.

I laughed as hard as everyone else along the way, be it watching Mick succumb to the power of acid that convinced him he was a rookie GI in Vietnam (he was eventually found sitting halfway up a tree, stripped down to his underwear, mud all over himself as camouflage. having spent the whole night out in the forest, on guard duty against a nighttime attack by Charlie-Viet-Cong) or anything else mental that happened.

On one gig, we had a crazy support act opening for us. It was a nutty guy who was carried onstage by two roadies while he was wrapped up tight inside a giant black industrial-sized bin liner. He was just dumped on the stage, and then a soundtrack of what sounded like Napalm Death blasted out at full live band volume as his backing music, complete with a full light show and loads of strobes and dry ice — so much so that Craig was in danger of having a Sisters of Mercy flashback. The fella on stage fought his way out of the bin liner, hand followed by hand, foot followed by foot, head next and then the rest of him. It took him ten minutes to achieve his freedom. He brought the fucking house down, we seriously thought Bag-Man was gonna blow us off the stage that night.

Craig was used to playing big, serious, full-production gigs with The Sisters of Mercy. He'd done The Royal Albert Hall and massive festival stages, and now, here he was in what was an accidental comedy show on a cartoon Punk-Rock'n'Roll tour. But he was cool beans, he was loving it and joined right in.

*

Mick Webb loved The Dead Vaynes. He loved the fun of the Holland gigs and knew we were a very good live band on our night. He wanted to help, so on the back of what he'd experienced in Holland, he managed to secure us the support slot for the entire upcoming Johnny Thunders European tour. He was happy to do it, he knew our hero was the former New York Dolls guitarist. He'd seen what a great combination Thunders and The Dead Vaynes had been at The Warehouse show back in '84 too, so it was a no-brainer to put us together as a package. It was an exciting time.

Arriving back home to Leeds, James Bullseye Vayne and Lucinda were both waiting for me at the flat. The dog went berserk as if he'd known me for years when I'd only known him for just a few days, and Lucinda made a proper fuss of me too. Not just because I was back in her arms, but also because of my grossly broken collarbone that still looked terrible as the bone still appeared to be trying to pop right through the tight-stretched skin. It did hurt, even though I'd kind of got used to it. Then again, I still had another four weeks' supply of the magic pills to tide me over.

I never let Lucinda move in with me, I didn't even give her a key. She had to arrange to come by in advance or take a chance and knock at the door to see if I'd answer it. Sometimes I would, but other times not. Don't get me wrong, she did spend half the week sleeping over, but I was careful to make sure that she always kept her place going and that there was no obligation to be with each other all the time.

216

It was a calculated setup on my behalf, but it wasn't because I was playing the part of some kind of control freak in the relationship and it wasn't that I was scared of actual commitment. It wasn't about anything like that. I kept things tidy and tight, probably more for her benefit than mine.

You see, the thing is, paranoid psychosis might appear in your life (seemingly overnight). You know, one day you go from curiously, innocently second-guessing what you think you might have just heard; was that simply a playful little dig, a joke at my expense, what did that comment mean? Silly little questions come into your head, but you don't want to be the dark cloud in the room, so you let it go, forget about it and brush it off with a smile or a forced snigger.

Then, all at once, a day comes along and BOOM — you're suddenly hearing everything as a vicious attack against you. You invent reasons why you're being attacked and why the attacker has a good reason to attack you. Then you try to defend yourself by being quicker and smarter, attacking back before the attack on you begins. Before you know it, you realise it's not just one or two *mates* sniping at you; it's the whole world attacking you relentlessly without restraint or respite. So the only thing you can do is close the world out, pull back the bridge and lock every door — hence the reason I kept Lucinda at bay.

My psychosis had begun in '84 before I'd even met her. The worst of it took place during '85, with the symptoms super-intense during the first six months and bit by bit reducing through the second six months. By '86, I was dealing with coming out of it, coping better some days than others. And in '87, things were starting to look much better in every way. So, because all that was happening inside my head, I needed my own space a lot of the time to deal with it. No matter how gorgeous Lucinda was, I wouldn't put her through 24/7 of my madness.

I shielded my mental issues from her as best I could, while she was happy to brush my mood swings off as being artistic — running hot and cold as an artist often does, highs and lows, the good with the bad, etc. My refusal to let her live with me a full-on committed couple would become a big problem for her as the relationship moved on, as months passed by. Being together but not living together was frustrating for her. She wanted it, she even started to get jealous of James Bullseye, hitting me with, "You love that dog more than you love me." And in all honesty, yes I did.

Eventually, the locked door would be our undoing, of course it would be. She had a good reason to be off-kilter about it, but that was only because she didn't know how off-kilter my head was. I could have opened up to her, I suppose I never really tried. That led to arguments and fighting — with me looking for a way to kill it off.

*

I was still selling speed, but now only grams or weights to mates. I wasn't up for hustling in the pubs and streets of LS6 to strangers because, besides anything else, I was quite well-known as the singer of The Dead Vaynes. Ever since *G.T.F.* had been released, we'd done bigger profile shows with great supports and good solid headliners. Our name had been on street billboards and posters, as well as in the national music press as a band of interest, a band to watch out for, and in the local press as a kind of niche, if relatively minor, celebrity. So I couldn't have people I didn't know saying to other people I didn't know, "Guess who I bought that speed off? The frontman from The Dead Vaynes, you know, that crazy guy who cuts his body up and gets naked on stage."

So I knocked the general dealing on the head but carried on selling grams to the immediate crew. At the same time, I cultivated a small set of satellite dealers who could shift an ounce every other week or two. It was more than enough for me; it was already proper dealing, more dealing than I wanted to be doing, too much dealing to want to be caught with. But it gave me enough action to be sure that I had gear available for whatever my needs might be, as well as moving a tidy amount of cash about so I'd have money handy whenever I needed it. I wasn't no gangster but I was active.

218

The lucky bust was just around the corner, and this is how the bust went down...

I had the drugs, wraps and scales all wrapped up in a plastic bag, pushed underneath the toilet and shower in a separate room located outside of my actual flat. The toilet and shower were in a communal shared bathroom that no one ever used, meaning it was handy for me to stash my stuff. My thinking was that if it ever got discovered, then I'd simply say "That could belong to anybody". OK, I wasn't convinced how well that would stand up, but it was an argument at least; it was a degree of separation, some "reasonable doubt". I hoped that the theory would never get put to the test.

Apart from the toilet and shower stall stash, on this night, I'd also kept four grams aside — two I put in my waistcoat pocket, along with about £300, and the other two grams I put with another £1,700 in a second stash which was underneath the carpet in the adjoining room in my flat. That room was empty, no furnishings, nothing, and I'd nonchalantly covered the stash with a pair of old curtains thrown on top. Not the greatest of stashes, but it looked so innocuous. My thinking was, if the police bust me, they'd think "only an idiot would stash something there", and I was banking on them thinking "dealers are scum but they're not idiots" — reverse psychology anyone?

If the carpet stash was found, I could claim personal use, and not trusting the banks. But if the shower stall stash was found, then I could be in a lot of trouble, that was proper dealing. And the only defence would be a "Hail Mary, not my property brother".

So on the night of the bust, I was in The Faversham, when out of nowhere eight firm hands grabbed onto me, holding my arms in a vice-like grip — two undercover members of the drug squad on each side. I was "bust" — it was early doors entertainment in The Fav on a Friday night.

The bust itself turned out to be a calamitous affair for the cops involved, especially the lead fella, DS Simister, who had a real hard-on for my dealer, "George The Red Indian".

George wasn't a Red Indian at all, he was a skinny white kid with long hippie-length hair that he topped off with a headband around his forehead and two feathers stuck in the back, like one of the Indians in a typical old John Wayne cowboy movie. I always referred to him as George The Red Indian; no idea where the name George came from, but he liked it.

Now, George might have had the long hair of a hippie, he might also have been very skinny, but he also wore big steel-capped boots and he famously could properly kick off in a scrap. He was genuinely a lovely, gentle fella almost all the time. He was also shifting a lot of gear, and DS Simister wanted him bad — not just because George was a drug dealer and DS Simister's job was to catch and take drug dealers off the street, but because he had busted George a few months earlier, catching him on his pushbike and finding 30 grams chopped up into individual bags stuffed into the drop-handlebars. It should have been an open-and-shut case — caught with 30 individual grams. He was charged with intent to supply, and the DS was convinced that George was looking at proper jail time.

When that bust went down, DS Simister was the happiest cop in town; he had his man, and he thought that George would probably lead him to much bigger players. By DS Simister's thinking, George wasn't a hardened criminal, he was a hippie freak, and the threat of jail time should force George to make a deal. If it goes that way, then bigger and better busts would follow. Only George wasn't a hippie, and he didn't get rattled easy — it didn't work out for the DS.

George, miraculously, got a hung jury, and the same again on the recall. By then, the story had been in the newspapers so much that the judge dismissed the case because no jury could hear it without already having been influenced one way or another. George The Red Indian was almost famous for a minute.

It drove DS Simister nuts, and hence he came after me to try and find a way to get back into court with George, or better than that, to try and get George to roll over and give him the proper criminals further up the ladder. Anyway, the bottom line was that I was being marched out of The Faversham with two cops on both arms; the haplessly innocent Lucinda was also being marched out right behind me.

In the station, all the cops seemed to play their part. The gruff, emotionless, unfriendly desk sergeant, who I had to empty my pockets to, including the two personal grams and the cash, while also alerting him to the fact that I'd already informed the three cops who had brought me in their speeding car from The Fav to the station of my personal gear and cash.

Next, they did a strip search. It's designed to make you feel small and knock your confidence. Even though it was obvious I wasn't out at The Faversham with a bag of shit stuck up my arse, they wanted to go through with this charade nonetheless. What they didn't know was that I didn't worry about exposing my bollocks. I'd often strip down fully naked when playing a Dead Vaynes show, so I whipped everything off without batting an eyelid. Once dressed, I was put in a cell. Nobody explained what was going on. It's all designed to unsettle you. I hadn't caught sight of Lucinda so far. I hoped that maybe they'd just let her go, meanwhile I decided to get my head down and have a kip, even though I was buzzing to fuck off of the speed I'd taken earlier. I still made the effort to try and ride the storm.

After a while, maybe an hour, the doors opened and before I knew it, I was back in the car, a second car full of cops following behind, but no Lucinda in sight — they had the paperwork to make a search of the flat.

My only concern was that they'd find the big stash hidden under the floorboards in the bathroom outside of the flat. If

they found that stash, then they would have a result —
dealing — and enough evidence to warrant jail time if
convicted. A guardian angel must have been watching over
me — they didn't find fuck all, not even the carpet stash. I
could breathe once again on the way back to the police
station. Now they had to run with Plan B.

Simister took a breath and went with his big roll of the
dice. "Right, listen, I want you to arrange a delivery of speed
from your dealer. We already know that you call him George
The Red Indian, so don't say you don't know him because we
know you do. We know he's been supplying you, and you've
been knocking it out around your way too, but we're not
interested in you. We want to leave you alone to get on with
your music career" — fuck me, does this mean that The
Dead Vaynes were really famous? — "to live normally with
Lucinda and all that." Little does this cunt know, the last
thing I want to do is live normally with Lucinda. "But we
have to get George off the streets. It's a lot of drugs getting
out and getting into kids' hands." Kids' hands? Is this guy
fucking mental? No kids were getting their hands on speed
around our way.

I'm thinking, "Shut up, you daft sod. You're describing a
criminal mastermind or somebody peddling at the schoolyard
gates, neither being true by a long shot." Simister went on,
"If you don't do it then I'm going to get interested in
everything you do. You'll not get a moment's peace. We'll
pull you every day if we have to, and every time you do a gig
with your band, The Dead Vaynes, we'll drug bust the venue
in the middle of your show. So cut the bullshit and do what's
right." He was shocked when I turned around and said, "Can
you really arrange to bust The Dead Vayne's gigs? I'd love
that, and it will guarantee that we get famous!"

Eventually, me and Lucinda left Millgarth. They'd kept
her in a cell the whole time, even knowing that she was
completely innocent. And me? They charged me with
possession. It's all they had. I thought of The Heartbreakers
doing the same thing back in '77, in this very same cop shop,

as they took my fingerprints — the thought of it gave me a little buzz, and I wondered how to get a copy of them to use on a future record sleeve as a connector between them and us, Thunders and me. Once out on the street, I got straight to a public payphone and called George to let him know that DS Simister was all over his ass so he should keep his wits about him. Then we got a taxi to my place and hopped into bed to fuck it all off.

George gave me the number of his lawyer, and I eventually agreed in court to cop for what I had on me at the time of being busted, resulting in a £90 fine which I paid in full there and then. Meanwhile, Mr Collins, George's lawyer, waived my fee to him because I'd given him enough info on Simister to make a complaint against him for harassment of his client and the harassment of associates of George like me. Mr Collins went on the attack and I never heard from DS Simister ever again.

So that was the story of my drug bust in Leeds, and when I say it was the best thing that could have happened to me, it really was — because although I'd got away with a small fine for two grams of gear that I'd claimed as personal, the reality was that it could have been much worse if the police had found my two stashes at the flat. It would have been life-changing; my music career, the band, would have come to a crashing end or gone on pause at least. Who knows where my story would've gone from that moment on?

For all my bravado, it was a big wake-up call. I promised myself, even on the very morning that Lucinda and I returned to the flat, that I was going to stop dealing right away. And I did, as I dropped the entire load of gear off to one of my crew at an easy clearout price.

That drug bust might have only resulted in a forgettable £90 financial cost at the time, but the reality was, the actual record of the drug bust and fine followed me around and haunted me for years after — especially once I started to travel to America, and even more so when the company I worked for wanted me to move to New York City. That was a "future me" problem though.

*

I'd been busted, now it was time to get busy. I was ready to get out on tour again, and so to finish the year off we did a bunch of headline gigs around the UK on our own which went pretty well, before playing a few shows as support to The Gun Club. This was an absolute honour for Mick and me because Jeffrey Lee Pierce, their leader, was another big musical influence on us as a band. We believed JLP was one of the world's most underrated artists and songwriters, a mix of pure emotion and power coupled with a swamp-infused brand of dirty Punk-Rock'n'Roll.

The biggest highlight of doing the shows with The Gun Club wasn't the actual gigs, which were great, but it was when both bands would hang out backstage together after the shows. Mick and Jeffrey would get the guitars out and we'd all sing outlaw country songs like "Sin City" by Gram Parsons/Flying Burrito Brothers, "Your Cheatin' Heart" by Hank Williams, or "Lay With Me In A Field Of Stone" by David Allen Coe, and many more like that. Just the two bands hanging and jamming — it was a massive privilege and thrill. I wish those sessions had been caught on film or audio — they were magic moments that have lasted a lifetime.

I have to highlight one other show we did on December 1st, 1987, the fifth time Johnny Thunders came to town. Of course we had to be on the bill, and of course that was a thrill for me. But for Mick, who had stood in the audience in '73, '76, '77, '84 — he was now a step closer to one of his idols, playing the same stage in a home town gig… boom!

But let me jump back just a few weeks and colour in the picture. Before any of those dates got underway, Uncle decided to hang up his drumsticks. Losing Uncle was as hard for me as losing Dil; alongside myself, he was the last of the originals, so it felt like the end of something. What had

224

begun with Uncle, Dil, Cyrus, myself, and CJ as my muse, was now gone forever.

I tried to convince Uncle to hold tight and stay the course. I gave him my script on the concept of being one of God's Sad Boys — but to no avail. He'd made up his mind; he didn't want to play drums in a band and thought his ability would limit our potential. I told him he would get better as we all got better, that he was my Jerry Nolan from The Heartbreakers or Paul Cook from The Sex Pistols, but it made no odds. I had to respect the fact that it was his call to make. Thankfully it all went down without drama and it didn't affect our friendship either — we remained the spliff sisters even if I hadn't smoked a spliff for a long while.

In place of Uncle came Nev, who had been the drummer in the brilliant Leeds Punk band Abrasive Wheels along with Harry on bass. I was super-excited to work with the powerhouse drum and bass rhythm section that had been so effective in the Wheels. However, as you already know, "bad luck/good fate" has a way of showing up just to mess with me, or so it seems, and as already mentioned, Sir Harry announced, out of the blue, that he too wanted to quit The Dead Vaynes.

As a parting gift, Harry agreed to do one last studio recording session with the band, which would be Prince Michael De Vayne, Sir Harry Vayne, Nev and myself. That was a killer lineup and we all got along really well as friends. I believe we could have done a lot with that four-piece combo, but que sera sera, it wasn't to be. However, we managed to record a fantastic EP called *Baby Cruel* in that one-and-only session which we released on our label via a P&D deal with Red Rhino.

It's another record that I sit, without question, alongside the records of my heroes, especially the title track "Baby Cruel". The *Baby Cruel* EP was probably the dirtiest, swampiest, Stooges-sounding set of tracks that we ever recorded — and we even tucked in an acoustic coda of me with a guitar singing a snippet of the original Punk Hank

225

Williams' all time classic "Lost Highway". We snuck it on unannounced, a curve ball, a hint for folk to get themselves educated on the origins P U N K, the origins according to my book at least. It's maybe my second favourite piece of vinyl, after *G.T.F.*, or maybe I love them like a mother loves all her kids — just the same, only different.

So anyway, Nev had agreed to join; he was a very solid drummer, a good musician but more than that he was a great guy who I'd known for years. As a bonus, Nev was drug-free but booze-enthusiastic, which had made the recording session a lot of fun.

The Dutch tour behind us, recorded product released into the market, Uncle and Harry gone, Mick and I regrouped — and with Nev already intact — we brought in Jessica Fischer on bass, and Gerry Famous on second guitar. This five-piece would become the settled band, the one that would give it a go in earnest, not just for kicks or just for something to do, but to try and get ahead, try and make it big. We became The Vaynes.

It was a good band. The other four liked one another; they got along and had a nice balance among them. As much as I don't like to say it, and indeed I don't say it as a negative, I felt a degree of alienation from the others. Not in a bad way, and not on a musical level; we were tight on that side, but insofar as friends hanging out for fun, we didn't socialise very much outside of the band stuff. Maybe I did with Nev, but Mick, Jess and Gerry, not so much. They socialised a lot together, they were very tight friends and much tighter with each other than they were with me.

I want to stress that this feeling, that reality, wasn't a negative; it was a necessary requirement, if I was ever going to have a chance to move from the gutter to the glitter. You see, I needed a degree of separation from them, and they needed the same from me, because the fact of the matter was, what with my internal voices and various vices, I was weird gravy. It was better for them to keep arm's length from my daily life of daftness and madness — it could have torn the band apart before we ever got going. I recognised that I needed a band who could play my songs at the required level they deserved to be heard at. These guys were the crew for the job, I needed them, they were a really good set of musicians, and they were all top-shelf people too.

12. VAYNE-GLORIOUS

The Vaynes debut album, and by extension the band's second album following on from The Dead Vaynes' *G.T.F.* release, was recorded in the summer of 1988. Mick named it *Vainglorious*, which I loved even more when he told me it was an actual word and explained its meaning — a boast of personal infallibility. It had the same kind of feel as God's Sad Boys. Of course, I took some artistic licence and changed the spelling to "Vayne-Glorious."

By this time we were swimming in a much bigger pond and the process of recording the new album for The Vaynes was far removed, as an experience, from the process of recording the *G.T.F.* album for The Dead Vaynes.

Before getting any further into the recording of the big budget album by The Vaynes, I should mention that we'd also recorded and released three other Single/EPs, as well as the killer *Baby Cruel* EP on Vanity/Red Rhino, in 1986.

Step forward "Mr Fix It", released on our own Vanity records, via Red Rhino P&D. This was the most sophisticated song I had written up until that point. It actually came out before the *Baby Cruel* release, even though the recording process might have been out of step with the chronological release dates.

It had an almost Goth flavour to it, with cool guitar hook lines, complicated bass and drum patterns, off-kilter chord progressions, and dark lyrics that told the story of a heroin junkie and his descent into the chaos of Wako-Land.

Here's a snippet: "Now the money's gone, he sinks down lower, picked up off the street by an old war soldier, he took it in his hand now he's a hooker, it's a low down show but he needs brown sugar. When he's chasing in the night, that dragon's fire don't burn so bright, now the devil's by his side, he said 'se march (walk), your soul's mine'. He's Mr Fix It, he's on the hook, he's Mr Fix It, hooked on drugs."

228

It was quite a long way from the basic dirge-repeat of "Dead Vayne Woman", but essentially it carried a similar message, that drugs carry a price beyond money.

The flipside had a song recorded with Craig Adams from The Sisters of Mercy and The Mission on bass. "Cinderella" was a rocker and became a live fave. We also slipped on "Midnight Gun" from the *G.T.F.* album as a bonus track, and as a reminder that our classic Dead Vaynes album *G.T.F.* was still out there.

Next up was a return to the more familiar Punk-Rock'n'Roll sound, with a release called "Rock'n'Roll Crime" on Vanity/Red Rhino, in 1987. It was the first time the lineup of myself, Prince Michael, Nev, Gerry Famous and Jessica Fischer had recorded together and it came out great.

The release also had an instrumental from Mick called "Night Shift", and included a stripped-down acoustic version of the last song from the Dead Vaynes' *G.T.F.* album, called "Cry Me An Angel". The game-plan was always about moving forward as a band, but keeping a connection to the *G.T.F.* album too. The acoustic version of "Cry Me An Angel" was also a great way to highlight the calibre of the lyrics that I was writing.

Allow me to blow my own trumpet... again: "Another crack inside my room, and all is dark and cold and cruel, life is sad when lies are true, and love has died because of fools. She will play her magic flute and dance across the floor, and I will hide my silent fears and wash my hands in tears once more, she plays her mandolin tonight, my body's her violin, we play with passion, play with hate, once more upon the stage... Cry Me An Angel Tonight."

I had been writing lyrics that I believed were very good — they were both dramatic and poetic, as good as anyone else's in my eyes, and to be truthful, they were probably too good for my own music —I was definitely punching above my weight class.

The final release was a bridge that represented where The Dead Vaynes had been, where The Vaynes were, and where The Vaynes hoped to be going.

It was called "Big Cities" and was picked up and released on the Red Rhino in-house record label, Ediesta. "Big Cities" was a taster in 1988 of what they hoped we would deliver for them going forward: we all believed that we were capable of gaining a bigger audience.

The song was originally outlined with a little bit of help from Dil and Sir Harry a few years earlier, and finally finished as a piece of work by me once I had a band that was smart enough to record it properly — although I did give Dil and Harry a full share of the writing in the credits. It's one of those songs that even if someone hated the band, they couldn't help but like the song. "Big Cities" was a driving Punk-Rock'n'Roll epic bit of storytelling, with a lean towards pop sensibilities… It was a glimpse of what might be. The other tracks on the EP were "Fun Parade", a song that would feature on the upcoming album, and included a conversation about life and death, "I'm not frightened of dying, I guess I'm petrified… and love? I believe that there is no greater love than the one between a Mother and her Sons." Then lastly, another acoustic number that was a throwback to my "daze of high paranoia" called "Speaking In Code".

Ediesta/Red Rhino covered the "Big Cities" budgets, they were happy with the results — they committed to us, and us to them.

They also fronted the money for the *Vayne-Glorious* album, and included promo and marketing budgets too. We were about to become one of their priority recording artists… we were on the move, we move on…

For the *Vayne-Glorious* sessions, we were going back into The Slaughterhouse Studios in Driffield, where their sound tech guy, "The Spaghetti Kid", would be engineering — as he had done for *G.T.F.* — but that's where the similarities of the two album sessions ended. *Vayne-Glorious* wasn't going to be rushed like *G.T.F.* had been. This was no half-live studio recording process where everything would be done "wham bam thank you ma'am" over a quick week. No, this was going to be us holed up in the studio and working hard, day and night over a few intense weeks.

In addition to The Spaghetti Kid on engineer duties, the record label hired Julian Standing, a very good producer who had also worked with us on the *Big Cities* EP, which was like a precursor to the *Vayne-Glorious* album. The label wanted to ensure that the recordings were up to industry standards. For me, this intense process of recording properly was a drag. It was slow and laboured, with everything super-considered. It was the correct way, the way *proper bands* worked in the studio, but for me, it was like pulling teeth.

Prince Michael loved it though, and at the end of the marathon weeks of recording, overdubbing, adding production elements, mixing and doing the master mix-down, we ended up with a quality collection of recordings. It was a bigger sound than we'd ever imagined we could produce. We had something that sounded like a proper recording — this session had delivered a higher grade of sound quality than the niche, raw recordings of albums like *L.A.M.F.*, *Young, Loud and Snotty*, or *G.T.F.*

The *Vayne-Glorious* album sounded professional, the songs came over as *proper*, and as well-crafted as anything else in the market. Well, at least that's how we heard them: that was our opinion, and we were never shy when it came to shouting the odds.

I was very proud of the variety of songs I had written; there was a lot of diversity running through the collection and so much intricacy. I had to pinch myself that I had written the songs I was listening to during the final playback session.

I'd worked hard over the last few months with long days and late nights, writing and rewriting music, hooks, lyrics and guitar parts. The hardest part is usually finding something to be inspired by, or mapping out a story that makes sense, and other times accepting that sometimes the

231

lyrics were not going to make sense there and then, but having confidence that at some point, the point would reveal itself as being worthwhile and explainable.

I'd delivered almost all of the tracks on the album apart from the most commercial song, "Alive and Kicking", written by Mick, but for which I had added the signature top-line guitar melody hook. Then there was the most bizarre track on the album, a music-only instrumental called "Paul Christ" written by Gerry Famous.

The rest were all me, save for two collaborations, "You're The Only Girl" and "Lick The Dirt", songs I'd written but had also encouraged Gerry to get involved with. I wanted some of his strange chord progressions to give a different dimension to my more traditional sequences and spin. He did a great job of it and so got credits on those two tracks alongside me. I also gave Mick one or two co-credits because he added some guitar hooks that set the songs off with a new flavour.

I was also impressed with the level of the recordings rendered, Julian's skills, and the actual performance of us as a band was eye-opening. But, that said, I have never been able to truly feel, or hear, any real sense of *attitude* in the album. There is emotion for sure, also some swagger — but, in my opinion, the proper Dead Vaynes attitude was always missing from the *Vayne-Glorious* album, at least for me. It was like the project was slightly too vainglorious in itself to be truly *Vayne-Glorious*.

I was the only one to feel that way, understandably really, as it was another band completely now, completely different from the one that had started back in the drug pit of Glebe Avenue four years earlier on that crazy night with CJ, Uncle, Dil, Cyrus and the crew. But it was in the can; everybody said it sounded great and that it represented a massive step forward in the development of the group. So it was what it was, and as it had now been delivered to Red Rhino, to be set up with a release schedule and a game-plan that included at least two supporting singles before the album itself would

232

drop — well, it seemed to be in good hands. I turned my focus back to touring and the next dates in the diary.

*

Before year's end, 1988, we were en route from Leeds to Dunkirk. We had secured the support slot for a European tour with Johnny Thunders — "I Got My Cock In My Pocket and I'm Speeding Down The Old Highway." Well, maybe not so much speeding, for once, but here we were, rolling along steadily in the back of a beat-up fifth-hand Transit van.

Smarter people than me had devised a way to load the amps, instruments, drum kit and personal baggage into the rusty van so that everything was spread out in a precise manner to create a flat base. That flat base was then covered with a thick double king-size mattress so we could catch some sleep as we rolled through the non-stop, never-ending journeys across Europe.

We had limited tour support for hotels and very little money for meals. Our tour manager, a sensible fella called Charlie, held our daily budget. He kept the bare minimum float around him so he could supply us with water and snacks between cities. We got fed by the venues on show nights, had a good drinks rider, and sometimes even a bed for the night in a hotel. Straight Guy Charlie also gave us each some paid dailies, known as PDs (per diems), pocket money — just a few quid, but enough. My PDs went towards getting fucked up in each town after each show. I wasn't a tourist learning about culture in a gallery, I was trying to live my reality in the underbelly of the streets.

It didn't bother me that we were travelling on Shanks's pony, more or less broke and living day to day, hand-to-mouth. I knew I could hack anything considering all I'd been through to get this far. Nothing was going to faze me. But as far as everybody else, if anybody felt like having a moan, I had one piece of advice: "We've really got a good thing going, come on, if you think we're gonna make it, you better hang on to yourself." Cheers, Mr Jones.

233

As you know, I'd dreamed of being in this position for years. On tour with Johnny Thunders, we were the lucky ones. Rough as it was, we knew we were in an enviable position. Bands from all over Europe would swap places with us in a second if they could, whatever the conditions. How many times in your life do you get to hang out and play on a tour with your idol? It's rare. It's something to cherish, all of it — the good, the bad and the bullshit too.

The Vaynes were on this tour because our label believed in us and was investing in us. We were there to support our music, our legend, and our product being released into the market. We would be side by side — my music, my band, my performance — standing alongside Johnny's band on an equal platform, believing enough in our music to know we could hold our own. Don't get it twisted, I was acutely aware that we were the support band to Johnny's headline. That was part of the thrill of it all, to see how our band would stand up next to his, how his crowd would react, for real, to our opening efforts. "You've got this, buddy." Bravado was right there with me.

Occasionally, Bravado would give me a friendly slap. "Who do you think you are?" He'd say it with a joviality that really said, "You know who you are, champ."

Of course, Jam would also try to tweak me, but I was ready for him, and I'd cut him down before he even had a chance to get started. "Fuck off, Jam."

I wasn't in the mood for any downward strokes. I was alright. I winked at that mirror: "This is The Midnight Gun, and I'm Packing Silver Bullets, Baby — Bang-Bang."

It was the time of my life. Every other night, we would be rolling across the countries of Europe, arriving in some place we'd never even heard of, as well as places we had only dreamed of, playing all over from small towns to big cities, underground clubs to major venues in premier locations like Berlin, Barcelona, Amsterdam, and London. We criss-crossed Europe, one place after another — France, Holland, Germany, Austria, Spain, the UK and so on.

At each stop, I would look for mayhem, girls and fun. More often than not, I would end up rocking some local girl in each place we landed. There's something about the "outlaw" that always seems to find a way with the women, and that usually meant a bed for the night instead of crashing out cramped in the back of the van with the others.

Funnily enough, the tour almost ended as soon as it started, as the van's engine blew up when we hit a place close to Dunkirk. We went from riding high on the highway to suddenly grinding to a halt at the back of a supermarket car park. Even worse, it was on a French Bank Holiday, so Straight Charlie's "international motor insurance breakdown assistance" wouldn't arrive for at least three days, which meant we would miss the first date of the tour, scheduled to be in Italy — a festival show we were all excited to play. But boom went the van, and suddenly Italy had to be abandoned.

If we were lucky, we would find a way to fix the van over the weekend. Well, I say we, but what I really meant was that our patience-of-a-saint tour manager Charlie would find a way. I had no doubts about Charlie, I trusted him unconditionally. Maybe because he never expected me to be anybody else but myself, he never tried to get in the way like Jam, and he never gave false encouragement like Bravado. He just accepted and respected me as me.

Our new plan would be to go directly to Munich, and from there we'd finally start the Johnny Thunders European tour. The bonus for me in Dunkirk was that I managed to snag my first road girl, a beauty I called Papillon because she had a butterfly tattoo'd between her breasts, and Mick told me the French word for butterfly was "papillon". We fucked right in the middle of a crowded room as if we were completely alone. Did I think of Steve McQueen, or should I say, did I think myself to be as cool as Steve McQueen while on the vinegar stroke? Sure I did, who wouldn't? He was the most famous Papillon I'd ever heard of and he was one of my idols too. It was a sign that this was gonna be a great tour.

Once in Germany, the first night of the tour in Munich was mostly memorable because Johnny and his band had had their own van issues down in Italy, which meant that his entire band — apart from Johnny himself, and his co-guitarist, Stockholm Stevie — wouldn't make it to Munich until the day after the show. But rather than cancel the gig and lose his performance fee, Johnny asked us, The Vaynes, to become his backing band for the night. It was like we were dreaming, like one of those unbelievable feel-good plot twists in a movie — but it was reality. Not only would we be Johnny's opening band — and we were very good ourselves that night — but we would also be Johnny's backing band.

Nev was nervous, he didn't really know Johnny's songs, but as long as he kept a solid beat, followed the bass and followed Johnny's lead, he'd be all right. Mick and Stockholm Stevie spent some time mapping out the songs to Nev between soundcheck and showtime. Given that Nev was solid with his sticks anyway, nobody worried about it, especially not Johnny himself.

Stockholm Stevie, who generally played co-guitar for Thunders, took over the bass duties, while our own Prince Michael got to live out one of his musical goals as Mick was actually playing the guitar in a Johnny Thunders band. It was as good as it gets for Prince Michael… Utopia, Nirvana, Shangri-la, all of that and more for The Vaynes guitar player. Something was happening, really happening, beyond all his expectations since joining The Dead Vaynes that night in The Fav when he'd tried to snort the giant line I'd given him in the toilets to celebrate. This was it — we were taking giant strides, from the gutter to the glitter. Here we were, stepping on to a stage in Europe, on tour with Johnny Thunders, as Johnny Thunders' actual backing band.

Johnny sang, led the band, and talked a lot to the German crowd in his New York drawl, but he mostly made his guitar sing and bleed at the same time. He was magnificent.

Me and Jessica sang backing vocals. It was more than enough for me; I had the best seat in the house, up close, right there on the stage next to the greatest Punk-Rock'n'Roller of all time. Gerry took pictures and shot video. He was well-chuffed to be the one to document everything. He had his little handheld camera running almost all the time, day and night, like a fly-on-the-wall documentary filmmaker.

Can you actually imagine it? We were his actual band on the first night of the club tour proper. Well, it blew my mind anyway, and it sounded great. Better than that, Johnny loved the fact that we'd saved his ass and saved his payday. That counted for a lot — that we'd stepped up when the chips were down. It also broke the ice between Johnny and me. We were all set to get along just great.

Johnny's full band, which he'd named The Oddballs, showed up by the next gig. They turned out to be a fantastic bunch of brilliant musicians, who lined up as a female bassist and female backing vocalist, both out of Manhattan, called Jill Wisoff and Alison Gordy respectively. Then there was Stockholm Stevie Klassen, the second guitarist, so-called because he came from Stockholm in Sweden, and who we had already met and played with by now. He had an amazing drummer from London, Chris Musto. He had been with Johnny for quite a while. Sometime in 1986 Mick Webb had asked me to find a drummer and a bassist for an upcoming Thunders tour in the UK and I'd set up a mate called Adam Pearson to go try out on bass as well as a drummer called Martin Batfish from the Batfish Boys to try out on drums.

Adam got in on bass and actually did two tours with Johnny before leaving to join The Sisters of Mercy. Unfortunately Martin hadn't made it on drums even though he was a very good drummer. In fact Mick Webb told me it had been mission impossible for Martin, because Johnny had already set his bet on Chris, even before the audition took place. When I heard Chris play, I understood why Chris got the gig, Chris was just an amazing musician. The surprise member of the band was another New Yorker on saxophone, the wonderful Jamie Heath.

237

I say surprise because my sense of Johnny, as a live artist, had always been based around a basic guitar, bass and drums setup. Adding a proper backing vocalist and an actual sax player was more in keeping with recording and production values. Clearly, Johnny had put together a band of top-notch musicians, rather than a crew of junkie fuck-ups. This was a band that could put his music over and convey how great his songs were (hey, does that sound familiar?). This tour was going to be based on playing the music rather than around Thunders being a wonderful but mumbling, cool and shambolic, beautiful Punk-Rock'n'Roll disaster.

Uncle was also with them, acting as a roadie and merchandise man. Tenni showed up once we got to Holland and Mick Webb would drop in and out of the tour depending on the show. Both bands and crews got along brilliantly, it was like we had been on tour together for years.

Johnny and The Oddballs were the seasoned pros. They had a bigger, proper, touring van with plenty of seats for everybody and no mattress on top of their amps and drum kits because each venue provided the backline for them, as per the technical rider's demands. Of course, they also had the luxury of hotel rooms and good hospitality riders, which worked well for us because they hardly drank. The only directive from Johnny was, "Hey Vaynes, you can drink everything, eat everything, just don't touch the vodka and the orange juice. Leave those for me." The Oddballs band didn't mind; Jill, Alison, and Stockholm Stevie hardly drank at all, while Chris and Jamie were happy to have me, Nev, Mick, and our roadie, Punk Elvis, for drinking company. The drinks rider was always substantial and we always left it spent. So while they were the professionals, The Vaynes were like the poor boy Angels With Dirty Faces band, spluttering down the A-roads of Europe in our battered, half-broken tour van. We weren't guaranteed any hotels, but sometimes we got them when we didn't expect to, and other times we were actually even assigned them in advance like a proper band.

238

Hotels, no hotels, it didn't bother me. I was pushing my luck every night with the women, which was an adventure in itself. One time I had to drop out of a second-floor window, mostly naked, while a cute lass from Vienna dropped my clothes down on top of me because her boyfriend came knocking at her door at 10am with coffee and croissants. It was a nice little wake-up surprise he had spontaneously decided to spring on her. I got away OK, but I felt sorry for the poor bugger. He didn't have a clue that his lovely cutie had been rock'n'rolling with the singer from the support band. It might have been acceptable if I was the singer of the headline band — or maybe not. She was young, I was young, he was young; it is what it is. Meeting girls was my favourite choice for sleeping arrangements, and I made it a mission to find a girl at as many shows as possible. What Lucinda didn't know, Lucinda wouldn't get bent out of shape about.

I could go on and tell a story from every night of the tour, but you get the general gist. For The Vaynes, it was a hard tour to do physically, especially for me because apart from being low on money with hardly any hotels and a broken van that made each journey last twice as long as it should've, I was also performing and singing. Any frontman will tell you it's the hardest and most intense role in the band, it fucks you physically and mentally. I state that in good faith, while admitting that I also partied hard every single night on the road too. The booze and lack of sleep left me dehydrated, tired and blown-out between stage times. But at least I was staying off the gear.

Johnny was off the gear too. His choice of hard drug had always been the much more serious and physically damaging heroin. But on this tour, and in his regular life too, Johnny was on the methadone treatment, while also drinking vodka with orange juice as a balancer. And to top it all off, more than anything else, he'd be smoking joint after joint, non-stop spliffing.

I can hardly remember one time when he didn't have a joint in his hand. I wanted to smoke with him, just so I could say that I'd done it while on a European tour, so one day I did. Despite knowing that dope didn't go well with me, I took a chance and took a toke when we were hanging out in Johnny's hotel room, just chatting and taking turns to play songs on his Ovation acoustic guitar. It should've been better than jamming outlaw country tunes backstage with Jeffrey Lee Pierce on The Gun Club tour. It should've been and would've been had I left the joint alone. But I dragged hard on the perfectly built spliff. It was a mistake, a big mistake.

The very first toke on the joint he passed me did the damage. It immediately re-triggered my paranoid psychosis. I suddenly heard everything wonky again, like everybody was speaking in code. I wanted to make an excuse and get out of the room, but my paranoia was saying to me things like "Everybody knows you're fucked". Jam was right in the thick of it: "Wait till they hear about how Thunders fucked you up with just one toke — you pathetic lightweight cunt."

Fuck me, it was a dream turned into a nightmare. I festered there, rooted to the chair, too scared to stick or bust. It seemed like forever; I could hardly dare speak while Johnny was chilled and joking about. I thought he was having a dig at me each time he opened his mouth: "Yo, you wanna Heineken beer?" sounded like "Hey lightweight, you need some Dutch courage just to hang with me, you weak-arsed prick". An advert for cat food came on the turned-down TV, clearly confirming that I was a pussy. A magazine had a photo of Steve McQueen smoking what looked like a rolled cigarette on the cover, obviously daring me to take another puff. Jamie Heath came by and that's when I managed to get out of Johnny's hotel room, risking safety and sanctuary in a bar down the street. I bought a bottle of whiskey with the last of my daily pay and opted for a sipping-glass for company instead. "Get a fucking grip!" I said it to no one, maybe not even out loud.

The heebie-jeebies are horrible at any time, and I sincerely hope that those reading this who have never had them never fuck themselves up to the point where they get

240

them. It's not fun and it's not for kids, that's for sure. But for those reading this story that have had them, well, I know I have your sympathy.

I knocked the idea of smoking dope with Johnny, or anybody, on the head right away — no more toking. I'd done it now anyway and I've just told you about it, so there you go. I wanted to be able to say "I've smoked a joint with Johnny while on a European tour". I did, and now I have.

I made a conscious choice to stick to sipping whiskey, drinking beer, and fucking whenever I got the chance. It was a fantastic tour with dates in places like Madrid, Amsterdam, Hamburg and Berlín standing out as some of the memorable nights. Playing The Marquee in London was another goal on the bucket list ticked off.

The first time playing at the London Marquee gave me the same thrill I'd felt when getting hold of the first record I'd made, *The First Cut* EP by To Be Continued, or the first copy of The Dead Vaynes' *G.T.F.* It was as exciting as the first fuck, the first dig; it even matched the 1984 Dead Vaynes & Johnny Thunders first ever gig together at the Leeds Warehouse.

The Marquee was a show that sent a signal to the band, as well as to other bands — and the industry itself. It signalled to everybody that The Vaynes were a band that had now fully arrived in the game, that we should be taken seriously, and on that first Marquee show, we smashed it. We felt like we were getting closer and closer to making it.

The venue had a good-sized stage with a great sound system and effective lights — everything top class. The Marquee always attracted a smart crowd that knew real Punk-Rock'n'Roll music when they heard it. Better still, this music-savvy crowd let us know that first night that they loved our music. We even got an encore, which Johnny encouraged us to play. That was a top thing for him to do, given that some headliners can be pissy to deal with. They give you no space on the stage, hardly any soundcheck time, a really short set length, reduced sound system volume in front of house, no access to the dressing room or rider and definitely no encore. Johnny was the opposite to all that, maybe because he was secure enough knowing that Johnny Thunders was Johnny Thunders, unique and untouchable as Johnny Thunders. Or maybe he was just a good guy giving a kindred spirit band a helping hand, or maybe I'm inventing a reason for his actions and the truth of it was that he just didn't care. But that's not true, Johnny was a good guy and we appreciated it. Better than that, Mick Webb told us that Johnny had told him to make sure that The Vaynes went back out with Johnny Thunders & The Oddballs on part two of the European tour, which would be scheduled to happen early the next year.

Funny thing, but even though we had done quite a few shows with Johnny by now, I was always thrilled to hear him say our name, The Vaynes. It meant a lot to me that this untouchable, who didn't need anything from us, felt enough of something about us to recognise our existence. Daft, but there it is.

*

Once back home in Leeds, with part one of the European tour done, we felt like conquering heroes returning triumphant from the front line. Everyone wanted to hear the war stories of being in the trenches alongside Johnny: what he was like as a person, whether he was straight or screwed up, how the gigs went and how we were received. I loved it. I'd hold court in one of the bars in The Royal Park, not as a pontificating bore but as an entertaining raconteur — honest, it's true. Given the love that Leeds, especially LS6, had for Johnny's legend, I had a captive audience.

The bonus was that the now legitimate, closer association between The Vaynes and Johnny Thunders also gave The Vaynes an injection of professional credibility. We were viewed as a real band, a proper band — not just another LS6 band trying to get ahead, but a band from Leeds ahead of many of our peers.

When we played our next show in Leeds, we felt it. The feeling in the air was tangible. As a band, we were different now. We were on-the-road touring-tight. The songs were bigger and more confident-sounding. Small elements of production and punctuation were performed as naturally as muscle repetition. We hit everything spot on. Everyone was impressed, but mostly, we were impressed with ourselves, proud of how we'd adapted and improved as a band.

And how was Johnny as a person? Well, this isn't a book about Johnny Thunders, even though he looms large in these writings and memoirs. He was a pivotal presence in my story and someone I got to call a friend. But how was Johnny? It's for others to say, people who knew him better, longer and more intimately than I did. My eyes are rose-tinted with John. He was a hero, so I can't be objective. But I've given you a taste. He was more than just a New York junkie with a guitar. It's written up in many books, reviews and spotlights of the man. I recommend that you go off on a journey of discovery if you don't know who he is. Read up on him, watch the videos and films about him and hear his music. I can only say that he was everything he wore on his sleeve — the ultimate Punk-Rock'n'Roll star. When it came to his musical persona, nothing about him was played out for show. He was who he was, Johnny Thunders, in a world that revolved around Johnny Thunders. He'd taken on the perfect legend with that name. Johnny Thunders, it couldn't have been scripted any better. It'll live on forever, and there'll never be another.

We were brought down to earth with a bang when Amanda told us that our record label, Red Rhino, had gone bust. But fear not, the sinking feeling only lasted a moment. Well, I say a moment, but that moment took about a year to turn into an album release date.

The good news was we had a new record deal with the super-hot label Native Records who had agreed in principle to pick up the *Vayne-Glorious* album masters from Red

243

Rhino's bankrupt catalogue as part of their compensation settlement.

Native Records had made national headway with bands like The Primitives and The Soup Dragons. The Primitives were even delivering hit singles and strong-selling albums for the label and now they were willing to take a chance on The Vaynes.

On top of signing to Native, we still had part two of the Thunders tour booked for the UK and Europe in early '89, and we were also invited on to The Mission's Scottish Highlands & Islands Summer–Autumn '89 tour as well.

The *Vayne-Glorious* album was finally set to drop sometime towards the end of '89 on the back of high-profile touring momentum. Things looked very rosy for The Vaynes.

All the Thunders dates were special because they were dates with Johnny. He loved us, took the band under his wing, and loved us being on the road with him. We all became so close, and for a short while, Johnny even lived at my apartment in Leeds, when he needed to chill out between tour dates in Europe and the UK. Lucky for John, I was in an attic apartment by then, near the top of Brudenell Road — the unofficial mainline artery into the heart of LS6. This was much better for him than the old gutter-level flat on Brudenell View. It was a favour to Mick Webb so he could keep an eye on him and hope he wouldn't fall back on the drug train.

It was a thrill for me to have Johnny take over my place for a while. It was also a thrill for the people of LS6, who all felt a strong connection to Johnny. It was beyond anything I had ever imagined, and years later, another Leeds band called Cyanide Pills immortalised it on their record with the lyric "Here they come, Johnny Thunders and The Dead Vaynes. I was down on my knees when Johnny Thunders lived in Leeds".

There's also a tape recording of Thunders playing an acoustic set at The Duchess in Leeds while living in my flat. During the gig, he chats with the audience about where he is

244

staying, poking fun at me, the colour of the bathwater, coming out of the tap yellow, and how cool my dog James Bullseye Vayne is. I might have been the brunt of the comic quips, but it didn't get any better than that for me. In my home town, in the Leeds venue that counted, Johnny was ripping and riffing on me — boom!

We eventually finished that part two tour after dates around the UK and Europe and finally closed out at The Marquee in London again.

The Marquee show was important for Johnny. Record labels were coming to see him, see his condition and see if they could take the risk of investing. The bottom line was that all labels wanted him, but they were mostly nervous about what they would get and how long it would last. Their biggest fear was, if they paid him an advance, what would he spend it on?

It was sad to think of JT having to audition, but it wasn't his music under the spotlight. He knew that, and all of us who had been on tour together through parts one and two knew he was on point, pretty clean right then and with a super-tight band of top musicians behind him. We all hoped and joked that a label would come to The Marquee and love both bands so much that they'd offer us both a deal with a recording-and-release schedule that matched so we could all keep on the road together. We had all had a blast, and Johnny loved the stability of it all too.

That night at The Marquee quite a few faces showed up: Mick and Craig from The Mission, Clem Burke from Blondie, John Perry from The Only Ones, Brix E. Smith from The Fall, who came along with Romy Mori of The Gun Club. Keith Richards' son, Marlon, was there with his mum, ex-Rolling Stones muse Anita Pallenberg, who had dated Brian Jones for a couple of years before having three kids with Keith over the following thirteen. There were loads of other movers and shakers, as well as various music industry bods. But the best of all was Stiv Bators from the legendary band The Dead Boys, who came to hang out for the night.

Johnny introduced me to Stiv; it was a special moment for me to be standing in conversation with Johnny on one side and Stiv on the other. There I was, side by side, on equal footing, with the two people who had influenced me the most. I thought back to moments playing their records non-stop, back at my mum's house, then at 27 Leicester Grove and down in Glebe Ave. I remembered giving my speech at the pub in Schiedam to my down-in-the-mouth band on that first date of that first tour of Holland, hitting the jukebox with The Dead Boys' "Sonic Reducer". Sure, by now The Dead Boys had been long gone for years, and Stiv had been leading The Lords of the New Church since '82. While I liked The Lords, I loved The Dead Boys. At that moment, backstage at The Marquee, chatting with Johnny and Stiv, it felt like I'd made it, even if I was nowhere, commercially speaking. I was happy to be nowhere, standing between these two legends, giants, rather than somewhere with anybody else.

We said our goodbyes after The Marquee. All the record labels were feeling positive about Johnny; it looked like a deal might be within reach for him to record a new album. Equally as good as that news was the talk between the two bands about the idea of doing part three on the road together again, hopefully sometime in 1990. Everybody wanted to see it happen, including Johnny, who'd joke, "You Vaynes are gonna be my European support band forever." It would have been OK with me.

Not long after part two, we were on our Highland fling with The Mission, which turned out to be a tour that both bands and all the people that travelled with it, including the 101 dedicated Mission fans called The Eskimos, came to cherish the memory of for years and decades to follow. Various members of The Mission band and crew often cite that Scottish tour as their favourite set of dates ever, which is remarkable given that The Mission are a band that played gigs worldwide.

The fun of the Scottish adventure was that it was Leeds LS6 going wild in the Highlands and Islands, accompanied by a convoy of Mission die-hard Eskimos. If you can imagine about 120 people, all in black, travelling in a conga line of cars and vans, crisscrossing the remote, countryside, one-track roads of the Highlands, to play in tiny hidden Scottish towns, in venues that could maybe hold a capacity of only two or three hundred. This at a time when The Mission could sell out five nights in a row at The Astoria in London or sell out in advance at Wembley Arena. It was a bizarre and fantastic time.

The Vaynes were a brutal live band by now. The natural effect of touring so much had made us a powerful force on any stage. Our songs sounded bigger than ever, still earthy, still sleazy, but played with confidence and pomp. We delivered our music with a sense of mischief and an air of menace. If it was a particularly good set, I would strip down to my low-waist, naturally-worn-through jeans, leather belt discarded, button and zipper pulled open — not quite exposed, but close.

Up on the Highlands and Islands tour with The Mission, I had started stripping down to naked again, as I had sometimes done during The Dead Vaynes days. I'd started making a habit of it leading up to the Astoria Ballroom Christmas show that we were scheduled to play. Jessica and Gerry weren't impressed with it, they thought it devalued the music and the band. My position was that it was my songs we were playing and essentially my band. The name Vayne means nothing without me, so I can perform how I want and do what I want. Yes, I had managed to get myself stuck right up inside my own arsehole by this point. I can't even blame the voices for leading me on, because by now all three of us were in cahoots together.

Things came to a head at that Astoria Ballroom show in Leeds. We're backstage after finishing our set, and even though I was drunk and drug-fucked before we'd even set foot onstage, the gig had been sensational and the crowd were demanding an encore, proving to me that whatever state I may appear to be in, whatever I do, one thing is always

247

constant: I always deliver come showtime. I turn the crowd up, engage and grab their attention, they never leave without an impression. I'd done it time and time again, on stages all over Europe. I was never going to be the weak link. This band was my life. As we were getting set to go out for the encore, Jessica said to Gerry, Nev, the room, and me, "If he strips down to naked, I'm walking off." Gerry concurred. Nev was non-committal, but I sensed he would swing towards the walk-off. Mick tried to take the edge out of the room and just said, "Come on, Let's Ride." And so we marched back on to the sound of cheers and approval from the crowd. It was a fabulous second reception.

We roared through the first encore song. All was great: the band and room were engaged and connected. The second and last song of the encore was a cover version of the Van Morrison/Them classic "Gloria", which was also a standard song in any Johnny Thunders live set. We were giving a nod of appreciation towards Thunders when we played this song live. Anyway, as we got near to the end of the song and the overall performance, I finally went full frontal — maybe I did it to spite the words of Jessica and Gerry backstage? In any case, if getting naked on stage was good enough for Iggy when he was in The Stooges, then it should be good enough for me in The Vaynes. If it were good enough for Stiv Bators when he was in The Dead Boys, then again, it should be good enough for me in The Vaynes.

So, there we have it. I'm bollock-naked and the crowd are cheering and showing their approval. Jessica walks off before we get to the end of the song. Gerry Famous follows. Nev keeps the beat for a couple of bars, finishes with a full-kit drum roll and exits the stage. Finally, Mick unplugs his big red guitar and follows suit, leaving me naked and alone on the stage, now throwing myself about to nothing but the sound of my own howling banshee voice, singing a final chorus of "Gloria" before ending the performance with, "Thank you and good night, that's the last gig The Vaynes are ever gonna play." And off the stage I danced.

Backstage, everybody is freaking out. I pull my jeans on, T-shirt, boots and leather jacket, turn around and walk out while having the last word: "That's it, the end of the line for The Vaynes. See you around sometime."

Despite my little display, the playing up of me, myself & I at that last show — or maybe that should be me, Jam and Bravado — looking back at the ending of The Vaynes, I can see that it was all my doing; I'd been a fool, acted like a dick, and worse still, I hadn't respected my band in the way I should have, and in the way they deserved to be respected.

They had all put up with a lot from me, and in truth, they had allowed me to be me, so I could be who I thought I was… what greater gift is there than that? While there was no doubt that I loved them, and I knew they loved me back just the same, I fucked up. I often wish I hadn't, and wonder what could have happened if I'd let the band run to its own destiny, rather than causing and forcing the car crash at the end. They were such cool people; Nev, Gerry, Jessica and my right-hand man Mick. I should have done better by them, and I'll always have a pang of guilt for what might've been had I not fallen for my own dark charm. I apologised to them many years later, we found a way to reconnect, and we even took a few rides together again with a series of special events. It's all cool beans x

"Cry Me An Angel" (EXCERPT):

The lights go down
The room is full
The script is bad
But the act is good
The stage is bare
When no one cares
And I break every golden rule.

In the moment of that last gig, I'd felt justified — if the band wasn't going to accept me, in my band, well, that was that. It is what it is and it was what it was… what kind of fool am I?

I know I haven't mentioned her for a while, but throughout all this time, touring and being away from Leeds, I was still seeing Lucinda. We managed to get through a few months more than two years altogether. I'm not sure how, but we did. But since I was cleaning house, I cleaned her out of the scene too. It wasn't as cold as that. The problem was that she wanted us to live together full-time, and as sexy as she was, I wasn't into it.

Lucinda could be moody and insanely jealous of any other girl I'd talk to — maybe with good reason. Although I wasn't unfaithful to her in Leeds, I was insatiable on the road. Anyhow, she kept starting rows and stopped being fun. She was great if it was just me and her in the apartment, but every time we stepped out for the night it'd end up bad. That wasn't my thing. I suppose ending The Vaynes ticked a box for me and earned an X for her in the process. People often say "It's been emotional". And of course it had, both with The Vaynes and with Lucinda it'd been emotional. And in retrospect, it had been emotional, with a capital *E*!

"Broken Heart":

I don't want you hanging around no more,
No, I don't want you hanging around.
They say I'm crazy at the bar,
I guess that's true, I really go too far.
Drinking vodka and wine, all the day and all the night,
And those other girls, well, they don't care,
They look real cool through eyes glazed with beer.
And when the money's gone,
You know you're gonna need someone.
I suppose, I suppose you could still be mine,
I suppose, I suppose I never really tried.
All I ever did for her was make her cry.

250

All I've got left, baby,
Is a broken heart.

Now let me say just one thing,
Don't let me be misunderstood.
Though you say I treat you bad some,
I gave you everything I could.
You said you loved me,
Yeah, you always would.
I started drinking,
You said you'd leave me when you could.
I suppose, I suppose I never really tried, no,
And I suppose, yeah, I suppose you could still be mine,
oh.
All I ever did for her was make her cry.
All I've got left, baby,
Is a broken heart.
Just a broken heart,
Poor broken heart,
Just a broken heart.

I don't want you hanging around no more,
No, I don't want you coming around.
I don't want you hanging around no more...

I want you coming around.

13. RUNNING WITH THE BIG DOGS

The '80s popstar Matt Goss from Bros was sitting two feet away from me. I was in a giant armchair and he was on a big plush sofa with a beautiful coffee table between us.

We were inside a gorgeous hotel suite, which must have been the best room in the house. Everything in it was over-the-top VIP style, super-opulent and grandiose. I can't remember the hotel's name, but it was a proper swanky joint in uptown Manhattan, not far from the entrance to Central Park.

The suite was so big that my downtown Lower East Side apartment would fit inside twice over. Matt probably wanted to make a point — "I'm still a big shot", maybe?

He did make a point, even if I didn't realise what it was immediately and even if it wasn't the point he had set out to make. A little later in our relationship he let slip that the suite hadn't been on his dime nor caused by his celebrity. It was, in fact, courtesy of his then-fiancée, the Latina MTV star Daisy Fuentes. She had travelled from LA to Manhattan for a high-level clothing range deal. The clothing company had paid for the trip, first-class flights and a 5-star hotel, laying on all the trimmings. Matt was the plus-one ride-along, brutal but true.

Of course, I had never met him before. How would I have? This was a guy who had hit record after hit record in the UK. At one point, he could have easily been listed as the most recognisable man in Britain, definitely the most photographed.

His band, Bros, created fan mania among teenage girls. Scenes of the Brothers Goss being chased by hordes of screaming fans were part of the everyday news cycle. Between 1988 and 1992, they were simply gigantic. They were proper popstars who racked up three top-20-selling albums and ten singles that reached the higher end of the national charts, including four number twos and one number-one bestseller. Bros were as big as pop can get in the UK. Let's put it like this, while I was trading in gutter-glitter

Punk-Rock'n'Roll, Matt from Bros was one of the biggest names in the UK music industry, a bona fide popstar with legions of teenage fans. The chances of him and I meeting were as remote as a one-legged man winning an arse-kicking contest, yet here we were.

Matt Goss is hopelessly good-looking — he has a perfectly symmetrical face with everything cut to the perfect size, perfect nose, perfect cheekbones, perfect everything. Matt Goss is straight out of central casting. Every teenage pop girl, mum and grandma had a twinkle in their eye and a tingle in their belly for him. To top it off, there were two of them, Matt and Luke, identical twins. If anybody had told me in 1990 that I'd be working with Matt Goss in the 2000s, I would have thought they were nuts. But life is strange, right?

Then again, I would have said the same thing about working with Latina superstar Shakira, Hip-Hop mega-mogul P Diddy, and the official estates of Bob Marley and the King himself, Elvis.

How did all this happen?

Well, I'd moved to NYC in time for the millennium, Christmas of 1999, transferred there by a company I worked for in London called MasterTone and its dance label subsidiary, MasterDanceTones. Remember the story right at the start of this journey with Daryl Pandy? Well, it was that London-based company that sent me to NYC to create specific dance music products for the US megastore chain Best Buy.

Yes folks, by 1999, I was — finally — fully involved in the business of the music business.

I'd dared "to be'" and now "I was".

I'd been running the MasterDanceTones record label for the MasterTone/Point Group in London for about two years, and was proper flying as an industry executive in the House music scene by the time I arrived in NYC. However, I didn't stay with MasterDanceTones very long after my arrival in the States — we'll catch up with what happened there a little further along.

253

First I ran a US-based label called 303 Records on behalf of Atlanta-based Ichiban Music. They were actually a Hip-Hop and Rap label, and I got to work on a compilation put together by two members of the mighty Wu-Tang Clan, which was a proper thrill for me, given that (in my opinion), they were one of the greatest acts ever in that scene, they always came over totally authentic and real. I also made a UK Garage album by groundbreaking UK collective So Solid Crew, again another thrill because, although they were young, they were the real deal. They pulled up so many trees that they were even the subject of political debate, they were considered a danger to the wellbeing of the feral youth in the UK. The So Solid Crew project was helmed by DJ Swizz and MC Romeo as a mix CD, along with another release I put together, an Electronic House music mix CD with the alter-alter-ego of the massively creative and influential DJ producer Green Velvet under his Cajmere persona. All three projects were special, and each one made an impact inside their niche. But it wasn't long before I parted ways with Ichiban and 303 to take on the top job at the coolest House music label around as I became the Legal, Business Affairs & Label Manager for the hot independent House music label Subliminal Records.

Let me take you on a detour with some of the major artists I ended up working with during this journey. We can start with iconic superstar Puff Daddy, AKA P Diddy, AKA Sean Combs, AKA a purveyor of cultural chaos and absolute scandal.

How Diddy will be remembered in the annals of history is the subject of global debate, as he went from famous to infamous very quickly due to the multiple "Freak Off Parties" that he hosted.

The accusations that were made against Combs were so bad that people openly compared him to suicide pervert Jeffrey Epstein, but all that would eventually come out much later in his personal story — over twenty years later in fact — whereas, so far as my interactions with Puffy are concerned, they were actually back during the early 2000s, when he was loved as a music superstar all over the world.

*

I'll always remember my first face-to-face meeting with him at his offices near Times Square in Manhattan.

He had fallen in love with House music, the energy of it and the freedom the music style gave artists. The culture allowed producers, programmers, DJs and vocalists to be creative, and collaborate with one another. I had always felt that House music had a DIY ethos similar to the original Punk scene that I'd grown up with as a teenager. Diddy probably thought there was a street ethos in House music similar to the original Hip-Hop scene from which he had emerged. Whatever the reason, he was interested and wanted to get involved with it.

So, Puffy contacted Subliminal Records, where I was the Business, Legal Affairs and Label Manager, through one of his assistants to talk about working on a track with one of our main artist-producers, Harry Romero.

Harry's name dripped with credibility. He was regarded as a super-producer for House music and Tech Beats. Lots of name artists wanted a piece of Harry on their tunes and records for his production sounds and name credibility. As the conversation started getting underway, it quickly grew into a bigger concept to work with the whole Subliminal team of producers: Harry Romero, Jose Nuñez and the main man himself, superstar DJ, artist and producer Erick Morillo, who also owned the Subliminal label and brand. Erick had founded and funded Subliminal after the success of his global hit record"I Like to Move It" — more about this track later.

Eventually, an appointment was agreed upon — Thursday at two o'clock. It worked for both Erick and Puffy. Well, we thought it was Thursday afternoon, but when Puff's assistant called back a couple of hours later to confirm, it turned out that when she said, "That's great, let's schedule for Thursday at two o'clock," she actually meant two o'clock in the

255

morning, not two o'clock in the afternoon as per regular office hours.

Puffy's reasoning was that he worked on a 24-hour clock. He slept when his body wanted him to sleep, but outside of that, any hour was an office hour. It seemed to make sense. We thought, "That must be how moguls work," so we decided to work more like moguls from now on too. "OK, 2am, that works out perfectly for us because in our world, on our clock, it's actually Wednesday evening, and we do our weekly Subliminal party in the city that night, so it's a great fit. Erick's spinning at 3.30am, just a bit further downtown, so just keep in mind that we have to be out of your place no later than 3am."

We felt chuffed. Our plan was to work late at the Weehawken office and studio. At some point, Erick would spring for a couple of Popeye's chicken buckets to be delivered from the famous Weehawken Bergenline Latino Street, rather than lose time going out for dinner. Then we'd clean up and spin over to Diddy's space in the city, and we'd have our meeting, before jumping downtown to the club. Mogul style, baby. Accommodating the 2am meeting also let Puffy know we had a similar mentality: we're always on, always on point and ready to roll. Yeah, we felt chuffed with our new mogul sensibilities.

Thursday "Mogul" morning came around and Erick Morillo and I went to the meeting together. Erick had some beats on a CD for P Diddy to hear. If he liked them, we would leave the CD and Puff would put some vocals to them. Then we'd build the track with Erick, Harry and Jose in the Subliminal Studios. If Puff didn't like the beats, then we'd take the CD back with us and call it a draw. We'd write it off as one of those things, a might-have-been idea that didn't come off as a project. Nobody would lose sleep. We'd all walk away, get on with our lives, and say things like, no biggie, it is what it is, a cute idea but it wasn't meant to be, etc.

256

My job was to ensure we walked back out of the offices with the CD of Erick's beats in my hand if Diddy didn't feel the vibe. I didn't know how to achieve that without appearing disrespectful, but that potential drama was in my head as we walked into the meeting.

We entered the lobby of what looked like a regular apartment building, only to find it was floor after floor of different office spaces and businesses rather than living accommodation. As far as I could make out, Puff had at least one entire floor, but it wouldn't have been inconceivable for him to have two floors or even the entire building. The man was a money-making machine, and we were immediately called up to Puff's receptionist and given the green light to take the lift to Puff Daddy's floor.

We went up, and a giant guy greeted us as the lift door opened. He wasn't very smiley, but I guess it wasn't his job to smile, given that the East Coast-West Coast Hip-Hop war was always raising its head, and those dudes weren't playing — they were literally taking shots at one another and some even got killed, Tupac and Biggie Smalls being the most famous, of course. Anyway, he and another guy just marginally smaller patted us down looking for weapons, also checking Erick's bag for the same. We were obviously clean, so the giant security guy ushered us through to the waiting area of the Puff Daddy offices. This was all new to us; guns and violence had little or no place in the world of House music, at least not between the artists, producers and labels. Club promoters and club security was another matter.

At this time, Puffy was doing an MTV show called *Making The Band*, the idea being that he would put together a brand new Hip-Hop band and set them on the road to stardom. Loads of hopefuls were battling each other week-by-week to stay on the show, praying they would get taken under his guiding hand. So, it's two in the morning, and in the massive waiting area of the offices, which had multiple giant flatscreen TVs fitted into the walls, were all these young Hip-Hop wannabes, maybe fifteen of them still left in the running with the chance to be selected. They were on permanent call per Puffy's 24-hour clock schedule.

The atmosphere was noisy but fun, with all these late-teen, early-20s Hip-Hop *kids* acting out, showing off, goofing about together, hoping to be seen, staying turned on just in case Puff was watching or one of his crew was taking notes, I suppose. Puff Daddy to these guys must have been like the *original* Iggy or Johnny Thunders to me when I was their age. I got where they were coming from, it was cute to see.

The TVs in the waiting room were all hooked up to the same MTV Hip-Hop channel and a cool but super-loud, top-of-the-range speaker system. Occasionally, a hot track would come on and the entire room would bounce up and start rapping along, dancing, high-fiving, almost turning the waiting room into a nightclub. It was really great, even if I hadn't a clue why one track was considered "da bomb" and another considered "whack" — it was what it was, great energy, and they were all having fun. Meanwhile I was thinking, "What the fuck is a council kid from the Whinmoor estate in Leeds doing here?" I enjoyed an internal pat-on-the-back chuckle moment with myself while Jam and Bravado also joined in, "Well done, I suppose" (thanks Jam), "Top of the World kiddo," (cheers Bravado).

Even though it was 2am, the offices buzzing with loads of people were on Diddy's Mogul Clock, and as people either entered or exited the room, they all seemed honour-bound to launch into "grand handshake greetings" and, just as grand, "handshake farewells".

It was a mix of hand-slapping, body-tapping, finger-clicking and fist-pumping. It looked complicated, so complicated that I debated it in a rhetorical conflab with Jam and Bravado… "What do I do when it comes around to me? When it's my turn to be introduced to anybody, introduced to Puff Daddy, do I go with the flow and attempt the grand handshake?"

I have to admit, I was pretty nervous about being able to pull it off, and even started to become a little fixated with trying to learn and memorize the sequence of the moves.

As we waited, all kinds of people walked in and out — artists from Diddy's labels, security people, MTV Hip-Hop types — all doing the gymnastic hand-dancing as they entered or left. Then there was a bit of a commotion at the door. The MTV cast went into double energy mode and in walked Puff Daddy, with the youngest man to ever win the Best Actor Oscar award, Adrien Brody.

It was 2003, and Brody had won the Best Actor Oscar at the last awards in 2002 for his lead role in *The Pianist*, an absolutely fantastic film with an incredible performance. (He was to win again in 2025 for *The Brutalist*.) It was clear that Sean Combs hung out and mixed with some very special heavyweight talent, be it Adrien B right here in his offices, or be it starring himself alongside Best Actress Oscar award winner, Halle Berry, and all manner of other global superstars, movers and shakers, powerful executives and political power players. This dude was connected from A to Z and back again.

Of course, the famous P Diddy Parties would become a story unto themselves a few years from now. Those parties would be outed and mired in pure scandal, with heinous accusations and political consequences, with more, more, more and more coming to light. Bedlam would erupt around the mega-mogul, Sean Puff Daddy/P Diddy Combs years on from this night. Of course, nobody could have seen that coming, least of all this council kid from the Whinmoor at a business meeting with the Hip-Hop heavyweight King of New York. Let's just say that for now, for me, the only thing that was on my mind, vexing me, was hoping to get the impending handshake ritual right — and the moment was almost upon me.

I wondered again, "What the fuck is this guy, who used to run down the Spotted Path to John Smeaton Middle & High School on the Whinmoor estate back in Leeds, doing here?"

Even Morillo has a global number-one hit to his name. It made me want to pinch myself to prove it wasn't just a dream. I did a sneaky pinch on my thigh and had another internal smile — more like a belly laugh this time, the three of us (Jam, Bravado and me) were proper back-slapping and howling.

So Puff Daddy makes his way towards us. It takes a few minutes as everybody goes through the hand-shaking ritual with him en route to Erick and me. I'm paying attention to the moves, playing them out in my mind's eye, practising them mentally. As he gets to us, we both prepare to respectfully greet our host. It's the first moment we have come face to face and Erick and Diddy immediately do a cool exchange of the hand dance. I'm next, and I think I'm ready. I tell myself I'm ready to roll. Diddy and I start moving towards one another, raising our hands, wrapped into fists — the first movement in the dance — and about to connect, when Morillo suddenly interjects and introduces me to Puff Daddy, "This is my Business and Legal Affairs Manager." I swear, if there had been a DJ playing vinyl, we would have heard the sound of a dramatic needle-scratch, that unmistakable sound when a DJ pulls the needle across the record to stop everything dead in its tracks — you know the sound.

Puff Daddy pulled up short, just as we were about to swing into it. Giving me full eye contact, he switched his hand shape from fist bump to open palm, having instantly decided to go for the respectfully cautious up and down businessman handshake. It was gonna be a "two shakes up, two shakes down", firm but casual grip and release, but it was too quick for me. I launched forward with the original fist bump starting position. It all happened in a split second, and before I knew it I was punching Diddy's fingers. We were still locked in with the eyeballs — it was like two drunk idiots having a staring contest. He switched back to a fist bump, but I automatically switched to a business handshake. Another collision. I was ready to try again — third time

260

lucky — thinking I'd double bluff and stay with the business handshake, but he'd had enough. He decided to bail on the game of rock, paper, scissors. We neither fist-bumped nor handshaked; I'd punched his fingers and he'd punched mine — I guessed we were gonna call it a draw. Puff suggested we walk with him and his female assistant to the studio to hear Erick's beats and have a chat.

The walk down the corridor went from bad to worse. First, we started with Erick front left, Puff's assistant front right, Diddy back left and me back right. So Puffy was directly behind Erick and I was walking alongside Diddy and behind his assistant — just take a moment to visualise our positions. As we walked down a never-ending corridor towards a big bulky door at the end where the studio was, Puffy looked across to me and simply said, in a cool, natural style, "Wassup, playa." Now, of all the answers I could have given, for some reason, it just popped out — words and actions together. I instinctively shaped the fingers on both hands into a sideways V position, flexed them in front of my chest and just said, "Chillin'."

He looked at me as if to say "What the fuck did you just pull?" Maybe I'd flexed a gang sign by accident? I suddenly remembered reading somewhere that he was affiliated to one side or the other, I don't know which, but I figured I'd ride it out and do it for a second time, with sideways V fingers in front of my chest, and a casual quip of "Chillin'." It was almost as if I was subconsciously saying to him, "I'm saying, I'm fucking chilling, what do you think I'm saying? I'm chilling, I'm fucking chilling, is that alright?" Leeds Leeds Leeds, it never leaves you!

Diddy rolled his eyes and let it go. But it got worse…

Erick and Diddy were quipping stuff back and forth, but Erick was straining to look over his shoulder and Diddy was talking to the back of Erick's head — remember, I said visualise the positions. I had a spontaneous idea to switch places with Puff. I moved and spoke simultaneously, "Let's switch sides so it's easier for you two to talk," and as I said it,

I moved from right to left, undercutting Diddy as I switched behind him. Now, don't get me wrong — Diddy went with it. He knew what was up and moved in front of me from left to right. However, when he walked, Puff had a Hip-Hop swagger, which manifested itself in a kind of one-leg-dragging limp — a pimp walk. As we both moved, my right foot collided with his dragging right foot and I accidentally tripped him so badly that he skipped and stumbled forward, having to move his feet quickly so that he didn't end up falling on his face. It was like an old black & white film, running-on-the spot comedy move.

I wanted the floor to open up, but at the same time, I had a gigantic belly laugh inside at the daftness of it. I couldn't believe I'd almost put Diddy arse over tit. "Oh dude, I'm so sorry, I caught your foot by accident." I regretted the "Oh dude" line as soon as it burped out. But truth be told, if he didn't have the one-leg-dragging limp, if he walked properly, then his right leg would have already been in its correct position and my right foot would have swooped through the space left behind it. At least he had a reason to limp now.

Puffy must have decided to get clear of me because he bounded forward towards the studio door. It was like he'd had enough of bumping, chilling and tripping. He swung the door open and motioned for us all to enter the studio. The next thing that happened, and this was also his own fault, 100% his fault, was he ushered Erick through the door and then his assistant. As I started to go through, as the guest in his house, he started to go through at the same time. I couldn't believe it. We were face to face doing a door-frame tango, an okey-cokey dance to see who goes through first. We were literally nose to nose, chest to chest and crotches feeling the static. I pushed myself through, thinking it was obvious it should be me. I was his guest and he was the one welcoming us into his crib, right? I got another set of eyeballs from him, I think that was maybe the fourth. I'd only known him for about five minutes.

I decide to sit quietly in the studio and say nothing unless asked. Erick passes the CD and gives me a look, almost as if to say, "Remember, if he doesn't like it, get that CD back, whatever it takes." Given the size of the security guys by the lift, I'm not sure I'll be able to force the issue, but I'm rehearsing my spiel internally just in case, as Diddy starts to play the beats.

I'm not kidding, it's some of the most basic beats I've ever heard — literally a kick drum and a snare in a four-four pattern, that's it. The last time I'd heard anything so monotonous was when Wayne Hussey from The Mission was producing a track in the studio with The Vaynes and he decided to listen to a kick-snare-four-four pattern for about three hours before deeming it ready to use. But Erick and Puffy are both tapping, head bobbing, acting as if it's gold dust. Diddy is saying things like "Those beats are nasty, nasty, nasty" and Erick is saying "Deep and dirty, sexy nasty beats". The assistant is bouncing her head like it's "da bomb" too. She purrs, "N-a-s-t-y" while I'm sitting quietly thinking, "What is this shite? Am I on *Candid Camera*? Is this *The Twilight Zone*?" Puff says to me, "Yo playa, you like those beats? Nasty, right? Nasty, nasty." I can't honestly say they are, so I say, "They're filthy and filled with bad intentions." I didn't even understand what the fuck I meant by it, but I got another set of eyeballs for the considered critque. The reality was that it sounded like monotonous nothing. Jam says to me, "For fuck's sake, what are they getting their pants spoiled over?" I had no good answer for Jam. Then Bravado chips in, "Not only have you earned another Puffy dead-eye look, but I think I even heard him suck his teeth. The cheeky twat. That's like him saying, 'Oh fuck, this dude, he don't know what nasty beats are.' Give this dickhead a slap!" I wisely ignored Bravado's slap suggestion, it wasn't a slapping occasion, plus that security guy was bigger than a house.

Bottom line, he likes what he hears. He's had countless global hit records in his career, so what the fuck do I know? They agree that the CD stays. Thank Christ for that. Puff says he will work on some vocals. There's nothing else to say for now, so it's time we got ourselves out of there. Puff Daddy stays in the studio, beats rolling again as we say our goodbyes. Then he's already on the phone with somebody and waves us away. As he closes the door, he gives me one more set of eyes for the road: "Yo, check this shit out, nasty, nasty, nasty," I hear the refrain as the door clicks shut and the assistant leads us back to the lift.

Some weeks later, somehow, Erick and Puff cobbled a track together. Puffy sent it over by messenger from his Manhattan office to our Weehawken office. He wanted us to hear his final pass at the track. He believed it was done, finished and ready to go. Now he wanted to hear what we thought of it. His idea was to premiere it at the Miami Winter Conference, the annual House music industry event where a House song can be broken, and kick-started on its journey to success, or where it can fall on its ass and land in obscurity.

Once we got the Puffy version of the track delivered to our offices, we all took a hopeful listen, and then Erick decided it wasn't good enough. It needed a lot more work, it needed some Harry and Jose magic adding to it. So Morillo says to me, "Call Puffy and tell him it's not cooked, and also tell him he can't perform it in Miami at the WMC." I was like, "Say what? What are you fucking talking about, Erick?" His basic answer was along the lines of, "It's dogshit. But don't tell him that, be diplomatic about it, but in reality, it's about 25-50% done at best and is nowhere near ready to present at WMC or release. Just tell him we need to work on it at Subliminal with Harry and Jose, so we can set it up to get ready for the Ibiza summer season from June and not rush it for the Miami Winter Music Conference in spring." Yeah, thanks for nothing Erick.

I put off calling Puffy. It was Friday afternoon, and I figured Monday would be a better day to deliver bad news. So I left the office in Weehawken and went home to the Lower East Side in Manhattan. I'd already planned for a bunch of friends to swing by my apartment on Ludlow &

Stanton. We were going to get lit and make a big weekend of it.

A few hours later, my apartment was full. My second wife, a Muslim woman from Tunisia, had been working in a French restaurant and all the girls there had become like our little crew. There were five girls of different nationalities and ethnicities: Tunisian, Polish, Japanese, Brazilian and French. Things were rocking pretty good. We were bagged up with cocaine, had various bottles of liquor and all the right stuff to make strong margaritas. Around midnight, just as we were about to hit the streets, my cell phone went off.

About my second wife: don't worry, I will tie it together and tell you how I went from the first wife to the second one. But let me just finish off with Puffy first.

So the phone goes. "Who's that?" I shout down the phone in a cocky manner. Well, I'm bopping on coke and margaritas by now. The voice comes back at me, "Yo yo, wassup, wassup, playa, it's me, Puffy. Can you spin by the office tonight? I wanna talk about the track."

Well, hold fucking the phone, pop-pickers. First of all, how did he find my cell number? It's Friday night at almost midnight, I'm en route to getting lit and P Diddy is calling me on a number I haven't shared with him or his assistant. He goes on, "So the track, it's nasty, right? That shit is damn nasty, playa. Can you swing by in about an hour?" — well, maybe it wasn't word for word like that, but it was pretty much the top and bottom of it, and all delivered in that super-cool lingo and style he has.

I'm signalling to the girls that Puff Daddy is on my cell phone right now. Everybody is like, "What the actual fuck!?" I've barely uttered a word past my opening line: "Who's that?" Puffy continues, "So what d'ya think? I'm gonna hit it in Miami, get the room lit with that shit. What d'ya think? Will E be down in Miami? We could even perform it together. I'll see you in an hour, right playa? It's on!"

Daddy is already set in his thinking: in his mind, the track is fully cooked and he's ready to debut it at the Miami Winter

265

Conference. To be clear, the WMC back then, around 2003, was the most important conference for House music in the annual diary. Tracks were presented to the industry there, be it at events or around the South Beach hotel pools. They could become hits or misses based on four or five days of hardcore promotion, selling and presenting.

I started going there around 1994. It was magical. The idea of flying out to Miami from the UK back in the early/mid-'90s was exciting, and the fact that the plane was full of people working in the dance music scene made it even more special. We were the executives of a new scene. We were on the business side of the coin, representing options and opportunities for artists, labels and the business of the music business.

Back to Friday night in the Lower East Side, I don't have the slightest inclination to go uptown and meet with Puff, so I tell it to him straight on the phone, "Sorry dude, can't make it tonight."

Unsurprisingly, my negativity doesn't go down very well and Puff starts babbling on about 24-hour clocks, being "on" at all times, the track is this, that, blah blah blah...

I also took a chance and went on to tell Puff Daddy that we didn't think the song was ready and that he should wait until we'd finished it before putting it out or performing it in Miami. Well, that went over even worse, and he starts insisting that he's gonna do his performance, and that the track is already perfect...

I backtracked a little, I didn't feel the need to get into a big debate with Diddy. I'd already put a few hours' work into getting my buzz going with the girls. We were veering off track, and that was only gonna fuck up my vibe...

"OK then, you do as you think best. I'm sure you'll smash it, but Erick will not be able to do the show with you. We've got our own show going on that night."

He wasn't happy, and he gave me a few minutes of "yada yada yada", but he rang off sharply, leaving me with a *fait accompli* demand, like a 50/50 settlement of sorts, "OK, OK,

266

tell Erick to keep working on the track for a summer release and I'll give it its premiere in Miami to start the ball rolling." He clicked off.

A few weeks later, we were all in Miami and Puffy went ahead and did his thing — the first performance of "Dance I Said". It wasn't a disaster, but it wasn't great either. It was kind of as we knew it would be.

His dance career didn't take off or explode into the success he might have expected. That first performance in Miami didn't help. But I have to say, Puffy gave House music a good go. He really gave it a good shot. He'd keep appearing at venues across Miami, New York and Ibiza as an unannounced but rumoured guest. He'd get on the microphone in the DJ booth in Ibiza and start to shout out hook lines from the tracks we'd worked on including "Let's Get Up & Let's Get Ill", "Dance I Said", or "My World". It was a spectacle because it was superstar and music mogul Puff Daddy/P Diddy inside a House music club, getting his freak on. But it was never great in terms of quality or performance, it was really no more than a talking point, a bit of drama at the party.

He never asked for expenses or payment, and of course he could've bought and sold us all 100 times over. He was just happy to be there and to be seen to be there. So far as energy and desire go, I was impressed with Puff in terms of his work ethic. It was insatiable, just unreal — I've never seen anybody like that before or since. But as for the tracks, it was like all his tracks were just one line of dialogue repeated over and over. He'd say, "It's nasty, dark and nasty."

Erick and Puffy started hanging out like pals. Puff opened the door to all kinds of options; through him, we managed to get supermodel Naomi Campbell to appear on a track and video for an Erick Morillo vs. Audio Bullys jam called "Break Down The Doors", released as a key single from Erick's *My World* album.

The album also featured the Erick and Puff Daddy tracks "Dance I Said" and "My World" — as well as an "accidental" but super-cool Yorkshire speaking vignette by yours truly. My broad Leeds accent always had Erick, Harry, and Jose in stitches. But then again, these guys never had a clue who I had been in a past life, my life before House music, and I didn't tell 'em either.

As usual, I went a bit off-kilter there — and I didn't finish up the story about Matt Goss.

But let's take a breather after that Puff Daddy rollercoaster ride, and we'll return to the brother Goss in the following chapters.

14. GOODBYE PUNK-ROCK'N'ROLL

You're probably wondering how I — a Punk-Rock'n'Roll reprobate — ended up at the top of the dance music world. Well, let's take the story back to '89 and the split of The Vaynes.

When The Vaynes split up, I jumped straight back on the horse and formed The Slaves, almost immediately — and along the way, I dropped Lucinda.

I loved sex with Lucinda, but she was becoming more and more moody, and I didn't think I was the type of guy she should get any further into bed with, so to speak. You could say I split with her for her benefit — I'm good-hearted like that, you see; "Maybe I'm bad, but I'm good-bad, not evil."

I also took over the second album clause in the Native Records deal, at their request, and recorded what I thought was a wonderfully introspective, but drug-fucked, album, that was both stripped down and chaotically brutal at the same time. I called it *Guarana*. I was told that Guarana was like natural speed, so the title was supposed to send a message that I was less chemically inclined and more natural these days. However, the cover is a full-face shot of wired bloodshot eyes, taken by Johnny Thunders' backing singer Alison Gordy, or maybe it was his bassist, Jill Wisoff. I can't be sure. I do know it was taken at some place in Europe where we were playing. So the album image kind of betrayed the album's title and its supposed subtle sub-message.

Native Records also released The Vaynes recording of *Alive & Kicking* under the band's name — a decision I played absolutely no part in. The *Guarana* album was released in the first half of 1990.

I'd started touring this new band to support the release. We were doing well, we all got along together and partied a lot with alcohol and speed — like I said, and as per the sleeve image, forget the Guarana "natural high hippie bollocks", I was doing lots of speed again. Anyway, somewhere along the line, I got together with Ann-Z, a

269

weird-strange American girl who was freaky-gorgeous, but who had also overstayed her UK visa by more than three years. She lived in the next street behind me in LS6 with Gerry from The Vaynes, but not in a biblical way, they were just great friends — or maybe they'd been biblical earlier on in their friendship but had morphed into real friends from there. They were both unique people with off-kilter thought patterns, real birds of a feather.

Anyway, I never asked either of them, and it didn't matter to me what their thing had been, because Ann-Z and me were destined to go down another path. After a few months of hard partying together, we agreed to get married and "beat the system".

On one hand, it would help her get a visa to stay in the UK. On the other hand, it might also give me an advantage to get a visa to live in America at some point as well, as I felt destined to be in Manhattan.

So yes, the inconvenient truth of it was that this was a convenient marriage. It wasn't a marriage forged in love, but there was love-making and sex. And, truth be told, she was open to the idea of being in love. As for me, maybe it was just thrill-seeking again.

We got married at the Leeds Registry Office. It was an amazing wedding day, as my old 27 Leicester Grove bedsit neighbour Chester, and his brilliant Rockabilly band, Pink Peg Slax, played a killer set of classics that had everybody rocking. Later that evening it got even better at the wedding party night, with loads of people descending on The Duchess, packing it out to the rafters. We had some great bands there too, including the ever fabulous Three Johns. It was some day, some night — and then a whole crew went back to mine for a mammoth 48-hour speed session. It was proper romantic, not.

Ann-Z was bang into the band, The Slaves. Now married and legal, she could work, which she did at The Royal Park. Somehow she found a way to use the pub's public phone for hours at a time while only putting in one 10p piece as payment. That Royal Park public phone became my office — Ann-Z and I managed to arrange a couple of tours for The Slaves using this payphone scam.

Johnny Thunders was touring again; half the shows were acoustic and the other half were electric with a full band. I was brought on as the support act for the UK leg, which included a couple of nights in Leeds, one an acoustic show at The Duchess and the other a full electric band up at the Leeds Poly. Given I had the Native Records deal and this Johnny tour, it properly vexed Prince Michael, but at least he was asked to play guitar for Johnny on the acoustic dates, as Johnny thought he'd hurt his hand and couldn't play. He could, of course; it was all psychosomatic and psychological — Johnny could be a right whiny dick at times. But Mick didn't care; it was a big thrill for him and he was happy to play, and I was happy that he got to live out one of his musical goals, playing guitar in the Johnny Thunders band.

The Thunders tour finished as usual at The Marquee in London with two dates at the end of May. Both bands had the full electric setup, these weren't acoustic shows — these two shows, and in fact all of the dates we'd done, be they acoustic or electric, had all been brilliant. Whenever I shared a stage with Thunders, it was like a dream come true, I could never fully accept it was really happening, even as it was playing out. I was a fan first and foremost and always felt incredibly honoured, and lucky, to be there.

I liked playing shows with The Slaves; it was different to when I'd toured with The Vaynes, more casual. With The Vaynes, it was always *more* — and in all honesty, there were times when the twin voices of Jam and Bravado had me convinced that I was being tolerated rather than loved. But that was just inside my crazy head — it wasn't true at all. They did love me, did care for me, and they showed that love and care with their incredible patience and general understanding of what my nature was.

With The Slaves, I felt respect. I'd already done things in the music scene that they were still dreaming of, I

271

represented something, maybe that something was as simple as "he's made an impact, we can make an impact too". Just as Abrasive Wheels were inspirational for me, maybe I represented a little bit of that to them?

One of the guitarists in The Slaves, Mick Lake, was a lad I'd known since my school days at Smeaton. I always felt love from him, and I'm sure he felt it back from me too. Sometime later, Mick got a taste of the proper "rockstar" life with a band he had called Death Valley Screamers, who were feted as superstars in Ukraine of all places. It's a story in its own right, but it's not one of mine to tell. Mick also ended up in a relationship with the incredible CJ, which was never an issue or problem for him, her or me — but let's not get distracted.

While touring with The Slaves was relaxed, a lot of fun — and touring with The Vaynes was more intense, more professional, but still with many moments of fun — neither were anything like the reality of touring with The Dead Vaynes. That had been pure chaos, mayhem, filled with side-splitting hilarity and non-stop danger. We would have all been committed, or dead, within a short time period had we stayed together — members jumping ship probably saved us from ourselves.

Let's just say, at this point, touring with The Slaves was a pleasure.

By the end of the year, on December 21, 1990, we played once more with the incredible Johnny Thunders at the London Marquee. He was incredible on stage at this show (maybe the best gig I've ever seen him play), and offstage he was even better: straight, lucid, fun, talkative, warm and caring, which was very unusual for him, it shouldn't have been, but it just was. At the end of the gig, the bands were saying their goodbyes once again. I remember being sat on the edge of the stage as bandmates and roadies cleared everything away.

Johnny came to talk to me: "Hey, Stevie Vayne, listen to me, listen to your big brother for a minute." He was in a really great mood, he had done a great show and was heading to Japan next. "I wish we could take you to Japan, but listen, I'm coming back and want you on the next tour across Europe and England, OK?"

Of course it was OK, better than OK, a pleasure. Remember what I said earlier, I was still a fan first and foremost...

"But listen up, you need to start taking better care of yourself, stop with the getting fucked up bullshit, don't become the next douchebag like me. You've got something good going on, good songs, good band. I can hear you, I can see you, Stevie Vayne."

I couldn't believe it, Johnny Thunders was giving me a pep-talk in the middle of The Marquee. Next thing, we're hugging it out and then he left me with, "Don't fuck it up, take it as good advice from someone who knows, OK?"

I nodded yes, before he continued, "OK, I gotta get out of here, see you around, Stevie Vayne, but don't forget what I'm saying, right?"

I loved it whenever Johnny would say my name, it meant so much to me to hear him address me as Stevie Vayne. But putting that aside, this display of affection was so unusual for John — being clean and straight really suited him, he wore it well. I was dumbstruck. I'd never heard him be sentimental in person before. In songs, yeah, but usually, he never really said much about anything. When he did, it would be goofing about or asking for weed, or cigarettes, or whatever.

He gave a playful light slap to my chest, emphasising the "see you around refrain", turned away, crossed the floor, and eventually that bird's nest shock of black hair was out of sight. It was just like the first time I'd ever seen him in the flesh, back in '84 — I honestly can't remember what he was wearing, he just looked cooler than anybody else, and I swear, I can't remember seeing his legs move or his feet actually step one in front of the other. He was here, then he was there, like he was floating... and gone.

273

I didn't know it right then and there, but that would be the last time I'd ever see him. On April 23 of the next year, 1991, he would be found dead in a New Orleans hotel. As tragic as that was, all the circumstances of Johnny's passing were muddy and full of half-truths. Drugs were involved, of course, but it was much more nuanced than another dead junkie overdose. Look it up.

For my part, well, between that Marquee night on December 21, 1990, and the news of Johnny's death on April 23, 1991, I hadn't taken his last words on board at all. I'd caned everything I could get my hands on, I was right back in the saddle. But once the news came over, and the details of that fateful New Orleans story were told to me, directly by his manager/tour manager, Mick Webb, I decided there and then to quit living life as an LS6 junkie — no more fronting for a Punk-Rock'n'Roll band.

*

I was 27 and I wasn't going to get any further than where I was. The future would be similar to Johnny's: touring, touring, touring, no major record deal, no major commercial success, just treading the boards and living hand-to-mouth. I came to realise: "Keep on like this and your death waits there. Quit this shit and get into the business of the music business properly, like you always wanted to do. It's time to stop messing about."

I split the band, told Native Records not to exercise the additional album clause in the contract, gave up my electric guitar and walked away from Punk-Rock'n'Roll. Maybe cutting out on the record deal would be the greatest mistake of my life, and maybe the next album would have been a game-changer for me — I'll never know. But I did know that another album would have been another year or two living the same way, and maybe I wouldn't have survived that. It only takes one mistake, I might've gone out just like Johnny. Or maybe I would've survived just fine but still not have kicked the can any further down the road. It is what it is, it is what it has been.

I realised, again, that I'd always wanted to be on the other side of the coin, the businessman rather than the artist. I knew, even from being young, that artists come and go. Some make their mark, some change the world, but most fade to grey. Executives, agents and managers seem to always be around and always rocking a good life. I had to get myself in hand and make a move. I was super-sad that Johnny Thunders was dead, but his last words rattled around my head: "Don't become the next douchebag like me." His passing was my signal to split. In all probability, Johnny Thunders saved my life.

After two or three months of drying out — no alcohol, no drugs, no music, just sleeping and doing a lot of nothing — I woke up one day and realised that the apartment was an absolute pigsty. Bags and bags of rubbish piled up everywhere, boxes and boxes of junk piled floor to ceiling. I'd never even really noticed it before. Some of it was mine, maybe 20%, the rest was Ann-Z's. As I sobered up, I realised I'd married into a mess, figuratively, literally, psychologically and physically. I started to try to rid the apartment of all the clutter. That's when Ann-Z revealed that she had a big problem. She was a hoarder, but not in a cute, jokey way — this was serious, in a psychological mental health way. I tried to take away just one of her boxes. It was only filled with old copies of the *Yorkshire Evening Post* newspaper, but as I made my move, she threatened to throw herself out of the top floor window. No joke, she was ready to jump rather than let anything leave the room, even a box of old newspapers. I'd never seen anybody so willing to throw themselves out of a window, whatever the consequences. There was absolutely no comedy to it — this was real-life drama.

I managed to get her seen by a doctor, just achieving that was another drama in itself, and she was diagnosed with something called "acute clinical medical depression" or some other jumble of words that amounted to the same thing: she was ill.

We discussed a way forward. I told her that I was definitely finished with being a fucked-up frontman, I wouldn't be changing my mind, I was breaking for the border with two pistols cocked and ready. I was gonna get a proper job, I was gonna claim my future — and once I had a job, with my first wage, I would buy her an incredible sewing machine that she said she wanted, a real piece of kit that had a high price tag to it, and I would help her enrol on to a serious Fashion and Design course that she said she dreamed of taking.

We agreed: she'd stop taking street drugs, same as me, and she'd also go through any course of prescribed drugs that could be required to get herself better. We also said we'd drink a lot less.

We made a deal, we agreed — we were gonna change our lives around and see if we could even make the marriage work in the real world.

To my surprise, I landed a job as the Events Coordinator of the Leeds landmark building, The Corn Exchange. I just blagged the interview by telling them I'd arranged tours, managed bands and ran record labels — all of which was kind of true — but I massively embellished the reality for effect, for the wow factor. It worked. I got a job that I had absolutely no idea how to do.

The first assignment was to carry on with the existing activities already booked and running. So, I started off managing the arts and crafts fairs, as well as the antique fairs on Saturdays and Sundays. It felt like a long way from Punk-Rock'n'Roll, especially at the start, and — truth be told — I had to dig deep to be fair with myself rather than letting my ego divert me from the road I'd chosen to take.

I was true to my word with Ann-Z. I blew my first paycheck on the Rolls Royce of sewing machines that she wanted, and I helped her enroll in a Design and Fashion course at one of the colleges. We repeated our promises to each other: we would change our ways and see how things worked out between us. I was willing to give the marriage a proper go, past the convenience and system-beating — I really, really was. However, it was a waste of time. She didn't even try to change. She never got out of bed, never took her prescribed medicine, and she didn't want to do anything apart from get fucked up on street drugs. She enrolled at college, went once and never went again. The incredible sewing machine sat dead in the corner, a waste of money, a symbol that trying with her was a wasted effort.

OK, I know I'm sounding brutal in the things I am saying about her, but that was my reality, how I was feeling her burn. In reality she was not purposely or maliciously being in a funk; she was ill and I wasn't mature enough to handle it. And besides that, I was in no position to waste anymore time — I told her I wanted a divorce. I'd made my break for the border but she hadn't even saddled up her horse, and still her junk kept piling up, more and more by the week. It got so bad that we had walkways between the boxes and bags, there was nowhere to sit down and the kitchen was unusable. Only the bed was spared. None of this had mattered before, or maybe it was never this bad before. I don't know how it got this bad, but now, I'd made an effort to make the switch, something had to change.

*

At this very moment in 1991, rave music and rave events were starting to explode across the country. I didn't know what the music was or who the artists were. The thought of a DJ's name being the attraction to an event was alien to me. No matter. After only a few weeks in the job, with a remit to bring some life into the old building and attract younger people to come inside and see what we were all about, I told the Corn Exchange manager, "We should put a rave on inside this amazing Grade II listed building." With a minimum of hesitation, the boss said, "OK, sort it out, but let's not call it a rave."

I'd never even been to a rave, never mind organised one. I didn't know who the famous DJs were or how to contact them. I'd been consumed by Punk-Rock'n'Roll since I was 14.

277

The clubs I went to over the last ten years were edgy, full of characters in freaky clothes or junkie Punks, they were Rock'n'Roll venues, none of this raving bollocks. House music, to me, was disco, music that straight people were into, folk in brand-name designer clothes and Vidal Sassoon haircuts. I didn't know what I was talking about when it came to talking about a rave.

Now here's a funny thing... You see, what I didn't know, back then, at that particular moment in time, was that House music was as Punk as Punk had ever been. Who the fuck knew? Not fucking me, that's for certain.

As mentioned, The Corn Exchange was a Grade II listed building, located in the centre of Leeds. It had been bought by some spivs from London and re-imagined as a speciality shopping centre housing about 50 small shops all selling "something special", be it House music records, rave posters, flavoured condoms, designer shoes, bouquets of flowers, fancy bath salts — and loads of branded designer clothes stores. This was so far out of my comfort zone it was unreal.

When the idea of turning the shopping centre into a club venue was first filtered around, the feedback was negative from the stores housed inside the magnificent building. The biggest voices were the older storekeepers, particularly the flower shop owner, and the idea almost turned to dust before it got going. But I had a brainwave: "We'll make it a fashion show and invite all the clothes shops in the centre to show their goods on the catwalk, but the runway music will be played live by great House DJs." Genius, eh?

I told the three restaurants/bars that they could run the alcohol sales — which was hilarious, as it turned out that the biggest seller on the night was water. Thanks to some cunning forward planning, I had snagged a space on the night to have a couple of young lads man a water stand for me and my security guy, who had been the one to give me the heads-up that "water is king at a rave", as far as liquid goes anyway. Again, who fucking knew? Not fucking me, but it were a great surprise to make an easy few hundred quid on a side hustle. Meanwhile, I told the record store and a few other shops that they could handle ticket sales.

These concessions changed the complexion of things completely. All the shop owners met and voted it through — we were going to have a rave, but we weren't going to call it that. My grand plan was to create a club event built around a fashion show, with the whole event running between 9pm and 2am, the traditional time when nightclubs were allowed to open back then. It was agreed by management in Leeds, and in London, to go full steam ahead. Now keep in mind that I had no experience in either fashion shows or raves, I needed to put a team together who knew more than I did while somehow not letting them know that I knew nothing.

The first thing I did was to go see Vidal Sassoon, the world-famous hairdressing brand, which had a store in the centre of Leeds. I'd never been near Sassoon's in my entire life. Everybody I knew cut their own hair, styled their own hair, dyed their own hair, or simply let their hair take on a life of its own. We'd never spent one red cent in a hairdressing salon. So I was going in blind, not knowing how to pitch it.

On top of that, my hair was what Sassoon would call a rat-tailed mess, not very trendy in the normal world. My attempt to look presentable in this new "normal" world was simply to tie my hair in a ponytail; high fashion it wasn't.

But sometimes the stars align just right because at Sassoon's there was a young woman, the same age as me, Dell, who was hungry and ambitious. She had just been promoted to the rank of Acting Art Director and she wanted to make her mark. When I approached her, she probably thought I was very unimpressive, but she was impressed by the idea of the project. Long story short, Dell changed my life. Once I met her, I knew I had done the right thing in switching lanes. Her enthusiasm, energy, creativity and relentless ambition were infectious. She was special.

We were from two different worlds. While she was in her natural zone, I was an imposter just blagging it. The more we

279

met to plan the event, the bigger the event became. We decided to invite other clothing stores from other trendy shopping zones in Leeds to take part in the fashion show. By final count, we would have 40 clothing stores involved on the catwalk. But more than that, we would have 40 stores promoting our event with a vested interest in making it a success — more genius, right? Of course it is, but I have to share that credit with Dell as she was becoming my partner in wild ambition.

By my calculations, we needed to attract 2,000 paying customers to buy advance or walk-up entry tickets. Before this event, I'd only ever done gigs for a couple of hundred people during the Punk-Rock'n'Roll days. Well, apart from a few shows with Johnny Thunders, The Gun Club or The Mission, which were maybe around a thousand a pop — this really was new territory.

Somewhere along the line, I was introduced to a cool guy called Glen Campbell. Like the country music star, the name was so strange on Glen because he was a well-built black dude whose father ran the illegal blues clubs in the Caribbean area of Leeds, Chapeltown. Glen was a really interesting guy. He came from a proper dodgy background, had a cowboy's name and spoke impeccable Queen's English, never swearing, shouting or raising his voice. He didn't need to, he had charisma. He also had a reputation for being hard as nails.

Glen Campbell was cool as fuck. He was also super-connected in the House music scene, and on top of everything else he was a fantastic choreographer for the catwalk models. I was talking to anybody and everybody, while never letting on that I knew nothing, all the time picking up names and connections as quickly as people were name-dropping them. So far as people were aware, I'd been in the rave scene since it had started, or at least since '88 or '89. I hadn't, of course; I'd been dressed in black or jumping around stages bollock-naked, as you already know.

Glen Campbell was the only person who knew that I was blagging; he wasn't slow, and Dell, well she didn't even think to question it. She wasn't slow on the uptake or naive, she was just the kind of person who saw the best in people. She believed in me, and she believed in us, she believed from day one that we could pull this off together. That inspired me, she made me better than I was.

Next, it was time to book the star DJs, a concept that was so *out there* to me, but it was what it was. I'd heard the names of Mike Pickering and Jon De Silva from The Hacienda being thrown about. I'd heard of the club because I'd once gone there to see a band called Blancmange, dragged there by the lass who became a soap opera TV star. They had a hit called "Living on The Ceiling". All I remembered was that I'd enjoyed the club but not the band. But I did know that The Hacienda, or The Hac as it seemed to be known to ravers, was supposed to be a proper player in this House music scene. Of course, I gave the impression that I'd been there loads of times without having to make a statement confirming it. I managed to get the right telephone numbers through Glen Campbell, of course. I made the calls and before I knew it, I'd secured them both. The young store owners, and everybody that was taking part in the fashion show, were all impressed.

My boss then informed me that we needed a special licence to cover the activity we wanted to host, which I had to apply for from the City Council. I needed permission to turn the building into a nightclub for the one-off special event. No licence, no fashion show, no event, no rave. But I knew I needed even more ammunition to have any chance of getting this licence, as one of the restaurant owners in the building had grandly announced that it would be "impossible to get the right licence". The flower shop guy also announced just as grandly, "I'm going to oppose this fucking rave at the hearing." Fucking wanker. So, another brainwave — another moment of genius! — I approached Yorkshire Television and asked them if they'd like to film the biggest fashion show ever presented in Yorkshire, starring 40 of the trendiest stores in Leeds, as well as the world-famous Vidal Sassoon, 80

281

models and star DJs from the House music scene, all under the glass-domed roof of the Grade II listed Corn Exchange building in the centre of Leeds. They only turned around and said, "We would be honoured."

Yorkshire TV agreed to bring a full team, all the salient broadcasting cameras, even one on a giant boom arm and another to capture the bird's-eye view. The DJs were booked: Mike Pickering and Jon De Silva from The Hacienda. I also had the owner of the Corn Exchange record store, The Listening Post, a respected DJ in Leeds, Steve Luigi, down to play.

Steve would be the first DJ to play the first records and the first set at The Corn Exchange. I also had another young DJ, Dean White, who would be the DJ for the fashion show along with a guy who would shout down the microphone — people called him an MC. I almost pissed myself that people would get so excited by a lad in a hat shouting "Put your fucking hands up".

All that was missing, for now, was the licence to do it. But I applied and got my day in the Town Hall of Leeds to make my case, stating that it wasn't a rave, it was a cultural event featuring dozens of businesses from Leeds and a global brand in Vidal Sassoon, as well as Yorkshire TV filming the event to broadcast as a special event the following week. It would be taking place in one of the most historically important buildings in Yorkshire. The event would galvanise the city centre and surrounding areas, showcasing that we were in tune with the moment. They granted the one-off special event licence. We were set.

The event was a great success. From there, I secured multiple licences, even making a near-Churchillian speech to get the first all-night 6am Leeds licence during that early '90s period. This paved the way for all the clubs in Leeds to operate on the same all-night hours I had secured.

Just to make a note here; many people have, or will, claim to have achieved the historic licence precedent. They're welcome to speak their own truth. But, somewhere, in the annals of Town Hall Licensing minutes files, there will be an incontrovertible record of my heroic pitch. Leeds, you're very welcome.

During those Corn Exchange years, I curated and managed some of the greatest House music parties the City of Leeds ever saw, more or less inventing the concept of the superclub event as I started to book lineups of three or four super-headline DJs on the same night, rather than just one or two headliners and a couple of warm-up supports.

Some amazing Leeds promoters came on board. Tony Hannon with his Up Yer Ronson and KAOS events, the lads from Ark who ran the Rave Poster Shop. I also brought up famous promoters from London, players like Charlie Chester and his Flying Volante event.

In fact, it was at that Flying Volante event in The Corn Exchange that Charlie Chester met a good pal of mine, Dave Beer, who was going through his own transition from Punk-Rock'n'Roll and live bands to House music and club events. Dave had just started promoting his own brand new party in Leeds at a venue just around the corner from The Corn Exchange. He called it Back To Basics, and went at it with wit, flare and a Punk sensibility and attitude.

His opening night fell on the same night as Flying Volante at The Corn Exchange, and the long and the short of it was that Dave's new party suffered with a very low attendance on its opening night. But given the fact that Dave had the Punk spirit of surviving against all odds, he sent a runner up to see me with a message... "I've got about fifty people here, if I close my party can I march them all round to yours for free entry, rather than send them home?"

Of course, given that Flying Volante was already officially sold out, and the fact that me and Dave had been very good friends for years, the answer I sent back was, "Absolutely, I'll be at the door waiting for you, and we'll funnel them all in as free guests, come on over, buddy." So that's what he did, he led them up the street and around the block like the Pied Piper. Dave Beer looked the dog's bollocks as he danced his people up the street and into the heaving, rocking Flying Volante at The Corn Exchange.

Nobody knew, at that moment in time, that Basics would find its feet very quickly, within the next week or two of that opening night, and that it would go on to become officially recognised as the longest running weekly club night in UK clubbing history.

Dave Beer himself became a legend of club culture, incredibly well loved across the entire global House music & party scene, and he and Charlie Chester would be like brothers from that night on. They're still thick as thieves as I write these words here today.

So how did I get away from Ann-Z?

One Christmas she fell pregnant to a guy I kinda knew — to be honest, I did kinda set it up. I'll say no more on that issue, but when needs must, needs must. We got divorced as quickly as we'd got married. It must have been maybe one year from start to finish. Being pregnant changed her completely. She bucked up, got busy, got straight and started making super-cool Rock'n'Roll hats to sell on one of the craft tables I let her have in The Corn Exchange. She sold a lot, she made a lot — she was finally doing OK. Everything had worked out. We threw all her junk away and I was free.

I learned to drive and bought a gorgeous white BMW car. Dell and I found ourselves growing closer every day — before long, we were together and soon after, we were in a passionate romance, taking holidays abroad to Paris, Antwerp and even America. But mostly, we did our courting driving the BMW up and down the country on weekends away. I'd never been materialistic in my life, but I did get a kick out of that car and, incredibly, I bought a small two-up, two-down back to back house just like the one I'd been born in.

We went to restaurants, spent nights in hotels — all the things that regular people did and more, more more, these were the kind of things I'd never even contemplated up to now. And we had money in our pockets to do it, both with decent-paying jobs and crucially drug-free at this point. Dell never touched drugs at all, but we did drink. Some years later she had to take personal responsibility and action to beat the drink out of her life. And God bless her, she won that battle. But at this time, when we met one another, we were raving and rolling all over the world and having a lot of fun.

Things were going great, the weeks and months flew by, and then out of the blue, she was offered the chance to go to San Francisco and take over as the Art Director for the West Coast salon of Vidal Sassoon. This was her working dream coming true in real life. There was no way I would ever attempt to stand in her way, nor was I the kind of person to tag along as a spare part. She had to go, and I'd have to wave her goodbye with a positive cheerio, "See you when I see you, go get 'em, kiddo."

And that's how it played out. It was like the Soft Cell song "Say Hello, Wave Goodbye" played out in real time. We'd been together less than a year, and more than being my girlfriend for a moment, she was my best friend in this new world, an inspiration who let me know that she believed in me; that was her greatest gift.

There was a delicious twist to Dell and I: we stayed the best of friends, no matter the distance between us, or the length of time between speaking to one another, and at one point, we actually ended up living two streets away from one another in the East Village. Her personal story is incredible, but that's hers to tell at a time of her choosing.

Not long after Dell had gone, I started to discover that these rave kids liked drugs, designer drugs, drugs like ecstasy, drugs like coke, and lurking in the background, drugs like crack. With no Ann-Z to deal with, now long gone from my day-to-day life and happy in motherhood, and now with Dell gone too — the righteous light that kept me occupied and away from the dark side of life — I was ripe to jump back into the fray. I kept on rolling all over the country in my White BMW with VIP invites to exclusive raves, after-hours raves, secret raves, big club events, wherever there was an

285

opening I was there, popping pills like they were chocolate smarties and sniffing Charlie in the same amounts as I used to sniff speed. It was a wild time and before long I progressed onto crack — there I was, smoking the crack pipe. What the fuck was I thinking? But like all drugs, if you have money, then drugs aren't so much of a problem; the problem is when the money runs out. I was strictly a weekend crack smoker, as I had my day-to-day job and the money it generated to protect — so I wasn't so bad... maybe. In my mind, I could take it or leave it each time. If I felt the urge to let weekends begin on Thursdays and last through to Tuesdays, sometimes I'd succumb but usually I'd pull back hard on the reins and tap out.

By now I was getting good at promoting and event management. I'd picked it up fast and made big money, more money than I'd ever had, producing events at The Corn Exchange and other venues in Leeds and around the country. I also started managing a couple of very hot DJs and producers who went under the name Cleveland City DJs. Before long, I was organising gigs for them in the UK and across Europe — I was really beginning to make waves in the music business.

At one of the Corn Exchange events, I also met a great lass who'd come over from Halifax. Molly was a proper raver girl, a bit younger than me but only by two or three years. She came over quite shy when I first met her, even though she came back to my Harehills house the same night. We started seeing each other as a proper couple immediately and within days she moved from Halifax to Leeds to live with me. We rocked it pretty hard together, but mostly only on weekends — and when I say rocked, we rocked; pills, coke, crack, sex, party, repeat, repeat, repeat.

At one of the Corn Exchange events I booked a two-piece band called D:Ream to do a PA. They were well regarded in the club scene but weren't a nationally recognised name in a commercial sense. I spent a lot of the night hanging out with the singer, Peter Cunnah. This was sometime in the summer of 1993 and they had just had a club hit called "Things Can Only Get Better". I asked him to let my Cleveland City producers give the track a new remix, promising him it would become a commercial hit if he did. My guys had already hit No.1 in the national commercial charts with another artist, Tony Di Bart, with a song called "The Real Thing", and all the club tracks we were putting out were massive dancefloor hits too. So I told Peter that he should let us remix his club hit, and if he liked it, then he had to pay us two grand; if he hated it, we'd bin it. But my prediction was that a Cleveland City remix would get massive support on Pete Tong's Radio 1 show, which would bleed on to other radio shows, leading to a Radio 1 playlist and delivering a commercial hit record nationally.

Maybe the Guinness played its part, and I must admit, I was feeding him without pause, but he agreed and lo and behold, that's exactly what happened. By December the song was moving, and by January it was No.1 in the UK charts having sold 600,000 copies; it stayed at that peak position for four weeks in a row.

On the back of this success, I was headhunted to take over a club in London's Leicester Square, the club was called Maximus. Even though I was doing great in Leeds, my personal aspirations were to get to the place where the streets were paved in gold. As The Clash once intimated, London was calling. So, me, Molly and James Bullseye packed a bag — just like Dick Whittington — and moved down to the Big Smoke. I rented out my house in Leeds to a lovely gay couple and I set myself up in London and began running the nightclub — again, just blagging and getting away with it. All of a sudden, I was the new face in the London club scene.

London seemed really warm to me, and within a year I was promoting a giant party with a small team of associates, including legendary London promoters Alan Warman and his business partner, Mad Tommy Mac, at the world-famous Royal Albert Hall.

287

I was also offered another job in London as head of A&R for an underground vinyl record label in Hammersmith, which came about purely because of the history I had with Cleveland City DJs — the two number-one hits by Tony Di Bart and D:Ream, along with a bag load of club chart hits we'd delivered.

I was riding high, life was good but I wasn't earning the same kind of money as I was back in Leeds. The streets of gold maybe weren't so true after all. Things always seemed to be hand-to-mouth rather than solid or stable, everything I might win tomorrow was dependent on the success of today. Everything you touched had to come good to keep on point — but even so, I sold my house in Leeds and bought an apartment down by Spitalfields Market, around the old haunts of Jack The Ripper and the Kray Twins.

Here's a funny aside, try and get your head around this: one thing that did have a global effect, or at least a major effect in the UK, was the remix of "Things Can Only Get Better" by my Cleveland City producers that had delivered the No.1 hit for D:Ream. It became such a piece of the everyday fabric of life that the New Labour Party leader, Tony Blair, decided to use the song in his party's election campaign. It galvanised the population so much that by 1997 Blair and Labour swept to power, the song delivering the Prime Minister's job into his hands.

Well that's my take on it anyway. The rest, as they say, is history…

Cool Fucking Britannia… You're also welcome… Maybe?

288

15. MAKING INTERNATIONAL MOVES

Things were fun — *loosely* influencing UK elections, running events in London, and putting records into the top of the charts.

But I wanted something a bit more stable, and I found it when I was offered the chance to work for a multimedia company called MasterTone which did most of its business in America.

They asked me to start up and run an imprint label for them, which we imaginatively called MasterDanceTones.

They'd become aware of the fact that the promoters and DJs, who were involved in rave and House music events, were producing bootleg cassettes of the DJ sets being played, and then selling them into independent stores nationwide. They were moving big numbers, especially for the mixes that featured *big name* DJs.

The other reality that they'd noticed, was that this street-level cassette bootleg business was moving relatively big numbers in deliveries and sales. In real terms we're talking anywhere between a min-max number of 1,000-10,000 units. They referred to each cassette as a unit, which was a new term for me.

In my personal opinion, being new to the business, it felt like the use of that word kind of relegated the grand art of a thing down to bare basics. By doing so, they took away the idea of art, and left it simply as a thing, a unit. A unit could literally be a unit of anything, be it a cassette of underground music that captured a cultural phenomenon, or as mundane as a paperclip, a coffee cup, a key chain, a piece of memorabilia. It was all about units, and how many were being moved. And so far as these cassette bootleg units were concerned, they all featured unlicensed music, which meant that they couldn't be sold into traditional, nationwide, worldwide, retail chains because they were illegal "product" — another new use of a word in this music business context.

289

MasterTone wanted to get in on the action. They wanted to do the same thing as the cassette bootleggers, create product and move units, but on a legal basis. They wanted to record DJ mix sessions in a studio, master and produce them on to CD, fully packaged with smart designs, full-colour credit booklets, and get them shipped into major retailers across the UK, Europe, Asia, anywhere in the world, but most of all, all across America.

"Do you think you can handle that for us?"

My answer, as always, was a great big smiley-faced, gigantically positive and enthusiastically confident "Yes I can!"

Look, I was a blagger, it'd gotten me this far — and I learnt quick once on the job. So yes, "Yes I fucking can!"

Of course, in reality, I hadn't got a clue what the job actually entailed, I didn't even know what "licensing a track" really meant. But they were offering me a very good wage, stable employment as a director of a record label inside a decent-sized global multimedia company — it was a "proper job" in the business of the music business.

I had arrived at Destination Zululand, soon enough I was gonna be swinging big in La La Land — but I wasn't nervous, "I'm Packing Silver Bullets Baby".

Before I knew it, I was making deals for the use of tracks with record labels from all over the world, producing loads of CDs for sale to major chain stores, travelling around Europe, and better still, travelling across America on the company dime to source "hot" DJs and produce a more tailored product for the USA.

On the personal front, I was loving life in London's East End. I could hardly believe that I owned a small flat on Commercial Street, just a street over from the world-famous Brick Lane and next door to the equally famous Spitalfields Market. Things with Molly were brilliant. She was never any problem, always great fun and up for anything, never clingy, never attempting to control things: she just rolled with the flow. I had a lot of love for her, these were fun times, everything was going really well.

Working at MasterTone, specifically MasterDanceTones, was amazing. Great people worked there, it was creative in so far as coming up with concepts, but it was mainly focused on moving product. Things were done with business in mind rather than sentiment. This was the business of the music business.

We did projects that featured some of the world's biggest names; The Beatles, Roy Orbison, Ozzfest, The BBC Radio 1 Studio Sessions series, as well as loads of catalogue product — what we would call "stuff". The word stuff was even lower in value than the word unit: it could be classical, marching bands, the sounds of the sixties, whatever. It didn't matter what it was, every piece of product/stuff had a unit cost, a market value, and a profit somewhere in between. We would buy catalogues of music and then compile them over and over again — as I said, it's what we called "stuff".

The only exceptions were the dance label that I ran, and which dealt solely in club/House music and all its sub-genres. And then there was the other special project, the production of various albums by the Three Irish Tenors which sold so many units in America that we even staged a concert at Madison Square Garden in Manhattan, NYC.

What a night that was! It's fair to say that it was a long way from The Staging Post on Whinmoor Way, with mates nicking the Orange amp from the band A Flock Of Seagulls so we would have something to plug our guitars into and practise with. We'd put two guitars and a bass through it at the same time, it was some piece of gear, that Flock Of Seagulls Orange amp! Sorry, Flock of Seagulls, but eternal thanks too. And just to be clear, it weren't me that did it, I weren't even at the gig the night it happened. I originally thought that our next door neighbour, and sometime bassist at the time, Taffy, actually owned it.

It's funny to think, but if somebody hadn't walked out of The Staging Post with that amp, then plugged it in back at

291

Mum's house the next day, we might not have carried on with our first band. Maybe I would have become a bricklayer in Oz with Jim — and then I'd probably have never been involved in staging a gig at the world's most famous arena, MSG, NYC, nor put on the first ever rave at the equally famous Royal Albert Hall in London. Life is a kick, right?

I told the company that I could do even better numbers with the DJ mix CDs if I was actually based in Manhattan. I thought, why not chance my arm and ask. Against all odds, they agreed!

So by Christmas 1999, Molly and I had moved to NYC.

Sadly, James Bullseye Vayne Esq was very old by 1999. He was 18 according to the vet, and by now he was well into a bad losing streak against the still unbeaten Father Time. He was blind, deaf, incontinent, and very, very tired, sleeping his way through his end of days. I was torn up beyond belief, so was Molly, so was anybody who'd had the good fortune to know him, CJ, Dell, Mum, my siblings, everyone. But I took comfort in the idea that the spirit of Vayne was probably running with the pack again, causing chaos down glorious bin-filled back alleys, or barking at the world from an open field, maybe back in Leeds — maybe even in the one where I'd first met him, opposite The Royal Park Pub and the Brudenell live music venue?

I have to say, Molly was a superstar when it came to the last days of my old pal. I still have him in my heart today, his photo is displayed on a particular shelf in my home and I ask him how he's getting along every now and then.

By the turn of the millennium, I was running the MasterDanceTones record label from an office on Broadway — "Yes, I said fucking Broadway!" Every day I had to check I wasn't dreaming. It was hard to compute how far I'd come, especially with all the distractions I'd gladly embraced along the way.

Unfortunately, as much as Molly and I got on together, now I was in NYC I turned into a workaholic. I didn't pay the attention to Molly that I should have. I was now inside my dream life, and I started to resent having to consider her in my day-to-day schedule — all I was interested in was ducking and diving and deal-making, 24/7.

It led to our separation, of course, all completely my fault, my selfishness. She didn't put a foot wrong, she really didn't, but I sent her back to the UK, broke her heart and ended things for no good reason.

She'd been completely loyal, from the night I'd met her to the day I said goodbye. She'd moved from her home in Halifax to live with me in Leeds, then she came to London with me, and from there we moved together to NYC... I should've been much more respectful of her, I should have admired her much more than I did. She deserved it.

But I was self-absorbed, a fool, blind. Not only did I let the boat sail away, I cracked the bottle of champagne across its bow and cast it off into deep water. I regret doing that to her. She didn't deserve it.

She gave me nothing but love. Was cutting her out of my life the biggest mistake I'd made up until that point? Who knows? Everything has consequences, everything happens for a reason. Things have a way of making sense in retrospect, forks in the road turn our journeys into adventures; good ones, bad ones, happy and sad ones too — life is a tapestry.

She did go on to have a full and event-filled life after we parted ways, as separating from me sent her on all kinds of funky tangents of her own. Her biggest prize being her son, her world. Good times came to her, and that makes me smile. I have nothing but happy vibes for her, and in fact our friendship made it through the other side of the chaos I caused.

As things went on I signed up a DJ called Bad Boy Bill to record a DJ mix session. He was introduced to me by the legendary Farley "Jackmaster" Funk when I was visiting him in his hometown of Chicago, The Windy City, where Bill was a massive star. A Bad Boy Bill mix CD would sell close to 100,000 copies in the USA, but he was almost unheard of in the UK, a market he wanted to hit. I promised him a UK tour in return for the rights to make a UK mix CD, but including re-import rights back to the USA through the Best Buy chain, who were the biggest retailers in America.

Bill agreed, and a few weeks later we both flew back to London and toured around the country on a handful of DJ dates. The last show of the tour was in London, and then we'd have three days off before flying back to the States. At the London show in the Yo Yo Mama Sushi Club and Bar Restaurant, a bizarre choice of venue to play, but strangely wonderful, my London office assistant, a lovely girl with a heart of gold, brought her roommate along, a lovely-looking Tunisian girl called Kenzi. We got along great immediately, just clicking and in tune.

It turned out that she was returning to live in her home country and moving in with her mother in four days' time, while I was returning to my apartment in New York in three days' time. After hitting it off so well on that first night, we arranged to meet again the following evening for drinks: we lost control and spent the night together at my hotel.

Then something crazy happened. Don't ask me how or why, but after two nights more together, as I was leaving for the US, I turned around and invited her to come and live with me in Manhattan. Why, I don't know, so don't ask, but I did. It just blurted out of me, maybe it was Jam or Bravado forcing their voice through, I don't know. Who said romance was dead?

She said she was definitely going home for three weeks but added, "If you still want me to come, if you want to take a chance on me, well, sure, I'm up for taking a chance on you too."

There was something so spontaneous about it that I was all in, and literally, a girl I had known for only three nights would soon be living in my New York City apartment, three or four weeks later.

As for the Bad Boy Bill CD, we sold thousands upon thousands of units back to the USA — MasterTone were happy and, more importantly, our biggest client, Best Buy, were over the moon as this gave them a massive foothold into the growing Electronic Dance Music scene in America.

After about a year, my brilliant new life almost came apart at the seams. The two owners of MasterDanceTone's parent company, MasterTone, willfully bust up the group, bagging all the money for themselves along the way.

It was alleged that they cooked the books to show a gigantic loss, and went into voluntary liquidation. The considered opinion of people within the now-broken company was that they'd scarpered off with millions.

The breakdown of the MasterTone company might have been inconvenient for the staff back on home turf in London, but it left me high and dry in NYC, without any cash, without any scraps to feed myself with…

Anybody with experience of knowing those two should have seen it coming. They were what you might call "charming tricksters and con men" — although very interesting dudes, and full of charisma.

One was German, nearly seven feet tall. One of his best moves was when the Berlin Wall came down and East Germany opened back up to rejoin the West. He bought out a CD-pressing plant that had gone bust in the East. Its value was something like a million dollars. However, the West heavily subsidised the purchase to stimulate activity in the old East, so it cost him about $400,000. But this was the genius of the deal; the plant already had two million units of classical music, in fully finished and packaged stock, which he then sold to Best Buy in America for $1 a unit. Best Buy then sold it at $5 a unit and paid us a 20% royalty on their net profit after recouping the $2m in costs that we'd charged them for the stock.

It meant that our company got $2m in advances, and another $1.6m in royalties, ($8mil x 20% = $1.6mil). So, a grand income of $3.6m, minus the $400,000 cost of buying the East German pressing plant, and that's $3.2m of profit, minus a negligible fee for slooooow-boat shipping and import costs. Well, let's just say that it was a *kerching* moment.

Of course the MasterTone company didn't benefit from this business, because the two partners got hold of it and claimed that after all costs, they hadn't made a penny… welcome to the business of the music business.

The other partner, who was even more spicy than the German, was quite famous for two things.

One was putting together a film that claimed to be actual footage of an alien autopsy. It was produced like a documentary with various talking heads arguing for its merits and others arguing it was a fake. It was brilliantly done, and every TV network carried it.

Was it real?

Was it fake?

It didn't matter, it generated millions of pounds.

The second crazy-genius thing he did was when he brought "The Birdie Song" into the lives of the Great British Public, taking an old piece of public domain English music and making it into a massive novelty hit record, again, making a boatload of money in the process.

And yet, somehow, the company went bust.

One more example of how these guys rolled. This one they did together:

They acquired a piano that they claimed had once belonged to John Lennon. They put the word out that it was the piano on which John Lennon had written "Imagine", and it was available to buy as an auction purchase via bids on eBay. The first thing people had in their minds was the white mini grand piano from the famous John and Yoko video. But, it wasn't that piano at all, it was an old, out-of-tune, stand-up piano.

As the auction began, people saw this beat-up thing and began to question the validity, asking questions like, "Why is it an old stand-up and not the white one in the video?"

Their answer was simple: the one in the video is just a prop; this is the actual piano John wrote the song on. They sold the piano for over £100,000, and made the buyer collect and ship it themselves. Things like eBay were brand new when they made that sale.

Maybe it was the real thing, maybe it was simply a piano they had bought in a Liverpool music shop, and perhaps Lennon had tinkled its ivories once upon a time — who knows?

Nobody really questioned it too hard, somebody bought it, I think it might have been an American super-fan collector.

There was a lot to learn from these two super-successful chancers — some good, some bad — but now, I was high and dry in the US, I was out of a job and should have been angry, but I wasn't. Jah was on my side and within days I was picked up by Ichiban to run the 303 Records imprint... Well, you already know how that twist in the road ran.

Things were super-cool with Ichiban/303 Records, but they were Atlanta-based, and kinda stuck in that zone, geographically and musically. There was chat about relocating me down to the Peach State, but I'd come to the US to take a pop at the Big Apple of NYC.

I took a chance and bought a copy of *Billboard Magazine*, hoping that maybe there would be a job for me in the jobs vacant section, and indeed there was. Subliminal Records was looking for a Label & Business Affairs Manager. I'd met the owner earlier in the year at the Winter Music Conference. His name was Erick Morillo, mostly famous for his Reel to Real hit record "I Like To Move It".

I'd organised the official opening party for the WMC in Miami, when Erick showed up at the door with a crew of 10-15 people wanting to get in for free. I heard somebody say, "Look, there's Erick Morillo." Something clicked inside me and I immediately welcomed him like a long-lost brother, even though we'd never met before. I opened the velvet rope and ushered his entire crew through into the club. We exchanged introductions, swapped business cards, and that was about it. I noted his name in case our paths crossed again in the future.

297

Hey presto, when I answered the job advert, I mentioned our previous encounter. It did the job. I was called to meet him at his offices in Weehawken, New Jersey, just one stop out of Manhattan across the Hudson River, and he immediately offered me the position.

We ended up doing great things together over the following five years, including my negotiation of the deal to feature "I Like To Move It" in the blockbuster animated movie *Madagascar*, which was worth millions.

*

So let's have a little recap…

Between 1991 and 1994, I did a lot of great projects at The Leeds Corn Exchange, including promoting the first-ever gig on the Jilted Generation tour by soon-to-be superstars The Prodigy, in Blackpool. I was also involved with two number-one hit records with Tony Di Bart and D:Ream through my management of Cleveland City DJs.

From 1994 to 1999, I did a bag load of cool projects in London, from running a central London Leicester Square nightclub to promoting a major dance music event at the immaculate Royal Albert Hall. I was also at the forefront of producing fully legal DJ mix CDs for high-street shopping. And, of course, I was involved in putting an artist on at Madison Square Garden, for a sold-out show with The Three Irish Tenors. I didn't do much, but I was in the team — and that's close enough for Rock'n'Roll.

Also, in between MasterDanceTones and Subliminal, I ran the 303 record label, financed by the Atlanta Hip-Hop label called Ichiban, where I'd been involved in a Wu-Tang-flavoured compilation, as well as the So Solid Crew-flavoured one, and the Green Velvet alter-ego Cajmere mix CD too. I was super-proud to have signed So Solid Crew to a mix CD project right in the midst of it all — it's a top notch on my belt, and I'm very happy to have it.

It was just a stop-gap piece of employment rather than a long-term deal, but let me just put in a little bit of colour to that detour.

By 2000/2001, I was running the hottest House music label on the planet. It was trendy when I arrived but was on another level entirely once I got the bit between my teeth. I worked tirelessly for Subliminal Records between 2000/2001 and 2005/2006, even delivering a top-15 hit record in the UK with "Shiny Disco Balls" by Who Da Funk. I also played a major part in discovering and showcasing the guys who became dance music superstars Swedish House Mafia.

The Swedish House Mafia story was about fate, chance and rolling the dice. It happened while I was tour-managing Who Da Funk for their appearance on *Top of The Pops*. Had Subliminal Records not had that hit record, and not been invited to make that TV appearance, and had we not stayed in that specific hotel, then me and these crazy Swedes wouldn't have met and wouldn't have set the tone for a friendship and working relationship that became the springboard for their global success just a few years later.

Was I a pivotal part of their story? I believe I am, but you'd have to ask them how they see it from their point of view.

Around 2003, Kenzi and I got married at City Hall, Manhattan. Why did we get married?

There was love involved, and there was a visa involved too as she was Tunisian — and now that she'd finished the MBA course we'd set up for her to do, her US foreign student visa would soon be running out.

Or, maybe we tied the knot because "fickle me" wanted to be able to say "I got married at City Hall, Manhattan, New York City". Getting married there had a charm about it for me, it had a strange old movie romance to it, a Stewart Granger coolness.

Or maybe we felt closer to one another, in love, as we had been through 9/11 in 2001 together, which was as sobering as it was unifying.

It's a day I'll never forget.

I remember seeing the fire department being cheered along their way down the West Side Highway towards

299

Ground Zero. Loads of New Yorkers lined the street, me included, clapping and encouraging, trying to play our part for them. They were in full kit, clean and determined to do their job. Across the highway in the giant warehouses, the hospitals had set up triage stations full of equipment so they could treat the wounded survivors quickly without needing full hospital treatment. They too clapped the firemen down the road to Ground Zero. All kinds of people in uniforms were moving up and down the road that day. We cheered and encouraged anybody who seemed involved in the effort to help. We felt we were part of it too, doing our bit simply by maintaining a sense of positivity, a sense of hope.

By late afternoon, around five o'clock, the atmosphere started to change. A wave of sadness seemed to creep up the highway as the uniformed heroes slowly made their way back towards us, moving away from Ground Zero. Men and women baked in dirt, so battered in dust and debris, head to toe, that most looked like they were made of clay. Only their tear-swollen eyes were visible on their grim beaten faces. A high-ranking medical man made his way across the road and held a conference with his counterpart from the fire brigade. I was quite close to them but couldn't hear the words. I didn't need to hear them. Everything became clear when the top medic returned to his team and gave them the news — there were no survivors.

The saddest thing I have ever witnessed was those doctors and nurses breaking down in tears on the curb of the West Side Highway. Their tears caused some from the fire department to shed their own, and even the cops struggled to hold it together. Us simple folk lining the streets lost it too — lost hope. Some people were wailing, screaming tears, in bits, crying so much that the only description that fit was to call it a river of tears. My tears were there too. I won't delve further into 9/11, other than to say that Kenzi and I lived only about one kilometre, maybe two, away from Ground Zero. It had a massive effect on us in Manhattan that day and it felt even worse for those of us who lived below Fourteenth Street, as Kenzi and I did.

Every year when 9/11 comes around, I feel the emotion of that day.

16. BROS GOSS

As promised a few chapters earlier, here's the full lowdown on my time working with Matt Goss.

Matt and I talked on the phone a couple of times and got along nicely. I'd negotiated a deal for him to put a guest vocal on a track with superstar DJ and House music producer Erick Morillo. It was supposed to be something on the Morillo *My World* album project. Aside from Matt, I also hooked up other guests to participate on the record too — artists like Boy George, Audio Bullys and Sean "Puff Daddy/P Diddy" Combs, as you already know. Matt was into it and we agreed on terms without drama.

Another vocalist I contacted for the album, and even spoke on the phone with about it, was Andrew Eldritch from The Sisters of Mercy. But that conversation went nowhere fast.

He was strictly about the money — no problem with that, but even money-heavy P Diddy was less precious. It's a pity I couldn't seal that deal with Eldritch; it would have felt full circle somehow, but ho-hum, you can't win 'em all.

It was the same with another blast from the past, Marc Almond, AKA the frontman vocalist of the brilliant original electronic duo, Soft Cell.

Even though Marc was open to collaborating on a track for the album, Erick couldn't really grasp what Marc was all about, or who he actually even was. It was a mistake by Morillo to not put in any effort with Marc — I really believed that there was a crossover hit to be delivered from that union.

Given Marc's enthusiasm to do something in House music, I managed to get our Subliminal hit-making duo Who Da Funk together in a London studio with Marc a little later on. Maybe they could find a song between them — or even re-record one of my all time fave Marc Almond/Soft Cell tracks "Memorabilia"?

But, likewise with Erick, the New Jersey born Who Da Funk duo were just as ignorant as Erick was as to who and what Marc Almond was — they had no idea of his standing in the music world overall. They missed the opportunity I'd put in their hands, neither of the Subliminal artists even bothered to research Marc's discography — all they could hear was a strange voiced off-kilter vocal, which they dismissed as "not very good".

Ho-hum, you can't win 'em all, and sometimes you can't even win just one of 'em.

Matt Goss lived in LA, but he was visiting NYC with his fiancée, the fabulous Latina MTV star Daisy Fuentes, who had her own deals to take care of around town. So while she was out, he invited me to meet him. Once there, we had a beer, chatted about the Erick Morillo project for a while, and then, surprisingly, he began to tell me about his life over the past few years, and his current situation as far as being an active artist. It quickly became clear that he had been struggling in his career; doors weren't opening for him in the same way they had back when he and his twin brother were delivering hit after hit to the top of the UK charts and beyond. He wasn't hurting for money; his royalty cheques must have still been paying dividends. But career-wise he was running into walls.

I liked him right away. He was a nice guy, obviously passionate and still ambitious despite the gigantic success and the heavy fall from the spotlight he'd experienced. Matt Goss was hungry for more: "I've been writing some songs, do you want to hear them?" he asked me. I expected him to put a CD on the stereo, but instead, he grabbed his acoustic guitar from the other room, returned to his sofa and began strumming and singing his songs.

We were two feet from each other, face to face. I'll be honest, it was an incredible moment to experience, because, despite his popstar background and his music style, he has an incredible voice, and he was singing with it at full volume, right up close, in my face — he sounded amazing.

303

On top of that, he is a fantastically handsome man, with piercing blue eyes that were fixed right on me, without blinking. His is a perfectly symmetrical face, like a work of art — I didn't know whether to shake his hand as the song ended or give him a kiss. It was a mesmerising performance.

The only vocal I have heard that was as enthralling at such close quarters was when one of The Three Irish Tenors sang for a private table of ten in a Hell's Kitchen steakhouse after the show we held with them at Madison Square Garden. Of course, that was a few years earlier when I was still working for MasterTone.

Anyway, after I'd finished complimenting Matt on his voice and his songs, he asked me right away, "Would you consider being my manager?"

Now I knew he was on his arse, it was a "Hail Mary throw" from him. Even though I had done well for myself in the dance music industry, and by now I was running Subliminal Records, the world's number-one House music label, I had no experience managing a celebrity popstar like Matt Goss from Bros. In my mind, I was still this council kid from Whinmoor, deep at heart, at least, and basically I'd found a way to make a career using only my wits, desire, self-belief — it was just a load of bullshit and bollocks, just bluffing my way through from job to job in roles I had absolutely no real experience, qualifications or know-how in.

Somehow I'd been getting away with it, and each time I moved jobs and companies I just seemed to glide upwards. I'd gone from Leeds to London to NYC, and eventually I would land in Ibiza too. And here was Matt Goss from Bros asking me if I'd be his manager.

Of course, you already know the answer I gave him: "Sure, I think I can do a lot for you, Matt, I'll get you back in the public eye. Let's do it!" And with that, we shook hands and I was now the manager of the '80s pop superstar Matt Goss from Bros. I'd work out how to actually do it as we went along, but I was in for 20% of the net on whatever revenue streams I opened up.

304

The first thing I did for Matt was get him out of a terrible deal he had signed with a management and production team in LA — I basically told them to stick the contract they had with Matt "where the sun don't shine", so far as we were concerned the deal was null and void because they had sat on their hands for two years, letting him fester away, and had not been acting in the best interests of their client.

I was just trying it on with them, shaking the tree to see what would rattle loose — and to my surprise they put up very little resistance to me, whereas according to Matt they had been making his life hell and refusing to let him walk.

Maybe it was my Northern English Leeds accent, or maybe it was the colourful "listen, you set of fucking robbing cunts" turn of phrase and words used, coupled with a kind of Peter Grant attitude and tone, or it could have been the fact that I was "an Englishman calling from New York", and that gave them a sixth-sense feeling along the lines of "Ufff, he must be a proper player".

Whatever it was, they decided something along the lines of, "Fuck this shit, we've not managed to do anything with Matt for two years, apart from invest money without any return, let's call it quits and move on rather than go to war with this English douchebag in New York."

I don't know what swung things. Maybe they were looking for a way out so that the next agreed advance to Matt wouldn't be payable (but let's not entertain that thought, eh?). Whatever the truth of it, they folded, Matt was ecstatic, and massively impressed. So much so, that he decided to refer to me as The Farmhouse, which, for him, represented some kind of symbol of strength, and protection, like I would give him shelter from the storm — it was a compliment, and I took it as one.

Matt's twin brother, Luke, was also living in LA; he had reinvented himself as a movie star and was doing really well, notching up plenty of roles as either the main support or the lead. Matt and Luke had gone from being joined at the hip, twin brothers and massive popstars, to cutting themselves off from each other completely — literally not speaking for years — which I thought was pretty tragic. Never mind anything else, they were still brothers, twins — but it was what it was.

I think Matt was jealous that Luke had forged a new career and was making a proper success of it. He had also resisted any overtures to get the band back together for a lucrative concert tour or album, leaving Matt alone with the memories but not much else. It was hard for their mother — she loved them both the same and they were both very close to her, but she knew Matt needed a lot of attention and gave him as much as he would call for.

Matt is an amazing white-soul, pop vocal talent. His voice is truly something special and he is a very good songwriter, much better than he gets credit for. It's no mean feat to write hit pop music, but he had done it time and time again. The only part of his career I couldn't get involved with was the publishing side — the simple reason being that he was already signed to a major publishing deal for his songwriting, including the back catalogue of his big hits. I'd say the royalties from his old records were keeping his bank balance healthy. You see, artists may come and go depending on which way the wind's blowing, but the songs, they keep right on working forever. Now, money is one thing, and when you've got a fair bit, it's no longer the driver, but fame, relevance, that's another matter. And the thing was, Matt Goss was a popstar, and he wanted to be back in the public eye again. What Matt was really asking was, "When Will I Be Famous, Again?"

He wanted to make it in the USA, but I knew we needed to reset him in the UK first — that was always going to be his main market, where all those original teenage fans would now be housewives or divorced single mothers, with grown-up or teenage kids of their own. The first thing to do was to rekindle that massive sleeping fan-base of now older ladies, as well as pulling their kids in too. Matt said he was "open to doing whatever it takes" — I took him at his word and set about it.

This stuff with Matt was all going on at the same time that I was running Subliminal Records for Erick Morillo, which included the Puff Daddy episode, as well as multiple club hit records we were working on, like: Gadjo - "So Many Times", Herd & Fitz - "I Just Can't Get Enough", Praise Cats - "Shined On Me",' Dero ft. Leee John from Imagination - "Illusion", Macy Gray - "Sexual Revolution", Junior Jack - "Thrill Me", or Erick Morillo & The Audio Bullys - "Break Down The Doors".

That's just a very small sample of Subliminal Records titles that were monster dance-floor bombs that rocked clubs and DJ booths worldwide.

We had well over fifty consecutive bangers in the House music world. And for each hot record, I'd license them to over twenty other labels and countless compilations too.

It's strange to think that just a few years earlier all I knew about running a record label was being involved in the A&R of a small independent underground vinyl label, and managing a couple of "shit-hot" producer/DJs.

I knew nothing about licensing music, or what it even actually meant. But now I was the head honcho in the game, looking out for all the licensing contracts, business affairs and actual label management of what was by now the hottest and most successful House music label on the planet.

We'd also had some crossover hit success, the most notable being the top-15 UK national chart position of the Who Da Funk hit record "Shiny Disco Balls".

The chart position of that record earned us an appearance on the legendary *Top Of The Pops* TV show, a music program that everybody in Britain and beyond had grown up watching.

Kids all over the UK would take their places in front of the TV, complete with cassette players ready to record the hits.

Every Thursday night, since its first episode was broadcast on January 1st, 1964, when I wasn't even two months old, this TV show dominated the weekly ratings. I'll take an odds-on guess that my mum would've had me sat in front of the old tiny black & white TV, bouncing on her knee, while the whole house watched it.

I never imagined that one day I'd be walking one of the artists I was involved with through the doors of the BBC Television Centre studios in London, loading them on to the actual *Top Of The Pops* stage itself. I wished that cuntish non-believing, unhelpful, careers adviser could have been there to see me that day — her idea of "my fantasy" was now "my reality".

Look at me now, missus, serve me up an ice-cold glass of champagne, and let's talk about the business of the music business!

I also met the two young producers/DJs, Steve Angello and Sebastian Ingrosso at our hotel in London that night. They were unknown, just grafting and trying to get signed, a couple of rum lads from Stockholm who were up for a drink and a laugh, and were big fans of Subliminal Records and Erick Morillo.

I took their demos back to the Weehawken offices in New Jersey and forced Morillo to sign two of their tracks from the many they had submitted. I was rewarding their effort more than anything. I also told Erick we should give them another break by letting them record a mix CD for the label, and on top of that, we should showcase them at our Miami Winter Music Conference event — as well as putting them on our Summer Ibiza lineups. He reluctantly agreed.

Steve Angello and Sebastian Ingrosso would soon become Swedish House Mafia, along with their other pal, Axwell. They got so big — so quickly — that they would headline their own show at Madison Square Garden and sell it out purely on the strength of their brand name.

All of that success happened for them not long after our first fateful meeting during that *Top Of The Pops* adventure with Who Da Funk…

You're very welcome, boys. You all deserve every slice of success you have carved out in your incredible careers, jointly and severally.

It didn't take very long from when I'd first joined Subliminal Records to reset the internal mentality of the company, and start running this very cool independent label almost like a major.

I created multiple surrogate Subliminal labels all over the world, and soon enough each third party label working with us began cannibalising their own product, with our much sexier Subliminal product becoming more important than their own label's branded releases.

It hadn't been done before in House music, but it was an obvious move to me.

I was either a music business *genius* — or simply naive and getting away with it.

Whatever it was, it worked. We were flying. At the same time, the touring side of the business just went from strength to strength. Morillo's DJ fees started going through the roof. He became the most in-demand DJ on the planet and the best-paid, earning football star wages.

Erick had been active in Ibiza proper since 1997, with Subliminal sharing a residency with another record label for a few years, Darren Emerson's Underwater.

Then, by 2001/2002, we all felt that Subliminal were ready to hold a night down on the White Island under our own banner and commit fully to summers in Ibiza. All the activity we had worked on with the label led to us securing a massive Wednesday Night Subliminal Records residency in the world's most famous and iconic House music club, Pacha in Ibiza. It was all courtesy of the club's visionary Music Director, Danny Whittle, who believed in us as much as we did.

The tiny island in the Mediterranean Sea off the coast of Spain was the global Mecca of dance music — and Pacha was its shining jewel. And, in so far as business goes, let's put it this way: if you could break a track, a party, or a DJ in Ibiza during the summer season, it meant that you'd more than likely broken worldwide as well. Ibiza and Pacha were *that* influential on the global House music scene. The success we had on the White Isle further elevated the label's music, the artists we looked after, and the star of the show himself Erick Morillo to the status of bona fide superstar DJ.

We were in Ibiza for the long haul and life was rocking. We felt like kings of the entire House music scene. One more nod of appreciation must go out to the incredible Danny Whittle for helping us achieve all that we did in Ibiza — he actually went on to do the same for quite a few others who were lucky enough to find themselves in his incredibly wise Pacha Ibiza hands.

*

So, while all that Subliminal stuff was going on, I was also working on the Matt Goss project on my own time. I convinced an old friend, Max Bloom, who had a label in dance music but whose personal history was in crossover pop music, to take a chance on the reset of Matt Goss. He was reluctant but curious and the idea of reaping the rewards of a proper Matt Goss revival of fortunes had him smelling the potential odour of cash. I could hear his "private" thinking process as loud as thunder in my own head.

"OK, let's roll the dice, but let's roll with a strict, controlled budget. I'm not a major label with major label money. I'm an independent with limited budgets. But we will make Matt our priority artist, and his album will be our priority project — if Matt will put the work in. Remember, we're starting at street level, we're not at Wembley, but we're willing to give it a go."

Matt couldn't believe that somebody was willing to take a chance on his new collection of songs, rather than simply wanting him to regurgitate his classic catalogue.

310

We agreed a deal.

A couple of months later, we had set up a tour. It was an awful tour for a star like Matt Goss to have to do — basically a chain of bars/clubs/restaurants dotted all over the country, most of them without even a proper stage. Sometimes he would literally be standing on top of a bar. This is a guy who had sold out Wembley Stadium in the past — hence the reference to Wembley by Max when pitching his deal. It must have been a brutal comedown for him, but credit where credit's due; he performed and sang his heart out as if he was in front of 80,000 at Wembley Stadium.

The reality was clear though: even in those low-end, no-credibility venues, there was an audience for him. Every single one of those shows was packed out with almost-middle-aged teenagers, still wetting or creaming their knickers at the sight and sound of Matt Goss — and they'd brought their adult teenage daughters, who looked like they were getting as giddy as their mums.

As crap as the venues were, they still had capacities of around 1,000 pax per night. We played something like twenty dates, and all of them were busting at the seams.

That hard, paying-your-dues tour led to his first newspaper headlines in more than a decade. Matt had sucked up the negatives, didn't moan along the way, stayed focused on the positives, and did his job. I loved him for that — it can't have been easy for him.

Then a stroke of luck. A new celebrity-led TV program came along, *Hell's Kitchen*, starring well-known shouty chef Gordon Ramsay. The basic premise was that a group of celebrities would stay in a building for a few weeks, learn to cook brilliant food, and deliver quality dishes to a restaurant of invited guests. The real show was watching the celebrities make it through the weeks with multiple cameras set up to record everything — their images, actions, reactions to stress, etc. As the tour had generated features in the press for Matt, he fit the criteria required by the production team. He was a prime candidate for what they were looking for — a

311

household name that wasn't at his peak but could *potentially* make a comeback.

Peter Andre was another '80s girly-heart-throb who had been a big popstar at one stage of his career, but he had faded almost out of sight for years until he did a similar type of TV show called *I'm A Celebrity, Get Me Out Of Here*. He became famous again from that show and even managed to generate another No 1 record off the back of it, and in so doing re-ignited his entire career. ITV and *Hell's Kitchen* were hoping for a similar result from Matt Goss — if they could sign him up.

Matt was adamant that he didn't want to do it. It was the first time he had pushed back and said, "No, let's pass on that."

I knew that refusing the opportunity would be a mistake, and that this TV show was a surefire way to get him fully back in the public eye. It would also be enough to trigger the new comeback album that Matt was obsessed with getting done.

A big TV show like this would mean that we could roll out our single release, alongside the show's promotion, and perfectly time the album release into the market in cahoots with major retailers. I'm not sure Matt understood the attention he would garner from having an involvement in *Hell's Kitchen*, or maybe he did, but it wasn't the kind of celebrity-based promotion he wanted. All I knew was that the benefits of promotion — pre, during, and post the TV show itself — were massively valuable, and the chance to put Matt straight into the living rooms of a massive audience of Matt Goss housewives across the UK was too good to miss.

The TV producers offered a good fee. I got them to raise it twice more. Matt would be the best-paid celebrity taking part if he agreed. Because I knew Matt didn't want to be on the show, I could push harder in negotiations and ask for anything I wanted — a win-win situation. No deal and Matt would be relieved; a big deal and Matt would be happy — if he finally agreed to do the show.

I had to gently sell the project to him, while distracting him with things that I knew he actually did want to do. To that end, we set up another tour, this time in some decent sized credible venues, including a few theatres that were carrying capacities of around 2,000 pax or more.

This tour was infinitely better with fixed fees, tour support from the label, good hotels, and a professional road crew — it was a proper Band On Tour situation, which he liked a lot. He liked it even more when I got Richard Steele from the band Spacehog to be his touring guitarist. He was a superbly gifted Rock'n'Roll axe-man who could rock out and add grit to Matt's general soulful pop sound. Given that Matt was somewhat obsessed with wanting to be credited as a serious artist, and seen as a "geezer, just one of the lads", the Richard Steele move was a textbook act of stealth. I was proud of myself... "Who's a clever fucker then?" Jam and Bravado spoke in harmony for once. Then the cherry on top — I got the record label to agree to bring Matt's LA session band over to do the tour rather than hold session auditions and then try to get a scratch band of strangers in shape for such a key UK tour. It was a big cost to take on for Max Bloom, even if it was recoupable from the fixed fees — but when I announced the news to Matt, he was ecstatic, but more importantly, he was happily distracted.

On top of all that good stuff — decent venues for a credible UK tour, flying in the LA band, and adding Richard Steele — we also set up daily access to a top-class professional rehearsal room, got decent digs for the musicians to base themselves in and also set Matt up in a super-cool flat in Knightsbridge, just next door to his favorite shopping venue, Harrods.

Matt was happy as Larry, and was focused on his upcoming tour dates, which had been set up via an old mate of mine from the MasterTone days, a lad called Richard Smith.

I just want to make a point of order here...

Matt gives Richard a much bigger role in the story of his reset in his autobiography, *More Than You Know*, than Richard actually played. To be clear. I was the manager. I put Richard in as his booking agent, via the Mission Control Agency. I made the record deal with Max Bloom to sign Matt up to his Concept label. I pulled in the publicity company, Emms, via my relationship with its owner, Stephen Emms, who I'd worked with on the Who Da Funk hit record and other tracks. I got Mr Goss out of his shitty LA management deal. I recouped the rights to tracks he had recorded for Universal in America. I told him we could — and would — sell out the Shepherds Bush Empire in London, even without any product in the market. And so on, and so on, and so on. Just saying.

I'm raising this point because in his book, he doesn't quite tell the story as it went down. He elevates the roles of Richard and Max, while sidelining my role to a couple of lines: "My manager at the time was Steve, brought up in Leeds but based in New York, and he came back to the UK with me. We often used to say the phrase 'coming back guerrilla style' — it was nice to have somebody like Steve who believed we didn't need a record deal to fill Shepherds Bush Empire. The funny thing is, doing that tour without a deal was liberating." And then he gives me one other line: "Richard, along with his colleague Steve." Well, that wasn't accurate: Richard was the agent for the live shows, an associate, but not a colleague in a management team.

Nothing would have happened for Matt at that moment in time had I not pulled all the moving parts together, had I not convinced Richard, Max, Emms, etcetera, to all run with the ball, and believe in the project.

But I'm digressing…

I had it worked out in my head that if I played my cards right, I'd have him in the media spotlight throughout his 2003 UK summer tour, then we'd get him straight into the studio to record his album. By winter I'd set up the release dates and promo campaigns for his singles, and all that would fall nicely for the album to land just as he went in/came out of the national TV show, *Hell's Kitchen*, in the summer of 2004.

With all that activity, including non-stop press and media snippets, reviews and features, he would be a relevant and active popstar.

Matt Goss would be what he wanted to be — famous all over again.

My plan was to give Matt 12 months in the spotlight, and after that, assuming the singles had been hits and the album had moved proper units, then I'd get him signed up to a major record label, get straight back in the studio to record a second comeback album, and be in a position to really hit the heights in 2005.

But, I knew that getting him signed up and committed to doing *Hell's Kitchen* was the key to everything.

I never told Matt this, but his mother took me aside after the incredibly successful theatre tour and its wonderful finale blockbuster at Shepherds Bush Empire, which was sold out completely and generated fantastic reviews. Well, she says to me, "I can't say anything to him one way or the other. I have to support whatever he says about it, but I'm asking you now, whatever he says, or even if I seem to agree with him, know this: I want you to make him do that *Hell's Kitchen* show, whatever it takes. Promise me you will."

She knew, the same as me, it was the way to open the door to the possibilities of everything.

"I promise you, he'll do that show. You have my word on it." She was a wonderful lady, a truly beautiful human being.

Then we got another bit of great news, something that was going to help the plan move along at a rate of knots. The Shepherds Bush Empire gig had created such a commotion that Mariah Carey's promoters, Harvey Goldsmith, contacted us and invited Matt to support Mariah on her UK arena tour in September of 2003. The biggest thrill was that it included a date at Wembley Arena — Matt was ecstatic.

I told him that he'd be back to headline Wembley Arena under his own name within 12 months. I also told him that

315

he'd play at Wembley Stadium itself within 18-24 months —
if he signed up for the TV show.

He politely ignored the comment, but we agreed to do the
Mariah Carey tour, which probably went better for Matt Goss
than it did for her.

The comeback single, "I'm Coming With Ya", was
released in November and charted at number 22 on the UK
National Charts. It was a top-40 hit, his highest chart position
in 12 years, in fact it was his first chart position in almost
eight. He was so proud, we all were — and what's more,
we'd done it without the support of any Radio 1 heavy
rotation or even any light playlisting. Instead, we'd been
forced to go the more difficult route and we'd done it with the
support of the regional radio stations. Matt had talked to
maybe 200 stations, ran competitions, did guest appearances,
phone-ins and everything else that was asked of him. He put
the graft in, and even though Radio 1 weren't supporting us,
despite their refusal to show him the rightful respect that his
name, standing and history was worth, it didn't matter — we
had fashioned a top-40 hit record without them (a top-22
record to be accurate) and it felt good, it felt *Punk*.

We'd done it guerrilla style, fully independent. We'd had
Radio 1 over, we'd beaten them, and it was a well won
legitimate battle — we soaked ourselves in the result.

To have a hit without Radio 1 showed that we had a real
audience — and not just their rotation hype. We received a
phone call that we had hoped for, but had not believed would
come through — *Top of the Pops* invited Matt Goss to
perform the single on the show. He had done this show 15
times during his heyday, and he honestly thought he would
never get back there again. But here he was, after one year
working with me, looking at his 16th appearance on the
iconic show. Even better, for Matt, this success had been
achieved as an independent artist, he felt credible — it was
his music working for him, rather than simply his image, or
hype and promotion. To say that he was happy would have
been a gigantic understatement.

316

Other Artists also booked on to that show included the legendary Pet Shop Boys and the super-hot American act The Black Eyed Peas. After the broadcast had gone out the viewing figures came in — and the numbers confirmed that the audience was up by over two million on the previous week's.

Matt Goss had made the difference, he felt like he was back… and I felt like I was becoming vital.

I kept my word to Matt's mum. Eventually, he enthusiastically agreed to go on to *Hell's Kitchen*. On signing contracts, he was all in. He aimed to stay in the programme for the full duration; the last three would be enough to stay the course and get maximum exposure for his trouble. ITV paid the entire advance up front; Matt Goss was their *star name* — the viewing figures were great and Matt actually did come in third, managing to stay on the show from start to finish. Taking part in *Hell's Kitchen* was the final trigger for Max Bloom to green-light the release date of the album, which we set up to drop as soon as possible after the show was scheduled to end.

We'd recorded a very good Matt Goss album in between touring, having a hit single, and getting Matt in shape to go on the TV show. The album is called *The Early Side of Later* and it's probably one of Matt's proudest musical moments.

He got to record an album, purely for the sake of making good music, without the pressure of chasing hits.

If hits were to come, then great, but that wasn't the driver, that wasn't the demand.

Sure, the budget should recoup, if possible. And it'd be even better, if we could do better than just recoup. Recouping, and more, is always good — but this wasn't formula popstar music. It was Matt finally being an artist, because no matter what opinion anybody might have of him, that's exactly what he is — a talented and gifted musical artist and songwriter.

In the meantime, we delivered another top-40 hit single, "Fly", which reached number 31 in the national charts. And although we didn't do *Top Of The Pops* this time, it was

317

enough of a result to get Matt invited on to all the daytime TV shows that ran on the national TV stations across the UK.

At the same time, I had him do a couple of tracks for the House music scene, with an Italian artist named Minimal Chic. Both successfully topped all the club charts across Britain and Europe, and one of them even charted at number 55 on the UK national chart as well — which was an unexpected bonus result.

We were really on a roll.

Being truthful, Matt's music wasn't my music, it wasn't Punk-Rock'n'Roll and it wasn't House music either, regardless of the Minimal Chic club hit. But the thing about Matt was that he was always pretty honest with himself, about the music he wrote — which was generally very well-crafted pop-soul-rock.

And Matt's vocals are undeniably good, incredible at times, especially on *The Early Side of Later* album, which was a collection of fabulously crafted songs that he now had on CD under his own name.

It had been impressive to see the songs on the album take shape. From that first meeting in NYC, with him singing them into my face from two feet away, they now existed as a piece of product in the marketplace, as a measure of manufactured units.

I must admit, bizarre as it may sound, it was quite an emotional moment to hold the album in my hand once it was fully delivered.

Going on *Hell's Kitchen* was his best decision in years. The public showed they loved him by keeping him inside the show right through to the final three. Aside from giving Matt a lovely stroke to his ego — as a career move he'd had three weeks of constant day-to-day promotion coverage to a massive TV audience of housewives, many of them ex-Brossettes — he had come over brilliantly in the show. The public were interested in getting to know him all over again, and the best part was — Matt Goss really is a genuine geezer, with a big heart. Let me give you an example…

One day, we were hanging out at the Knightsbridge flat. At that time I used to wear three gold earrings through one piercing in my left ear — nothing special, there was no value to them and no sentimental story behind them either.

Matt had noted it all the way back when we'd first met in the plush NYC hotel, asking me why I had three rings in one hole. I didn't blink: "Once a Punk, always a Punk." Fast forward to the London flat, and Matt comes over to me, and just helps himself in taking out my three cheap gold earrings.

It's an odd thing to do, but I'm not vexed — I'm willing to let the scene play out. Next thing, he takes a small, beautiful, diamond-encrusted, rich-gold single ring out of his own ear and clips it into my now empty pierced one.

It's a beautiful earring that's worth some dough. I'll tell you a secret — I've never taken it out since that day. If you bumped into me in the street right now, it'd probably be the first thing you notice. I don't wear it for sentimental reasons, I'm not somebody who really has a thing for jewellery. It stays where it is because I've never had a reason to take it out, it replaced the old three, and so there it hangs: but I do like it. Anyway, that's the kinda guy Matt is — sometimes.

All the Matt Goss exposure brought people out of the woodwork. Everybody wanted to work with him now. After not giving a damn for the best part of a decade, they suddenly thought he was great again.

Peter Andre's managers approached him, a male–female power couple double act, with a meeting over dinner arranged with Matt, myself and them. It became clear to me within a few seconds that Matt had already spoken with them before this get-together; it was a set-up for Matt to announce that he was dropping me to go with them. I must admit, I was sadly surprised that Matt would be so quick to jump ship at the first sight of a shiny penny, but he did.

I could have said, "Well, sure Matt, you can have these guys looking out for you, you can drop me. But don't forget to pay me my 20%, we are contracted together."

319

I could've sat there and sung the old football chant to them, "Where were you, where were you, where were you when he was shit, where were you when he was shit?"

I could have asked Matt if he had forgotten that after the best part of a decade in the music industry wilderness, with not one person giving a rat's arse about him, that it was me who had gotten him out of a soul-crushing, career-stagnating, mismanagement deal in LA. That it was me who had secured him a booking agent, a publicist, a record label, that it was me that had caused tours to happen, features in newspapers and appearances on TV programs to happen, including three weeks on a peak-hour show…

I could've pointed out that I had been the puppetmaster who'd given him the team to deliver two top-40 hit singles, an album and two House music club hits — not forgetting, God forbid, the emotional return to *Top of the Pops*, as well as a sold-out Shepherds Bush Empire show and a Wembley Arena gig with Mariah Carey. And never mind that I had also delivered a book deal "to tell his story"…

In short, all the good stuff that had happened to him over these past 15 months or so had been caused, plotted, manipulated, and delivered by me, the Mother Fucking Farmhouse.

I could have stood up, created a scene, made a grand speech: "Did you forget that your dream of making a credible artist album might never have happened but for me Matt? Or that your career might still be stuck on hold, stinking up a toilet somewhere back in LA, but for me — maybe?"

But I didn't. I didn't have time for people who would cut you loose for the shiny penny at such a quick drop of the hat. I was disappointed in him, but I wasn't mad at him. Those people — I can take 'em or leave 'em each time. I just looked him in the eye, smiled and said: "Go with God, Matt. You're back, and you're gonna do great."

At the end of the day, I guess I wasn't as vital as I thought I was, and Matt wasn't as nice as I believed him to be —

notwithstanding the kind and generous gift he gave me of the beautiful, diamond-encrusted, gold earring.

So far as the book deal we delivered, the ghost-writer, biographer Martin Roach — a lovely fella — wrote it up quickly. Matt got to tell his story without any input or influence from anybody but himself. Once it was released, it became an instant bestseller, as I had said it would: you're welcome, fella.

Since my resetting Matt and putting him back in the game, he has gone from strength to strength.

I don't think he stayed with Peter Andre's managers for long, but due to his improved profile in the UK, and his own pure talent and desire, Matt managed to land a residency in Las Vegas, a one-man show on the world-famous Strip.

Somebody was very smart with that move; they have a massive Brit audience of middle-aged tourists over there, including the "Matt Goss Housewives".

Matt got hired, delivered a spectacular show, singing classics and standards, and became spectacularly successful as a Vegas showman.

So successful, that his show ran for over a decade, becoming one of the most popular events on the Strip.

At the same time, Matt's brother Luke had continued with his successful rebirth as a Hollywood actor. He was being cast in more headline roles, after delivering well-on a whole bunch of strong supports and cameos.

Both brothers had proved that they were each, individually more than just Matt & Luke Goss from Bros, which, ironically, led to them producing a one-off reunion show as Bros in London.

But it was more than a one-off show; the project saw them also make a documentary set against the backdrop of a 20,000 sold-out gig at the wonderful London O2 Arena. It was a massive success, and the documentary won a bunch of awards too.

The show itself was a stunning piece of then-and-now storytelling, and it cemented Matt as an icon of British popular culture.

Matt also signed up to participate in one of the biggest Shows on TV in the UK, *Strictly Come Dancing*. It's a mark of how far he has come back into the public domain.

Matt is a bona fide star, as he should be. I'm proud of him, and I'm proud of the work we did together, despite anything and everything, and how it ended as quickly as it had begun.

I am probably forgotten from his story by now. I'll take a guess and predict that I'm not even a line of memory in any updated version of his autobiography these days.

What can I say… that's the business of the music business, folks.

*

Things didn't go so well for Erick Morillo in the long run. When we split up our working relationship there was no way of knowing what the future held for us both.

Erick was one of the top ten DJs in the world when we went our separate ways. I moved to Ibiza and took on the massive role of Multimedia Director for the Pacha Group, with plans to repeat the successful game-plan I had concocted and delivered for Subliminal…

Create catalogue, exploit the product, both as individual releases and as tracklisting tunes on multiple mix CDs, as well as negotiating licensing & label contracts on a global basis — I had devised a method for success.

Before long, I was arranging Pacha Recordings label showcase events all around the world: we were taking off quickly.

Then, through sheer frustration with the label's DJs, namely that they wouldn't deliver Pacha catalogue-based DJ sets at the Pacha Recordings branded parties that we were booked in to, I decided to learn how to DJ myself, so that I could play the shows, under the alias name of DJ SYX. But, before getting deeper into that, let's just close things off with Erick.

322

For reasons unknown, the man who had the world seemingly within his grasp started to get more and more into drugs. Simple party drugs and social drugs to start with, things like MDMA, or E's, as they are known, found their way past his natural "work work work" defences, and straight to the top of his daily routine. He couldn't get enough of the buzz, and was bringing about a change in himself — and who he wanted to be.

Erick was having a wild time of it — and by that I mean he was having a wild time of it with anyone who wanted to have a wild time of it too. I'm not talking about partying with the people from the Subliminal team. He suddenly surrounded himself with all kinds of waifs and strays and hanger-ons — one week this group of dickheads, the next week another group, until soon enough he had a group of different dickheads set up all over the world.

Meanwhile, the Serious Businessman was sidelined, given a leave of absence, consigned to a tiny seat all the way back in the smallest corner of the furthest compartment inside the Superstar's head. It was a whirlwind of non-stop partying inside the greatest clubs, the best hotels, and the most amazing villas to be had — all over the globe.

The partying became more important to him than the Subliminal Records label. Don't blame me, don't blame the Subliminal family — none of us could even get near him, he was always somewhere else and out of contact, and, no surprise, things started to grind to a halt.

He moved to Miami as his main residence, buying a big villa in a swanky neighbourhood of millionaires. He also bought a super-impressive pad that was built into the side of the mountains overlooking LA. Smooth spy James Bond, or more likely smooth US spy Matt Helm, would've lived there if they'd been real people and not just over-the-top movie characters. That's how epic that pad was. Plus, he still had his Manhattan skyline view Weehawken apartment in NJ, and of course he also had a massive villa in a gated community in Ibiza.

As a DJ, he was in demand all over the world. He was on a non-stop binge of gigs, parties, girls and drugs; he was living high in the saddle — right up until the kind of drugs he was taking, inevitably, got more serious.

Eventually, he was shooting up ketamine, lots of it — something I had never imagined him ever doing: Erick Morillo shooting up shit? You couldn't have predicted it. But that was the reality, and it got so bad that he ended up hospitalised and nearly losing his arm: in fact, nearly losing everything.

At some point, the owners of the Pacha Group put the DJ & event bookings of Pacha nightclub in Ibiza itself on to my desk as well. Because, in their ridiculous wisdom, they'd decided to create a falling-out with the incredible Danny Whittle.

Danny, being an ex-military man, and an ex-fireman, was a guy of proper standing — he wasn't gonna take bullshit from anyone, and decided to walk.

Hey presto, all Danny's jobs landed on me.

One of the first things they told me to do was to drop Erick Morillo and Subliminal Sessions from their weekly roster of summer parties. After 13 seasons, that's 13 years, they just wanted him gone, and it was my job to deliver the news and replace him. It didn't go over well with Erick and it was a horrible experience for me. I argued with the family that owned Pacha and tried to make them see it made no sense to drop Subliminal, it was a fantastic event and a great moneymaker. I have to point out, at this stage I had no idea that Erick was shooting ketamine, that all came out a little while later.

If I'd known he was shooting ketamine I would have been the first to say let him go, because there's no way you can invest millions in someone when they're investing thousands into shooting ket into their veins.

Regardless of everything, personal feelings aside, at the end of the day, I was being paid a massive salary, it was my job to act for the company and deliver what they wanted. They wanted Erick out, they paid the bills, and I did my job.

Erick took it very badly. We spent three days on the telephone from Miami to Ibiza. He went through every emotion with me, from anger to tears, threats to bribes. The Subliminal Sessions season at Pacha Ibiza meant a lot to him, in fact it meant everything to him. But Pacha was adamant, so the decision held up and Erick was out.

A few weeks later, I got word that Erick was so far gone on drugs that he had been escorted out of the DJ booth during a prestigious gig he was supposed to play. This was unheard of for Morillo, and was a scandal across the entire scene because Erick had always been regarded as a top professional who always delivered an amazing set... The wheels were coming off and the whole industry could now see it.

Soon we heard that he was under physical and psychological supervision, badly affected in everything he was doing by the ketamine he was shooting. Inside Pacha, the feeling was "We dodged a bullet". Not by me though; I was worried for his health and life. I knew a thing or two about how destructive shooting drugs could be. My underlying feeling was nothing but empathy.

Miraculously, after many false starts, Erick finally turned the dial around. Kicking the drugs and focusing on reinventing himself as a more underground and edgy DJ, he got himself a manager and an agent to set him in a new direction. And things were going well. He was making new fans and becoming underground cool beans, building brick by brick into a new phase of his career. Until the roof came tumbling down again — Morillo was accused of sexual battery.

An incident happened at his place in Miami, and he was accused of and charged with a terrible crime. If found guilty, the sentence could be 15 years or more in jail. The thought of jail for Morillo would have been the stuff of nightmares. One night would be too much, he wasn't mentally built that way to stand doing time locked up as a criminal, especially as a sex-crime criminal.

Now, I don't know what happened that night. And what little I do know about it, I don't believe it's my place to share or pontificate on as it's third party chit-chat, comment and gossip. All I know is that I worked alongside him for nearly seven years and never heard of anyone making accusations about him during that time. Many strong women also worked alongside him and they too never heard anything or accused him of anything. On the other hand, since he was accused, up to ten other women came forward and have made similar claims about him. What really happened, I don't think anybody will know apart from Erick and his accusers, because one commonality that prevails in all the accusations made against him, it comes down to "he said/she said". None of the accusers have actual witnesses.

Morillo denied the accusation in Miami that he was charged with, even though there was positive evidence of sexual contact in a DNA Rape Kit test. He denied any contact at first, then he claimed that there was contact but that it was consensual, not forced.

I can't say what happened that night, I wasn't there. But what I do know is that the woman involved was somebody else's fiancée, the serious partner in life with another guy, and more than that, the guy she was hooked up with was a friend of Erick's - and a friend of mine too. I'd made a mix CD with him all the way back in 1994, and I've worked many times with him all over the world in the decades that followed. Erick shouldn't have been anywhere near the woman. But he was, and it brought the entire house crashing down to rubble in the aftermath.

Erick Morillo died of a drug overdose three days before his trial was to be heard; he was up on a charge of sexual battery, accused in the media of rape. He was neither convicted nor cleared of the accusation or the charges against him.

Erick was a major talent, not just inside the global House music scene, but way beyond that, he had a gigantic personality, natural star quality and real charisma. Some say that he was the greatest House DJ of all time. Today, he is both immortalised and also forever tainted. RIP Erick Morillo, but only if your true conscience allows you to…

"Violent Dream":

Positive President
I expect a lot
A week of laughs
Maybe Shangri-la
Each child's got a story
Many wait in fear
Violence becomes routine
You're lost inside me
Inside of my
Sweetheart oh sweetheart
Come over me
New year bride
Well she wants to look so good clean
African American
Give them all to me
I am king on
A holiday
You're lost inside me
You're lost inside
I hate the smell
Of a clean embrace
Like Uncle John laid out to rest
On his coffin day
He looked his best
On his coffin day
He looked his best
You're lost inside me
Inside my violent dream

327

My violent dream
Ooh my violent dream
Ooh in my violent dream.

"Love To Hate":

They're sweeping down from the sky
I'm coming down
Because they're coming down on you and I
They're coming at me from underground
Crawling out of the sewers and into my mind
They've all got a piece of the action
That's what I say
They all need satisfaction
And they love to hate
The blood suckers are everywhere
They're wanting souls
And they want 'em bare
They tried to take all the things I need
My liberty, security, my state of health
They've all got a piece of the action
That's what I say
They all need satisfaction
And they love to hate
Yes they do now
Yes they do
Yes they do now
Love to hate.

"Graham Said":

The monkey's gone
It jumped off my shoulder
Must've weighed about forty stones
It clung on with three different claws
And, there's an albatross hanging round my neck
I gotta get it fixed

328

Vainglorious: A Punk in the House

I try direct inject
Graham gave me some good advice
He said
"Stevie, live your life, before you die"
Graham said, do what you gotta do
Graham said, be who you gotta be
Graham said, hey live it fast and live it free
Graham said, he said "life, don't let it get you down"
There's a dog fouling up in the sidewalk
Hey no-one cares or even notices
With all the shit dropping out of the sky
And all the garbage on the subway line
Oh Miss Dee she said nothing but she spoke a lot
And Miss L's eyes are open but her mind is shut
Little Jeannie hit the ice with a bottle and a knife
She said "hey, live your life, before you die"
Now Graham Vee is dead and gone
But he's not forgotten
He lived his life right up to the end
He would not take the cop-out
He gave me some good advice
He said
"Hey Stevie, just you live your life
Live it fast and live it free
Live your life just like you were me"
Graham said, do what you gotta do
Graham said, be who you gotta be
Graham said, hey live it fast and live it free
Graham said, he said
"Life, don't let it get you down
No don't let it get you down
Don't let it get you."

329

17. ROCK IT, SHAKE IT, BREAK IT

The whole period of living in New York and moving to Ibiza, as well as growing up in Leeds and the London years too, was like living in a movie. Things were happening to me, around me, because of me, or despite me — all the time.

In fact, there was so much glitter in the air that every breath I took tasted like it was being spoon-fed to me by a naughty harem of Vestal Angels in the form of a delicious golden nectar that had been gifted to me from the gods. Which gods? All of them, of course!

Just in case you're curious, my Angels were just like me — good-bad, but not evil.

Jam and Bravado were riding the wave, or should that be riding the storm, we were all getting along nicely — well, apart from when Jam was being a spiky little downer bastard, or when Bravado was being a cocky little over-confident cunt. But thankfully I was present during those periods, which meant I could keep shit tight... OK, OK, loose-tight. Sometimes things were loose, but most of the time, mostly tight — tight-ish at least.

In contrast, my Leeds years coming up on the Whinmoor, and then discovering life through the lens of 27 Leicester Grove, Glebe Ave, the Brudenell and the LS6 music scene in general — not forgetting my adventures in Europe — were a whole different ball-game. Probably because those years were part of what we might call the journey's grind, me paying my dues, as the saying goes.

Of course, even in those days, I was around some incredible people, folk who were amazing and often inspirational, characters like CJ, Ronaldo Racoon, Fisherman Moore, Skum, Franky, and all the others in our cool-as-fuck crew. I'll not shine a light, nor will I pour petrol on top of fire, regarding Evo, and what became of him, other than to say, if it were true, what they said, then I hope he never sleeps well

330

again. But, as I wasn't there when it all went down, it's not my place to add to the chit-chat and whispers. I'll leave it there.

I'd also had the good fortune of having had a whole array of fabulous, and patient, band mates — from Uncle to Prince Michael, Sir Harry to Cyrus, Dil, Smelly, Toddy and Martin, through to Jessica Fischer, Nev and Gerry Famous, and anybody else I may have missed or who came around in another lifetime. They'd all been the willing canvas to my Jackson Pollock style of being. And I'll include the incredible Craig Adams, AKA Craig SuperHero, Space Cadet No1, from the brilliant band The Mission into that wave of thanks and praise.

If London, Manhattan and Ibiza were the glitter, then you might think Leeds to be the gutter — and for the sake of poetic licence, its role here is likened to that: it's the start, and we weren't born rich: ergo, the gutter.

We weren't supping on golden nectar back in those days, but there was always a lot of shit to go around. That's not to say we had it hard, because in truth we didn't. Even if things were relatively shit, at least our mums found a way to serve it with sugar on.

There's a lot of people who live in dire straits, born to poverty, even slavery, in far-flung lands — they hold on to belief, they don't hope to die before they get old, but in reality many actually do. In comparison, my reality was that I came from a big industrial city in the North of England, the third biggest one in the country at the time. Whatever hard times I imagined I had as a kid were just the consequences of other people's choices. Dad fucked off, that cut our legs off from below the knee, but then they grew back ten times stronger. Any shite times I might of had as a young adult were all of my own doing: nobody told me to stick a needle in my arm, I did it cos I loved it, I wanted it all, I gorged myself on it — no complaints here.

I'd also come in contact with two of my musical heroes while still scraping away for attention in Leeds. Back then

331

my dreams were limited to finding my way into the business of the music business. What that meant in reality, I hadn't really processed — well, not beyond the initial desire to do it. My heroes seemed to be so far away from my reality that I considered them to be untouchable.

People like Johnny Thunders, Iggy Pop, Stiv Bators, and David Bowie — they may have walked on the same earth as I did, but they lived on wholly different planets.

However, fate and chance often have ideas of their own, as they seemed to have for me. I was a lucky fucker, going all the way back to the start — "shit 'n' roses", my mum would always say.

I managed to become friends with Johnny Thunders... the idea of it was so abstract to me, but I even had him hanging out at my apartment back in Leeds when he needed to chill out between tour dates in Europe and the UK.

I also got to meet Stiv Bators, which was another cool moment, especially as it was Johnny Thunders who introduced me to him. On a darker note — a bizarre twist — I even ended up sleeping in the same Parisian bed that Stiv had actually died in while he was holed in Paris.

As for Iggy Pop... Well apart from that moment at the Leeds Warehouse, where we both showed our appreciation to the new band on the scene, The Sisters of Mercy, I also had a funny 'three-way' moment with The Ig during the glitter years when we were both living in the Alphabet City part of the East Village of NYC. Not that Iggy knew. He was an unknowing participant, while the other two in the threesome, Rita Margarita and me, were both fully cooperating players. There were also some strange collisions with people like Dee Dee Ramone at the Chelsea Hotel, or Chris from *The Sopranos* at a Suicide gig in Manhattan, as well as Giorgio Moroder playing DJ sets for me at the world-famous Pacha nightclub in Ibiza. And then there was the time Menzi from The Angelic Upstarts slapped Max Splodge backstage in my dressing room at The Marquee in London. Menzi was convinced Splodge had played the drums better for me at the

332

one-off Johnny Thunders Memorial Show — where I'd enlisted him via Matt Dangerfield of The Boys — than he ever had for The Upstarts.

Other notable highlights to stash away in the memory bank included the incredible tours and backstage singalong get-togethers with the late great Jeffrey Lee Pierce and The Gun Club. While not forgetting tours and concert dates with local lads, The Mission and Abrasive Wheels, as well as the push-and-shove disagreement with the iconic Rock'n'Roll Metal God Lemmy, outside the Alice In Wonderland Club, Soho, London.

There have been loads of other collisions that I haven't even mentioned in these pages, the list could go on and on and on.

For example, I almost accidentally knocked David Bowie on his arse when we smashed into one another in a London street, just around the corner from where the famous Ziggy Stardust Telephone Box image was caught on camera. Bowie even spoke to his starstruck fan, "You alright there, fella?"

I was too starstruck to say anything back to *the great one* — I just gawked, open-mouthed, the thought flying through my mind of how bizarre life is, every step that he and I had both taken in our lives had led to that collision — I thanked "it" for that moment in time.

Talking of great Rock'n'Roll photos, there have probably not been many better at catching gold dust through a lens than the late great Mick Rock.

I'd never thought, or dreamed, that one day I would meet the world-famous photographer, but fate and mutual friends made it happen. We got along great right away and became friends, or maybe friendly acquaintants would be more accurate, while we were both living in New York. Whatever, we were friendly enough to arrange to meet up for casual drinks, or brunch, or just coffee and a chat.

To convey why meeting Mick Rock was such a thrill for me, you have to consider that when I was a teenager, I'd lie on my bed listening to the genius albums, Iggy & The Stooges' *Raw Power* and Lou Reed's *Transformer*.

I knew every word, every drum beat, bass line, guitar riff, of every track on each album.

But it's not just the tracks on the albums that made them masterpieces, nor just the performance of the artist or the band — it's also *those front covers* which can be placed right up there among the best covers of all time.

Iggy walking on hands above the crowd. A deadpan Lou in a strange negative silhouette…

The photographer — Mick Rock!

As I held those albums in my teenage hands, reading every last word of the covers, the idea that 25 years into the future, I would be sitting in an American diner opposite the world-famous Flatiron Building in Manhattan, NYC, drinking coffee and chatting about music & Rock'n'Roll culture with the man that shot the '70s, Mick Rock, didn't even get a fleeting moment of thought-time from yours truly. Why would it? What were the chances of that ever happening for this Whinmoor council kid. Zero — yet there I was.

I first met Mick down at BarOnA, introduced via the Brit contingent in the East Village. Mick, being a Brit himself, had taken photos of the Leeds band Spacehog, who were a sensation across the USA on the back of their top-selling Billboard hit "In The Meantime". He was also friends with the whole crew at Toni & Tina Cosmetics, where my then-wife Kenzi also worked, and we kind of hit it off.

Mick knew I worked in the music business, not just in A&R and concerts but in the wider sense of the serious industry. I'd told him about the projects I'd worked on with MasterTone and Best Buy, things like The BBC Sessions, The Beatles *One* project, Roy Orbison, and other things like The Irish Tenors and various CD/book projects. The one he liked most was The Beatles *One* project that we did for Best Buy. We made a deal where we would package the *One* CD inside a massive box and include four never-seen-before photos of The Fab Four. The result was that Best Buy, which

334

had 30% of the retail market, was suddenly responsible for 50% of all US sales of that Beatles album — that's a lot of units.

Mick asked me if I had any idea what he could do with the classic photos of pop and rock royalty he had in his files. "Come on, dude, make a coffee table book — you'll clean up." So, I gave him the idea, introduced him to some old contacts on the multimedia side of the business, and…

Well, I'm not claiming all the glory, but not long after, Mick did indeed release a few critically acclaimed and commercially successful coffee table books of his photos.

Just to underscore exactly who Mick Rock is, his work included classic shots of Syd Barrett, David Bowie, Queen, Waylon Jennings, The Sex Pistols, Thin Lizzy, T Rex, Lou Reed, Iggy Pop, The Dead Boys, Blondie, Roxy Music, The Ramones, Joan Jett, Spacehog, and many, many more. His album covers included classics like *Transformer* by Lou Reed, *Raw Power* by The Stooges, *We Have Come for Your Children* by The Dead Boys, *End of the Century* by The Ramones, *Deuce* by Rory Gallagher and even *Plastic Hearts* by Miley Cyrus, just to name a handful.

Mick had released one book prior to our chat, 1995's *A Photographic Record*, which he told me hadn't done anything in terms of sales or financial reward. But after our chat in late Summer 2001, he went on to release 13 books between 2003 and 2010. Personally, I think that's ample evidence to suggest that I played at least some small role in Mick going on to find commercial success.

Well, I'm claiming a little bit of influence in it all, and I think I'm justified — like it or not.

Another artist I came in contact with was the Latín singer and dancer Shakira…

Not long after arriving in Ibiza in winter 2005 to take over the record label for the Pacha Company, I set about creating content. I saw that the brand was releasing mix CDs but all the tracks on the CDs were licensed-in music. That meant that Pacha had been paying third-party labels for a one-time

335

use of a track on a mixed compilation CD. The argument many people had was that the tracks on the mix CD are what sells the mix CD, something I agreed with for major labels chasing gigantic commercial sales numbers. But it was something I passionately disagreed with for independent labels who were using the mix CDs as an income stream and a secondary marketing and promotion tool for their brand.

I viewed Pacha as a brand, much more than just a nightclub. The Pacha brand was, in my mind, much sexier and more appealing than a music track or a DJ. People collected the brand, invested their time and energy into being associated with the brand and they trusted it. They believed that what was inside would live up to the brand name on the outside, whether it was entering the club, a piece of merchandise, a special event, restaurant, hotel, or, of course, a Pacha Mix CD.

Why pay third-party labels to fill our Pacha CDs with music? The way ahead, as a business, was to create content — lots of it — and inside that content, create some special eye-catching moments. Enter Shakira!

One night, I was introduced to a guy who claimed to be the brother of Shakira's husband — not the Barcelona footballer Piqué, but her first husband, the one she left for Piqué. I had no reason to disbelieve the guy, I took him at his word, and we started talking about clubs and the dance scene. He told me that Shakira wanted to "get into House music".

At this time, I was running Pacha Recordings, but I was also involved with running Subliminal Records — I had my hands on both rudders. The guy said that Shakira would love to do a collaboration of some kind with Subliminal Records and Erick Morillo. She'd seen we'd remixed a big track for Jennifer "J Lo" Lopez, had also remixed the global hit "Lady" for Modjo, had done an original track with Macy Gray, and of course, tracks with Puff Daddy. I was certain Morillo would love the idea, especially as they were both Colombian.

Well, what do I know? Erick just dismissed the idea, spitting out dumb comments like "Why would I want to do something with Shakira?" My answer to that stupidity was an old Leeds expression: "If you don't know, then I can't tell you."

I was pissed off with him. The rest of the chat went something like this:

Me: "I'll make it easy… if you don't do it on Subliminal, then I'll do it on Pacha instead."

Him: "Why would Shakira want to do something with Pacha?"

Me: "Let me repeat. If you don't know, then I can't tell you."

It was clear that Erick didn't have his head in the game like he used to — in the past he would have seen the massive benefits of having a global superstar associated with the label, the same way that we'd benefited from having Macy Gray and others on Subliminal before. Yet, here we had Shakira, who was one of the biggest names in the game, and he decided to be pissy, brushing away the idea of Shakira doing anything with Subliminal. It didn't make good business sense — it didn't make any sense at all.

Of course, with Erick passing, I went ahead and made the deal between Pacha and Shakira. It was the perfect attention-seeking project for Pacha Recordings as we set about creating a catalogue. Shakira was all in — and she agreed that Pacha could release the collaboration on vinyl as well. Her record label, Sony USA, were not as excited about it all because Shakira had selected one of her biggest hit records for the Pacha All-Star Remix Team to rework.

The track was "Los De La Intuición", and she even did various re-versions of her original video for the project as well.

Even though Sony wasn't happy, they didn't want to upset Shakira. What she wanted was what she got — a House music rework of one of her classic hits.

I made similar Shakira–Pacha type deals with other big hitters including Bob Marley's "I Shot the Sheriff", Asia's "Heat of the Moment", Paul Hardcastle's "19", as well as creating some choice cover versions of some of my own personal favourite songs, including a fantastic House-style cover of the classic by Black, "Wonderful Life".

And on top of all that, an album of Graceland-approved Elvis Presley House music remixes arrived on my desk looking for a home too. Of course, I released it — and yes, maybe I went with it just so that I could say my name in the same breath, the same sentence, as The King.

"Elvis fucking Presley & Me — motherfucking careers advice woman, suck my motherfucking dick!!!"

The label was off to a flying start and before long we were releasing ten Pacha Mix CDs per season in Ibiza and maybe twenty more mix CDs a year via label deals I'd made all over the world — basically following my own Subliminal Records blueprint of exploiting brand and catalogue. It was viewed as a spectacular achievement within the Pacha Company, and the cherry on top was earning a Silver Disc for sales in the UK. To be fair to Pacha, they compensated me very well, and they also opened up my role inside the company so that I was free to explore many other areas of business on their behalf.

Before long I was handling all kinds of projects that were outside of the core label business, interesting and exciting concepts… from negotiating marketing and promotion deals with global drink brands like Red Bull and Coronita Beer to making deals to create Pacha branded TV channels, radio shows, and all kinds of one-off special events.

It was an exciting time, and in all honesty, I'd often flash back to Whinmoor and Smeaton, then through the junkie years of Punk-Rock'n'Roll and wonder, "How the hell did you get here?"

I mean I had no formal qualifications or advanced education. I'd probably made every bad choice there was to make, personally and professionally, in the years between leaving school and hitting 27. I'd survived it all, I'd been a lucky guy. And then, somehow, from the age of 27 onwards, I seemed to be even more charmed. It didn't matter what I said I was, because whatever I said I was, "I was". From the chaos of drug-induced paranoia, multiple voices fighting to be heard inside my head, and whirling towards a certain Johnny Thunders ending, I'd managed to step up from the inverted glamour of the gutter and landed on some kind of nirvana terra-firma. Maybe on wobbly legs for a while, during the early days of second chances at The Leeds Corn Exchange, but it wasn't long before I'd got myself standing up straight, rocking and raving my way through the gold-paved streets of London Town, and on to the bright-light possibilities of Manhattan, NYC. And now, on the famed White Isle, I was dancing as if I was a cocktail of Nureyev & Nijinsky, my glitter-feet making their mark across Ibiza and the world. Rather than — as might have been — lost, crawling through goo-goo muck, with an out of tune electric guitar spewing out its feedback, while laid prone and naked on a floor of spilt beer and discarded cigs. Or, more simply, just dead.

I'd made myself, made my name, I was globally renowned and respected in the business of the music business — and for ten years more I excelled within the Pacha Group.

What a life I was leading, what a life I was having! From the estates of my home town in the industrial North of England, Leeds, to the Big Smoke of London, across the pond to the streets of the East Village, the Lower East Side and Alphabet City, and landing on the island paradise of Ibiza, via the Dominican Republic (the DR is another story), with hundreds of stops across the world along the way…

I'll never forget arriving in Ibiza and feeling immediately at home. Of course, I had first visited the island a bunch of times in the early '90s, and Subliminal had been running an annual summer residency there since around the turn of the millennium. But I have to say, while visiting Ibiza is a buzz, living in Ibiza is another feeling completely.

339

Knowing that Ibiza is your home gives you a different sense of wellbeing.

You kind of appreciate that you're one of the lucky ones. For me, arriving in Ibiza, but not as a tourist, was the first time that I'd ever felt like planting proper roots, and making a home for life.

I had good money in my pocket, enough to buy a brand new model car straight off the production line. I also bought a cool motorbike, adopted a couple of dogs and cats, and moved into a *finca* in the *campo*, where we had a swimming pool in the massive wild-grown garden. There was sunshine almost every day of the year, and to top it all off, I was given a company credit card for schmoozing and entertaining clients and business connections.

You could say I was living the dream.

*

We — me and Kenzi — had landed in Ibiza in time for Christmas 2005 and I started work at Pacha at the beginning of January 2006. We rocked the hell out of Ibiza in that first year, but by 2007 we were divorced. I'll not go into the whys and wherefores, especially after all we had been through together — her moving from London and Tunisia to the East Village of Manhattan, going through university and collecting an MBA, while I was taking over the House music world with Subliminal. Then there were the problems, the access to *everything* and eventually moving to Ibiza. And so on and so on… we had crammed in a lot of living together — but, by 2007 divorce was sadly unavoidable.

As strange as it may seem, despite our divorce, the friendship lasted. We came through the other side of it in good shape — she even worked for me for several years in sales and distribution, and in fact, we are still friends. Her mother also still talks to me almost daily; she still refers to me as her "son", and I call her "Mother of Tunisia". She never forgot that I paid off the mortgage on her apartment in Tunisia when Kenzi and I divorced. I didn't have to, but I knew it was the right thing to do, and besides, I loved her just like a mother. It's maybe the second best thing I've ever done in my life.

Over the next ten years at Pacha I created a massive label catalogue, sold millions of units via the global label deals I'd put in place, and travelled all over the world as a DJ hitting up booths from Japan to Sri Lanka, Qatar and Dubai to Egypt and Morocco, everywhere in Europe, all over the Baltics, Scandinavia, back to the USA and as far as South Africa and Mexico, as well as Ukraine and loads of times all over Russia. I also played in the coolest DJ booths of Ibiza. But the thing that gave me the most pride wasn't based on my work achievements, whether in Leeds, London, NYC or Ibiza, or the fact that I had made a life for myself in the music business. Nor was it that I had become friends or associates with so many famous names from different corners of the music and entertainment world, or that I had managed to buy, sell and own properties. It was that I had done well enough to buy my mother's house. It meant that I could give her somewhere that she loved, to live in without stress, with cash in her bank account too. It allowed her to enjoy her later years free of worry and with money to spend on herself. That's the first best thing that I've ever done in my life, no question about it.

My mum, Lila, took the bull by the horns, and embraced freedom — she took loads of holidays every year, sometimes visiting me three, four or even five times a year in Ibiza, as well as all her other trips to places like America, Tenerife, Tunisia, Morocco, and wherever else she danced.

I nick-named her Liam, a jokey little reference to the Oasis Rock'n'Roll hellraiser Liam Gallagher, because she wouldn't go on holiday to chill, she went on all her holidays to raise hell! Soon enough everyone would refer to her as Liam and she ended up with her own catchphrase, "Live like Lila". She was still riding on the back of my motorbike through the hills of Ibiza well into her seventies. Live it hard and live it free… "Live Like Lila."

341

As I mentioned earlier, my good friend Danny Whittle, who had brought me to Ibiza and set me up at Pacha in the first place, left the company, and I was handed the role of DJ & talent booking director, on top of my other roles.

I was now handling multiple jobs inside the Group, and was managing budgets of €15 million a season, turning over gross numbers of around €40 million in income with the goal of making a profit somewhere in the middle. This was relatively big business in the music business.

On top of that, I became part of a core team of four that created and delivered the incredible Destino Pacha Resort, a super-luxury hotel, restaurant and events space, where I would program superstar DJs to play daytime and evening open-air sessions. These were fantastic occasions, where between 3,000 and 5,000 clubbers would show up to start the party under the sun and end it under the moon. My favourite event from the Destino Pacha Resort productions was by the maverick electronic superstar Nicolas Jaar — what a sensation to bliss out to the underground maestro as day turned into night, leaving us with a light show of the stars and the moon, pure Ibiza vibes, just perfect.

And this, Ladies and Gentlemen, Heathens and Brethren, is where we return to the start — at a place in time:

"How did I end up as a DJ making my debut in Moscow?"

Well, as the label manager of Pacha Recordings, I had to find ways to promote and market the music we were releasing. But since I didn't have a traditional budget to invest in billboards, press, magazines, online campaigns or hype chart manipulators, I opted to go back to basics: tour, tour, tour and take the music to the masses.

The idea was that I'd sign five artists to the label, each on what I called a "Triple Five Deal". That meant I would advance €5,000 to each of five selected DJ/producers. But to collect the advance, the selected DJ/producers would have to deliver five original records (each with a flipside version) and, they would also have to remix five tracks out of the catalogue being created by the other four DJ/producers in this setup. So, €5,000 for five records (including a flipside version) and five remixes of their label mates' records — hence the Triple Five Deal. Of course, they would also get a royalty, based on recoupment first, and also a 50/50 publishing split. But the main benefits were that they were on Pacha Recordings, and given that I was releasing loads of mixed compilation CDs in Ibiza and around the world, that meant that the tracks were going to get fully exploited, and their names were going to grow. Even better, it also meant that they would earn decent money from touring the label Pacha Recordings all over the world — multiple gigs booked on the back of the label rather than trying to book gigs based on their "unknown" DJ name. They could earn something like €250 to €500 per gig. Maybe not fantastic money, but if they did between five and ten gigs a month each, that would mean they'd be earning, relatively, a decent amount of money. And on top of that, they could also do whatever other gigs or recording projects came their way because I didn't want to tie them down to any kind of exclusivity.

I call that a pretty cool deal!

Well, let's just say this, in my opinion, it was a cool, funky and fair deal for a DJ/producer with no pulling power of their own.

I was laying it on a plate for them, so far as I was concerned, even if the Pacha owners thought I was being too generous. The only stipulation they had to adhere to was when DJing at the Pacha Recordings touring events they had to play 50% of their DJ set with tracks or remixes taken from the Pacha Recordings catalogue. Why? Because that was the whole fucking reason we were touring at all — to promote and highlight the product for sale on the actual record label, as well as getting supplementary income for the DJs and the Pacha Group itself. What could possibly go wrong?

Everything started smoothly, and everyone praised the business model as a smart move. The DJ/producers got to work in the studio, delivering their first records complete

343

with flipsides. They also began remixing each other's tracks, building up a label catalogue and establishing a stable of label mates for touring. I then had them mixing the CD compilations and I got various booking agents engaged to start arranging tour dates around the world. Before long, we had gigs lined up in places like Sharm el Sheikh, Moscow and other cities across Russia, Milan, Rome, Naples, London, New York, Dubai, Qatar — the list goes on and on and on. You'd think everything would be fine and dandy, right? But unfortunately, the DJ/producers didn't see the big picture as clearly as I could.

Like I said, all the DJs had to do was play at least 50% of their sets from the Pacha catalogue we were creating and commercially selling. Simple, right?

Well, it turned out the DJs couldn't grasp that these events were booked on the strength of the brand, the world-renowned Pacha legend, and not on their "unknown" DJ names. They just had to show up, play the set as required, have fun and get paid. But every one of them wanted to play their sets according to their own professional sensibilities — acting as if *they* were the stars of the show, when in fact, the real star was Pacha, represented by Pacha Recordings and the music on the label.

But no matter how many times I told them, the penny just wouldn't drop, and they'd end up playing maybe five Pacha tracks out of a set of 25-30 — it just wouldn't do.

Eventually, I lost my temper. I decided to buy two CDJ decks, a DJ mixer, and a couple of speakers. Then, armed myself with an insatiable determination to deliver the Pacha Recordings live events as they were supposed to be, even if that meant mixing the DJ sets myself.

Being honest, I had no idea how the machinery worked, but I'm a quick learner. I set myself up and practised relentlessly — over and over, repeat, repeat, repeat, not just the technical aspects but also the skill of building the sets. It turned out I had a knack for it, or maybe it was a throwback to an old lesson I'd learned all the way back from my childhood, the bit the public don't see — the practising. That discipline is always the key, and helpfully, I loved it. I couldn't wait to get home

I started off playing out with tiny steps, taking one DJ with me to the Pacha Recordings parties. I would select the tracks to be played, they would do the DJing, with me passing CDs to the DJ with instructions like, "Track five on this CD, then track four on this one." From there, I started getting my fingers on the controls, manipulating the EQs, adding dynamics with effects, interacting with the crowd and even grabbing the microphone to MC or sing over the vocal tracks we were playing — I was starting to really get a feel for it.

I ended up DJing all over the world for nearly ten years, rocking crowds in every type of venue. Whether it was small lounge bars or massive concert halls, opening sets or closing sets, all-night marathon sessions or after-hours gigs. I got really good at it. I could hold my own next to any DJ, go back-to-back with the best and play multiple styles within the House music spectrum. No matter where I played, I smashed it. But it all started in earnest at my very first solo show in Pacha Moscow.

Start at a moment in time:

I'm in the DJ booth of Pacha Moscow, 2010 — I want to make an announcement... The tech guy hands me the mic.

The crowd looked up towards the DJ booth, and I led the room in a round of ecstatic applause for the "incredible" resident DJ. It felt like we cheered him for ages, but in reality it was probably only a minute. I ignored the negative inner voice of Jam, "Oh, you're screwed now," maybe because Bravado kept my ego going, as I gave credit to the local hero, "We're cool beans, buddy, we're cool beans."

I cued up my opening track. Could I pull this off? I addressed the crowd, and it just blurted out of me: "This is the Midnight Gun, and I'm Packing Silver Bullets, Baby." I

345

hit the echo effect… "Baby, Baby, Baby, Baby, Baby". The room roared in approval and I dropped my first record, Pacha Recordings' remix of Bob Marley's "I Shot The Sheriff". I could hardly believe it, but everyone went wild. I yelled into the mic "Bang Bang" and everybody was instantly bouncing.

Three hours later, as I was closing out the night, the room started to chant my DJ name: "Syx, Syx, Syx", intermixed with shouts of "Pacha, Pacha, Pacha" as well as "Ibiza, Ibiza, Ibiza". They wanted one more tune.

My set had been a hit and the energy in the room was electric.

With everyone chanting for "one more tune, one more tune", I turned to another Pacha Recordings track, our cover version of the classic song "Wonderful Life", originally a global hit by Black. The entire room seemed to know every word, every face seemed to be singing along with me as I sang the lyrics over the top of the track via the tech guy's microphone. The dancers, the resident DJ, the tech guy, the owner — and Uncle Tom Cobley and all — surrounded me in the DJ booth. As I faded the music out, I sang the refrain again as an acapella.

No need to run or hide
It's a wonderful, wonderful life.

Take it from me, it really is if you go out and get it. Thank you all so much, goodnight and God bless.

To Be Continued…

Maybe.

EPILOGUE

I had an incredible relationship with my mum, Lila, or as I called her sometimes, Liam.

On that night in Moscow, I want to tell you something that happened that's not included anywhere else in the book. I actually called her from the club:

"Hi, Mum, what're you doing?"

"Hang on, let me turn the TV down — nothing much, just watching telly, I've paused it now. Where are you?"

"I'm in Moscow."

"What, Moscow… Moscow, Russia?"

"Yes."

"What're you doing there?"

"I'm about to DJ, I'm shitting myself."

"What, you're DJing?"

"Yeah, DJing — I might just do a runner though."

"You can't do that!"

"Yeah, I know. Actually, I'm in a toilet cubicle right now having a toot — you should see these toilets, they're incredible!"

"Drugs? You don't want to be doing any drugs, you've got to go DJing in a bit."

"I don't think I can do it, I think I might have fucked up."

"Don't be swearing horrible like that, course you can do it. Get out there and give it all you've got."

"Not sure I can, I might just pretend I'm too ill to play."

"You bloody won't, you'll get out there and you'll be great, I've got every faith in you. Now go on, get your arse in gear and knock their bloody socks off."

"Ufff. OK, I'll go and give it a go, nothing else for it really, is there? I'm off, wish me luck."

"You'll do it, you'll be OK. What do I always tell you? You'd fall in a bucket of shit and still come out smelling like roses! Remember, there's no party without Punch, give me a bloody black eye! That's the way to do it!"

"OK, Let's Ride. Love you, Mum."

"Love you too, big kiss."

Me, Jam and Bravado made our way back to the DJ booth and had a life-changing moment together. It was wonderful.

Now, you may have noticed there's been one or two voices ringing through my head throughout this book. I thought that the voices would come to some sort of conclusion and fade away, but in fact they've always been there, even before I first heard them. I just didn't know how to listen. I'm not recommending it to anybody, but maybe drugs opened the door on that. The voices have stayed with me and they're still here today. The fact is, it's just consciousness, and it's a gift to be conscious, not a curse. Be conscious of *glorious contentment* when it comes around — you don't want to miss that x

Live Like Lila

Secret Page...

I can't finish this book without giving the last moment to Johnny Thunders and myself — here goes:

When I got the news that Johnny had died, I put down my guitar and said to myself — and to all those around me — "That's it, I'm out!" And I meant it.

But Mick Webb called me up and asked if I would do *one more show* — headlining a memorial concert in honor of Johnny at the London Marquee. "Just one more time, for Johnny, for you." I couldn't say no. I would have regretted it for the rest of my days.

It was a fantastic gig, and it was one of the honours of my life to play it out for Johnny just a few short weeks after his passing.

It's an occasion I cherish every day in memory.

After that show, I kept my self-promise and didn't play another gig. In fact, I didn't even keep a guitar in my apartment — I either gave them away or sold them. This was a first for me. I was practically born with a guitar in my hands, and I can't remember a single time, up until that point, when I hadn't strummed out a song as a matter of course practically every single day. Johnny's passing had hit me hard.

Ten years later, in 2001, I was doing well in NYC — dining out on my super-successful position and achievements at the very heart of the global House music scene.

Then one day, I got a call from a guy I had never met or heard of — and whose name I can't even remember today — but he knew me. He knew all about Stevie Vayne, The Dead Vaynes, The Vaynes, Stevie Vayne & The Slaves. He says to me:

"It's the ten-year anniversary of Johnny Thunders' passing in three weeks' time. We're organising a Remembrance Concert in his name at CBGBs. We'd love for you to co-headline the event along with Lenny Kaye and also LES, the Lower East Side Stitches. There are bands playing all day

349

long from mid-afternoon, and then the last three headline slots will be Lenny Kaye, then yourself — Stevie Vayne & His Band — and finally, LES will close the event out. Are you in?"

I'll not bore you with the ins and outs of the conversations that followed, but the bottom line is that I agreed.

I was truly honoured to be asked, especially given that I was a Leeds transplant in NYC, not part of any Manhattan scene or any CBGBs history either. But the fact of the matter was that I had played more times on tours supporting Johnny over the final three years of his life — at least in the UK and Europe — than anyone else so the organisers believed I would be a wonderful guest star co-headliner for the occasion.

I agreed to do the show — Ride one more time, for Johnny.

The decision was made easier because it was going to happen at the world's most famous live music venue — CBGBs. This was Mecca for a Punk-Rock'n'Roller from the Whinmoor estate, for a Punk-Rock'n'Roll wannabe star from the LS6 scene — Leeds would ride again.

I didn't have a band, but I'd get one — and I did. Reality bit hard. Even after ten years of sobriety from the Punk-Rock'n'Roll world, the call of the wild was too much for this werewolf hunter to resist — I was in.

I put another scratch band together, myself and two other English guys I was mates with: drummer Griff and bassist Martin, and me on guitar. On the day of the show, I went down to CBGBs early to enjoy the vibe of the event, and by chance, I came across a shit-hot guitarist in one of the other bands playing a mid-afternoon slot. I asked him if he'd like to step up onstage with me. To my surprise, he was a fan — he had the *G.T.F.* Dead Vaynes album and was ecstatic to be asked. I knew all I needed to do was hand over the solos to him at any given moment in the songs we were going to play and the room would go nuts. I did. He delivered. They did.

The gig was everything and more — better than I could've ever dreamed it might be. And I had dreamed of playing CBGBs almost every day and night between the ages of 13/14 and 26/27. I did Johnny Thunders proud. I did myself proud. I'll take it to the grave.

It was a just ending to the story of Johnny & Stevie — The Boy Looked at Johnny, indeed!

RIP Johnny Thunders.

And that's Rock'n'Roll (Don't Try This At Home Kids!)

Age 17 - 'Who Takes the Blame' - Stevie, wound up like a Clockwork Orange, looking for the key to his destination - at 27 Leicester Grove, Leeds.

Stevie Vayne - Get Totally Fucked or Get To Fuck - your choice - I'll blow my own balls off

Stevie Vayne is a f**king Rock Star - You Better Believe It Baby - Leeds 1989

352

Stevie Vayne live at CBGBs NYC, co-headlining the '10th Year Memorial' of the passing of Johnny Thunders - this is April 2001

In-between Punk-Rock'n'Roll & Raving House 1991/1992

Pacha Moscow 2010 - getting set for a monumental night ahead - "I wanna make an announcement"

Stevie Hulme - Rolling Deep on the White Island of Ibiza - Summer 2013

Holding Court in my bathtub at The Chelsea Hotel NYC.

353

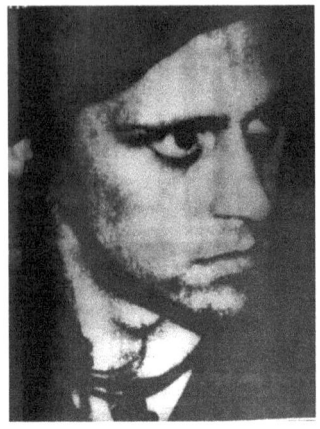

Royal Park All Dayer Leeds 6 -
Stevie Vayne 'Cover Star'

I put it on the same shelf as L.A.M.F.
and Young Loud & Snotty - I don't care
if you don't put it there too! - 1985

Stevie Vayne On Tour -
Holland - Dead Vaynes

Original G.T.F. Album Cover The Dead
Vaynes - Artwork by Shaun Slater.

354

"C'mon now touch me babe" - Stevie stakes his claim at The Faversham Leeds.

Ibiza Chilling...feeling metrosexual somewhere in Ibiza...

Stevie Hulme - Here and Now - We Made It Baby!

Looking At Manhattan from Butcher Bills Grave (maybe) NYC 1999

Mantra For Life - "Live Like Lila"

355